Politics under the Influence

POLITICS UNDER THE INFLUENCE

Vodka and Public Policy in Putin's Russia

ANNA L. BAILEY

CORNELL UNIVERSITY PRESS
ITHACA AND LONDON

First published 2018 by Cornell University Press

Printed in the United States of America

Library of Congress Cataloging-in-Publication Data

Names: Bailey, Anna L., author.
Title: Politics under the influence : vodka and public policy in Putin's
    Russia / Anna L. Bailey.
Description: Ithaca : Cornell University Press, 2018. | Includes
    bibliographical references and index.
Identifiers: LCCN 2017048070 (print) | LCCN 2017052221 (ebook) |
    ISBN 9781501724381 (pdf) | ISBN 9781501724398 (epub/mobi) |
    ISBN 9781501724374 | ISBN 9781501724374 (cloth; alk. paper) |
    ISBN 9781501724404 (pbk.; alk. paper)
Subjects: LCSH: Alcoholism—Government policy—Russia (Federation) |
    Drinking of alcoholic beverages—Political aspects—Russia (Federation) |
    Alcoholic beverage industry—Government policy—Russia (Federation) |
    Vodka industry—Government policy—Russia (Federation) | Russia
    (Federation)—Social conditions—21st century. | Russia (Federation)—
    Politics and government—21st century.
Classification: LCC HV5513 (ebook) | LCC HV5513 .B35 2018 (print) |
    DDC 362.292/5610947—dc23
LC record available at https://lccn.loc.gov/2017048070

CONTENTS

Acknowledgments

I am very fortunate to have benefitted from the wisdom and expertise of some exceptional scholars at the School of Slavonic and East European Studies, University College London. I owe a special debt of gratitude to Professor Alena Ledeneva, who has played a significant role in my development both as a researcher and as an author. This book would look very different without her insights and guidance. Dr. Peter Duncan, another SSEES stalwart, is a loyal and dependable source of advice and support and a master at facilitating discussion of Russian politics—whether in the Post-Soviet Press Group or the pub.

I am grateful to the Economic and Social Research Council for sponsoring my research and additional language training. Without their award, this research would not have been possible. Professor Andrey Korotayev and Maria Shteinman at the Russian State University for the Humanities provided helpful institutional support to facilitate my fieldwork visit to Moscow.

I would like to thank all of my respondents for their time and knowledge, and perhaps most of all for placing their trust in me, a British stranger. I am particularly indebted to those respondents who gave me several hours of their time and helped me enormously by providing contact details for additional respondents. Anonymity does not permit me to name them, but they know who they are.

I also extend my thanks to the organizers of the "Alcohol in Russia" conferences at the Ivanovo branch of the Russian State University for the Humanities. The conferences provided me with useful opportunities to get feedback on my early research findings as well as invaluable networking opportunities, and I am particularly grateful for the financial assistance toward my later visits. Mikhail Tepliansky is not only a scholarly and visionary conference convener, but a warm and generous host. I will always remember with great fondness the various cultural activities that were laid on for us foreign guests. Translator Dmitry Fedotov and his family welcomed me into their home like an old friend, and took Russian hospitality to new levels. The great feasts they laid on were cut short only by the need to get up for the conference the following morning.

I am extremely grateful to Dr. Mark Lawrence Schrad of Villanova University for his incredibly useful feedback on the numerous iterations of this book manuscript; it is much improved as a result. As a fellow researcher on Russian alcohol politics, Mark could not have been more supportive. It is reassuring to find that, while we have always conducted our research entirely independently of each other, our findings and conclusions are usually mutually supportive. I would also like to thank the two anonymous reviewers who provided useful suggestions and corrections during the publication process. I learned a great deal from Dr. Tomi Lintonen of the Finnish Foundation for Alcohol Studies, who provided useful conversations on the alcohol research literature.

Special thanks must go to my Russian-speaking friends who tirelessly answered my endless queries on translation and interpretation. Thanks to the medium of Skype—and my addiction to spending summers on the beach at Samara—Maria Kavalerchik has been an ever-present source of support. I hardly dare to imagine how many hours Masha has spent checking my translations of Russian bureaucratese and political rhetoric, but she is the reason that I have complete confidence in the translations contained in this book. Olga Semenova taught me my very first words of Russian, way back when I was a student of nineteenth-century British history and the idea of me researching contemporary Russian politics would have seemed crazy.

Neither of us could have imagined then that Olga's work as a volunteer language teacher was the start of a journey that would lead to me publishing a book on alcohol in Russia, but we have remained firm friends throughout. Irina Armitage did an amazing job of preparing me for my fieldwork interviews in Moscow—another inspirational language teacher who has become a great friend.

Most of all, I thank my family for their love, patience, and support. My mother, Angela, has seen me through many an academic low point with her words of wisdom. My husband, Paul, has had to share me with Russia for all the years we've been together, but despite the numerous months-long absences, he has always embraced it as part of who I am. Paul has been with me through all the ups and downs of study, research, and writing a book, and I am very lucky to have him at my side.

Politics under the Influence

INTRODUCTION

The Contradictions of Alcohol Policy

"You know just how serious a problem alcoholism has become for our country. Frankly speaking, it has taken on the proportions of a national disaster."[1] So declared Russian president Dmitry Medvedev in 2009, prior to launching a new government initiative to lower alcohol consumption. The media quickly labeled the new policy direction an "antialcohol campaign," drawing parallels with Soviet leader Mikhail Gorbachev's notorious dry law in the final years of the USSR. Alcoholic beverage producers braced themselves for new restrictions on one of the world's most lucrative alcohol markets.

It seemed natural that Russia should have an antialcohol campaign. The old superpower was experiencing a demographic crisis: a falling population and male life expectancy at just sixty-three years. One of the country's leading narcologists estimated that 26 percent of all deaths (30 percent of male and 17 percent of female deaths) were associated with alcohol.[2] Case studies by Western academics had produced similarly horrifying figures. Forty-three percent of deaths in men aged twenty-five to fifty-four years in the typical Russian city of Izhevsk were found to be due to "hazardous drinking."[3]

Another highly publicized study found that, over the period 1990–2001, 59 percent of all male deaths and 33 percent of all female deaths in the age group fifteen to fifty-four years were attributable to alcohol.[4] It was logical that the Russian authorities would wish to take action to preserve the population and reduce excessive alcohol consumption.

Or was it? At this point, history presents us with a problem. If the new antialcohol policy direction was a direct response to excessive consumption, why did it begin only in 2009 rather than ten or fifteen years earlier, when consumption was even higher? Digging a little deeper, we can begin to question some of the assumptions underlying this naive view of policy formation, according to which governments act to remedy self-evident problems in society. Why should we assume that a government has a vested interest in halting population decline or, indeed, that governments always act in the best interests of their people? Who decides which states of affairs constitute problems and how best to tackle them? What if the various actors within government are themselves divided on which policy direction to take? Political science provides the tools to analyze these complex factors shaping the realities of policy formation. This book combines insights from policy studies, comparative politics, and sociology to provide a more nuanced account of the directions that alcohol policy has taken in post-Soviet Russia. In doing so, it reveals the complex web of interests, attitudes, and influence shaping policy formation under the Putin regime.

The Complexities of Policy Formation

The idea that tougher policies on alcohol were a straightforward result of the Russian authorities' desire to tackle a population-level health crisis rests on a rather naive view of policy formation. In reality, policymaking is much more complex, combative, and haphazard than such a simplistic model would allow for. Public policy is formed through the competitive interaction of all those with an interest in that policy. A useful way to model this process is provided by the advocacy coalition framework (ACF) of policy formation. The ACF represents the competitive interaction of policy actors as forming a "policy sub-system."[5] Actors that share similar beliefs and policy preferences form "advocacy coalitions," which compete within the policy subsystem to try to get their preferred policy enacted.[6]

Rather than consensus on policy within the state, we should actually expect disagreement. This is because the state is not a single, unified actor but made up of individual departmental bureaucracies that, by definition, have narrow sectoral interests (for example, finance, law and order, health). Different departments and agencies compete with one another to pursue policies that promote their own interests and departmental ideologies[7] and to protect their policy territory or turf from encroachment by other bureaucratic departments.[8] Governments and bureaucrats are thus neither neutral arbiters of other actors' policy preferences nor benevolent guardians seeking to promote an agreed-upon national interest, but are actively pursuing interests and preferences of their own.[9] Numerous examples of this phenomenon are presented throughout the book. For example, the antialcohol campaign of the Gorbachev era was undermined by departmental interests within the state. The current federal alcohol regulator, Rosalkogolregulirovaniye, is a law unto itself, and has been accused of acting to skew the market in favor of certain business interests. A major 2011 law on alcohol was subject to such interdepartmental wrangling that it took nearly two years to enact, as individual ministries fought bitterly to ensure their preferred policy stances were the ones adopted.

The competitive wrangling of advocacy coalitions—including bureaucratic departments—is just one reason why high alcohol consumption does not automatically lead to a policy response. Another factor is how exactly that consumption is problematized. Social problems are not objective phenomena but rather are ways of thinking about and understanding certain real-world conditions.[10] The same state of affairs can be viewed and interpreted in many different ways. Even the ways in which Western academic and medical communities have problematized alcohol have changed over time, from a focus on alcoholism as a disease in the immediate postwar decades to a public health concern with average per capita consumption that emerged from the 1970s onward.[11] Thus, viewing high alcohol consumption as a demographic threat is only one of many possible interpretations of that phenomenon. Indeed, public health is still a relatively new and developing field in Russia compared with Western countries—a legacy of its neglect by the Soviet regime.[12] As chapters 1 and 2 show, alcohol consumption was problematized in various ways throughout the Soviet period, including as a challenge to state power, a public order problem, and a threat to economic productivity—but public health concerns were notably absent. Unsurprisingly, this legacy continued to shape alcohol policy in the post-Soviet era.

Policy responses to perceived problems are also shaped by the fact that policy space is limited. That is to say, a potentially infinite number of circumstances could be characterized as problems in need of state action, but decision makers have the time and resources to consider only a small proportion of them.[13] Thus, as a very minimum precondition for state action on alcohol consumption, that consumption would need to be interpreted as a priority problem area by an influential policy actor. As chapter 10 shows, this was not the case in post-Soviet Russia until at least the mid-2000s, partly because the transition from communism was bedeviled by a succession of acute political and economic crises.

The Ambivalence of Alcohol

So far we have considered the policymaking process in general. But alcohol as a product has one fundamental attribute that affects the development of policy regulating it: the ambivalence of its effects. That is to say, alcohol consumption has both positive and negative consequences, and this results in mixed attitudes toward it among both the general public and policymakers. This uncertainty is reflected in indecisive, uncohesive, and sometimes contradictory state policies.

The ambivalence of alcohol starts at the level of the individual. It is well documented that alcohol consumption can contribute to a range of health conditions, including cancers, cardiovascular conditions, liver cirrhosis, and diabetes.[14] But the balance of scientific evidence suggests that total abstention results in worse health outcomes than moderate consumption. There is a "well-established finding in the medical literature" that moderate drinking reduces the risk of coronary heart disease, and from middle age extends overall life expectancy.[15] Alcohol can act not only as a relaxant but also as a depressant and has been implicated in suicides.[16]

At a societal level, drinking is linked with numerous aspects of communal well-being, including sociability, in-group identification, social rituals, celebration, relaxation, and the enjoyment of food.[17] However, it is also associated with violence, crime, and other forms of antisocial behavior.[18] This ambivalence of alcohol is reflected in public opinion toward drinking: the Russian opinion polls analyzed in chapter 9 reveal hugely contradictory attitudes toward it. Drinking is seen as a problem, yet robust measures to

tackle it are unpopular. It would seem that people can neither live with alcohol nor live without it.

That alcohol consumption reaches into many areas of life means that issues related to alcohol are handled by a range of departments and levels of
government, even when they are not explicitly recognized as alcohol issues.[19]
The state's interests in alcohol can be categorized into four broad areas: fiscal (revenues raised for the exchequer from excise duty and other taxes); economic (production, trade, and inward investment); social policy (including
health and demographics); and public order (crime and the maintenance of
law and order).[20] The wide-ranging nature of the state's interests in alcohol
means that alcohol policies tend to be highly differentiated across government structures. In 2009, regulation of alcohol in the Russian Federation
was the responsibility of no fewer than seven separate ministries and departments.[21] There is nothing exceptional about this figure: one study of British
alcohol policy identified sixteen national government departments as having
some responsibility for alcohol issues.[22] Thus, state alcohol policies tend to
be highly ambivalent in their aims and effects. It is often doubtful whether
a single alcohol policy can be said to exist, as different sections of the state
bureaucracy have different priorities, interests, and departmental ideologies
and so often act in unilateral and contradictory ways.[23] In particular, the exchequer tends to have an interest in high consumption due to the revenues
generated, while law and order and health departments have an interest in
reducing consumption due to the externalities it creates. This problem is not
confined to modern states. The vodka historian David Christian noted that
the conflict within the state between reducing consumption and increasing
government revenues had resulted in "contradictory and ambivalent" alcohol policy in Russia since the seventeenth century.[24] Christian was writing
in 1990, just before the fall of the Soviet Union, but as will be shown throughout this book, these inherent tensions in state alcohol policy have remained
present during the post-Soviet era.

This brings us back to the task of explaining the initiative to reduce consumption launched by the Russian government in 2009. It turns out that this
single policy development cannot be understood in isolation. Rather, it needs
to be analyzed in the context of an ongoing history of Russian state policy
toward alcohol, and Russian political economy more generally. The analysis
contained in this book reveals the many ambivalences in Russian alcohol
policy: the conflicting interests within the state, the effect of informal power

networks in shifting policy away from official goals, and the need to respect the Russian population's own contradictory attitudes toward drinking.

Overview of the Book

For better or worse, the legacy of Soviet alcohol policy has continued to influence Russian thinking on alcohol policy throughout the post-Soviet period. One cannot fully comprehend these attitudes without understanding their historical roots. Throughout Russian history, alcohol revenues consistently provided a major share of the state's income. How, then, can we explain the various points in history (1914, 1958, 1972, 1985) where the state (to a greater or lesser degree) chose to cut off a key revenue source by dramatically cutting the supply of alcohol? And why, having been passed, did these dry periods tend to be so short-lived? These issues are addressed in chapters 1 and 2.

The newly independent Russian state's surrender of control over the alcohol market in the early 1990s can hardly be considered a dry period. Indeed, it is widely regarded as the opposite—the lifting of controls and the dismantling of the state monopoly on alcohol flooded Russia with cheap vodka. But this development shared one important similarity with the fleeting Soviet dry periods: it again represented the voluntary sacrifice by the state of its alcohol revenues. Chapter 3 shows how, from 1993 onward, the dominant theme in Russian alcohol policy was the state's attempt to regain control over the alcohol market that it so hastily surrendered in 1991–92, and thereby restore those revenues. But these efforts were severely undermined by a phenomenon of 1990s Russia that political economists have labeled "state capture": private individuals, firms, and groups (including the *mafiya*) extracting enormous privileges, or "rents,"[25] from the state due to its institutional weakness.

Chapter 4 describes how a significant change in the Russian political economy took place around 2000, coinciding with Vladimir Putin's election as president. State capture gave way to increased state control in the economy, as Putin's government moved against noncompliant oligarchs and seized control of strategically important industries. The state holding company Rosspirtprom was formed to recover federal control over alcohol assets, a move that can be seen as part of President Putin's reestablishment of the "power vertical" (centralized federal control) in view of the high value of alcohol revenues to regional authorities.

Yet formal state ownership of alcohol production assets was far from the only way in which economic interests and alcohol policymaking collided under Putin. Chapter 5 provides a case study of the complex kleptocracy in the Russian political economy. The interests in vodka production of some of Putin's most high-profile cronies—and their perceived influence on state policy—are analyzed in the context of *sistema*, the informal network-based system of governance in Russia through which allies of Putin are rewarded with business rents.[26] Understanding the interaction between the formal and informal aspects of the alcohol political economy in Russia is crucial to explaining the actions of the federal alcohol regulator Rosalkogolregulirovaniye (RAR) (chapter 6).

Despite the enduring popularity of vodka in Russia, a new beverage has enjoyed a dramatic growth in popularity in the twenty-first century: beer. This development has had a huge impact on alcohol policy formation, with the struggle between the vodka and beer industries for market share in Russia giving rise to lobbying and counter-lobbying (chapter 7). A further twist in this tale is provided by United Russia Duma deputy Viktor Zvagelskiy, who represents a fascinating case study of an alleged "vodka lobbyist" operating at the highest levels of lawmaking (chapter 8).

How much do Russians actually drink, and why are antialcohol policy measures popular in theory but not in practice? The difficulties in satisfactorily answering these questions are the subject of chapter 9. Chapter 10 looks at how alcohol has been constructed as a social problem in Russia, and why the large consumption peaks in 1994–95 and 2002–3 failed to provoke alarm among the ruling elite at the time, in spite of efforts by public health activists to problematize the issue.

In the mid-2000s, a new small but influential antialcohol movement emerged: an alliance of key members of a civil society elite including the Russian Orthodox Church, Public Chamber, and public health professionals. Chapter 11 shows how this new elite was able to seize cultural authority over the definition of the alcohol problem and thus set the antialcohol agenda where previous attempts by public health lobbyists had failed. It is vital to the survival of the political superelite that they are seen to act in the national interest. Once the "alcohol as demographic problem" was in the public eye, this included taking action against drinking. This led to the launch in 2009 of a new antialcohol initiative overseen by President Medvedev, which is analyzed in chapter 12.

Brewing executives working for companies that have major stakes in the Russian market, such as Carlsberg and Heineken, may legitimately wonder why rafts of increasingly restrictive legislation on the production and sale of beer have been passed by the Russian parliament. The commonplace explanation is that the government ordered such legislation as part of the so-called antialcohol campaign of 2009. However, this would be to fundamentally misunderstand the mechanisms of policy formation in Russia. The development and passage of the major 2011 law on alcohol regulation provides a pertinent illustration of this. The law did indeed implement many of the policies instructed by President Medvedev as part of the drive to reduce alcohol consumption. But crucially, the finer details were a perpetual battleground between the numerous policy stakeholders, and the final version impacted the beer industry much more harshly than originally anticipated. The stages of the bill's passage provide a case study of how the alcohol regulator RAR seemingly worked in tandem with Zvagelskiy to push its preferred policies, and how antialcohol rhetoric was used to provide moral cover (chapter 13). Chapter 14 shows how, even after the passage of the 2011 law and the fading away of the alcohol problem from public discourse, the same fiercely contested policy battles between advocacy coalitions have continued to shape alcohol regulation in Russia.

I conclude by assessing how the case of Russian alcohol policy can improve our understanding of policy processes, and what it can tell us about Russian governance more generally. On the evidence provided in this book, merely studying formal institutions and policy channels is insufficient for a full understanding of public policy in contemporary Russia. Rather, the kleptocratic nature of the Putin regime means that analysis of vested interests and informal sources of power—and how they interact with formal institutions to produce real-life policy outcomes—is essential.

Chapter 1

Feeding the State

Vodka from Tsarism to Communism

Just how did it come about that a clear, intoxicating liquid provided the economic foundations of the Russian state? Vodka distilling appeared in Russia some time before the beginning of the sixteenth century. Beer and mead predated vodka by several hundred years, owing to the less sophisticated technology required by brewing as opposed to distilling. These weaker drinks had already acquired a sacred role in important ceremonies and celebrations, and so were regarded as untouchable by the state for revenue-raising purposes. By contrast, vodka distilling emerged just at the time when the monarchic Russian state had taken shape as a strong authority. Thus, unlike beer brewing, vodka distilling never became an economic activity of the Russian working classes, instead quickly becoming monopolized by the Russian state and the feudal gentry that supported it.[1] The historian David Christian argued that the institution of vodka production—through such mechanisms as monopolies and tax farms—actually served to redistribute wealth upward from the working and peasant classes to the social elites.[2]

By the early eighteenth century vodka generated up to one-tenth of government revenues. From the middle of that century the fiscal contribution of vodka rose further still, and in the nineteenth century it became the largest single source of government revenue, providing up to one-third of revenues by the early nineteenth century and as much as 40 percent in the 1850s.[3] Indeed, the vodka historian William Pokhlebkin went as far as to state that "if vodka had not existed, it would have been necessary to invent it, not from any need for a new drink but as the ideal vehicle for indirect taxation."[4]

The exact means by which the Russian state extracted its vodka rents from the population changed over time. In the early nineteenth century the tax farm was the defining feature of the system: vodka production together with the collection of taxes on its sale was leased out to private entrepreneurs known as *otkupshchiki* (tax farmers).[5] The tax farming system was abolished in 1861, the same year as the emancipation reform that abolished serfdom. This was significant as both reforms represented major moves toward a modern form of government, with coercive powers belonging exclusively to the state rather than "contracted out" to social elites.[6] The excise duty system that replaced it lasted only a generation, however, for at the turn of the century a state vodka monopoly was introduced by reforming finance minister Sergey Witte. Rolled out in stages between 1895 and 1904, the monopoly was a retail one: the government became solely responsible for the wholesale and retail sale of vodka, buying it from both state and private distillers. The government claimed the motivation behind the reform was to reduce drunkenness among the population. As Witte stated, "The reform must above all serve the pursuit of national sobriety, and only after that the interests of the treasury."[7] Only by controlling the supply of vodka, the thinking went, could the government regulate consumption levels. But in doing so, the monopoly not only substantially increased state revenues from vodka but also *increased* rather than decreased consumption among the population.[8] The "drunken budget" was growing drunker still.

The tsarist state's alcohol monopoly naturally provided a rallying point for the various opposition groups that flourished in early twentieth-century Russia. Opposition politics and the Russian temperance movement became closely intertwined.[9] Vodka, claimed socialists and democrats from across the spectrum, not only propped up the finances of a parasitic regime but also ensured the working classes remained submissive and oppressed. The First All-Russian Congress for the Struggle against Drunkenness (1909–10) was so politically charged that some groups walked out, while other delegates were harassed by police, arrested, or prevented from delivering their reports.[10] The Bolsheviks, however, were awkward participants in this movement. Karl Marx and Friedrich Engels had scornfully dismissed "temperance fanatics" as a bourgeois attempt to support capitalist society by detracting from the true cause of alcoholism—capitalism itself.[11] Thus, although the Bolsheviks railed against the tsarist alcohol monopoly as exploitation of the working classes, they did not sit comfortably within the mainstream Russian temperance movement.

By 1914, even Sergey Witte was publicly attacking the state vodka monopoly that he had created some twenty years earlier. In a speech before the State Council, the former finance minister lamented, "The real object of the reform, the suppression of alcoholism, was pushed to the rear, and the object of the monopoly became the pumping of the people's money into the government treasury." "What have we done for the suppression of alcoholism, the great evil that corrupts and destroys the Russian people?" asked Witte rhetorically. "Absolutely nothing."[12]

The State's First Hunger Strike: Explaining Prohibition, 1914–25

Mark Lawrence Schrad has stated perhaps the most intriguing puzzle of Russian prohibition of 1914–25 as follows: "How do we explain that this bad policy was in fact the *only* policy agreed upon by the ultraconservative tsarist government, the liberal Provisional Government, *and* the revolutionary Bolshevik government?" The explanation would appear to lie in the fact that, despite the radically different ideological outlooks of the three governments, they shared highly centralized, autocratic policymaking institutions that allowed the personal beliefs of the individuals who headed them to override the financial interests of the wider system.[13]

The tsar himself, Nicholas II, appears to have been converted to temperance ideals on humanitarian grounds as early as 1910,[14] and his intervention led to some measures restricting vodka sales being adopted in peacetime, such as the option for local authorities to declare themselves "dry areas."[15] However, World War I was the trigger for tsarist prohibition to be implemented. Like the major restrictions on the sale of alcohol introduced by many other European countries at this time, prohibition was deemed necessary to ensure social order during wartime.[16] The policy naturally caused a massive blow to Russian public finances, since vodka revenues had accounted for between a quarter and a third of all income to the imperial treasury. However, the imperial policy-making institutional structure was prone to the "Emperor's new clothes" syndrome: if the tsar was committed to a policy, Russian ministers dared not tell him that they thought it would fail. Thus, Russian army officers "repeatedly offered the tsar glowing reports about the effectiveness of prohibition in facilitating rapid and orderly war mobilisation, despite widespread evidence to the contrary," while finance officials assured the tsar that the budgetary difficulties were only transitional.[17] In the end the government was forced to resort to printing money to fill the gaping hole in its finances, which triggered hyperinflation. Prohibition also disrupted the traditional trade cycle between urban and rural areas, creating grain shortages in the major towns, which fueled urban insurrection. Thus, it was arguably the case that through its unintended consequences, prohibition served as a catalyst to revolution.[18]

The subsequent events of 1917 were among the most important in the annals of world history. Wartime shortages—especially of bread—and the perceived incompetence of the regime led to strikes and demonstrations. In March, members of the Imperial parliament, the Duma, declared they were forming a provisional government to take charge of the country. Nicholas II was humiliatingly forced to abdicate his throne—from the carriage of his train, which had been halted by disloyal troops. But if the first revolution of the year had been achieved relatively peacefully, bloodshed was to follow soon after. In the October Revolution of 1917, the Bolshevik Party, led by Vladimir Lenin, overthrew the Provisional Government and seized power. However, the formation of a White Army to oppose Bolshevik rule led to a bloody civil war (1918–21) that cost literally millions of lives.

The War on Moonshine

The influence of Marxist-Leninist ideology on policy formation in general in the USSR was greatest in the early postrevolutionary period (until the early 1930s),[19] and alcohol policy was no exception. The early leadership, in particular Lenin and Leon Trotsky, had prohibitionist sympathies. The Soviet ideology on alcohol was that alcoholism resulted directly from capitalism, as the working classes turned to alcohol to escape their squalid living conditions and hopeless existence. Accordingly, alcoholism should die out naturally as socialism developed. The role of Bolshevik ideology in shaping alcohol policy was illustrated by Lenin's declaration at the Tenth Party Conference in 1921 that, "unlike capitalist countries where they use such things as vodka and other dope, we will not allow that to happen, for however profitable they may be in terms of trade, it will lead us back to capitalism and not forward to communism."[20] Trotsky publicly declared in July 1923 that "to develop, strengthen, organise, and complete the anti-alcohol regime in the country of reborn labour is our task. Our cultural and economic successes will increase as alcohol consumption falls. There can be no concessions."[21]

The new Bolshevik government did indeed retain outright prohibition in its early years, not just because of an ideological motivation but for more immediate practical reasons. The decision to preserve the dry law that had been introduced by the tsarist government in August 1914 was made with an eye toward the law-and-order situation.[22] Alcohol was seen as a military problem that threatened Bolshevik victory in the civil war. Sergey Gusev, chair of the Military Revolutionary Council, declared, "When the Communist gets drunk, the Menshevik can celebrate."[23]

The dry law inevitably led to widespread moonshining, creating a whole new problem for the Bolshevik government. The government had introduced a policy of forced grain requisitioning, which faced considerable opposition from the peasantry. The production of *samogon* (traditional home-brewed vodka) was seen by the Soviet authorities as direct rebellion against their attempt to enact socialism: a way of using up the grain for the peasants' own enjoyment rather than handing it over to the government for transportation to the cities.[24] *Samogon* production was thus problematized by the Bolshevik authorities not only as a cause of drunkenness and related consequences but as a threat to the establishment of a socialist economy and society.

In December 1919 the government passed the decree "On the prohibition on the territory of the RSFSR [Russian Soviet Federative Socialist Republic] of the making and selling of spirits, strong drinks and other alcoholic substances." The decree made the consequences of home brewing harsher still: the distilling of any amount of alcohol of any strength was subject to a punishment of "imprisonment with forced labour for not less than five years." Drinking *samogon* or appearing drunk in public was punishable by imprisonment for not less than one year. Yet despite the Party Programme of 1919 having declared that alcoholism was a "social disease" that the new regime would tackle as a matter of urgency, the decree actually represented what historian Helena Stone called "a quiet retreat from the dry law," since it also authorized the state production of alcoholic beverages up to sixteen proof. Over the next few years the maximum alcohol content of state-produced alcohol was successively raised, reaching forty proof before the end of 1921. The Bolshevik government was desperately trying to discourage people from distilling grain into *samogon*,[25] but it was also already getting a taste for the alcohol revenues that had sustained the tsarist regime.

The widespread persistence of moonshining among the peasantry was the result of massive disparities between urban and rural prices.[26] Grain distilled into *samogon* fetched a price that was several times that of grain in its natural state. *Samogon* at this time of high inflation became a highly valued commodity often used as a form of wage payment. The government, however, saw it as deliberate political opposition to the requisitioning policy, and it placed the moral blame for the famine of 1921–22 squarely on the moonshiners. In 1922–23 Soviet authorities conducted a blitz campaign against home brewing, the timing of which, according to one historian, "was very much influenced by fear for the food supply in a time of famine."[27] The Commissariat for Justice asked the courts to organize show trials in rural districts to shock the peasantry into abandoning moonshining; in some districts of Moscow special moonshine courts were set up to fast-track the judicial process. In the summer of 1923, over half of the prisoners in Moscow jails were home brewers.[28] Police searches for *samogon* distilling were also stepped up dramatically. Yet despite the draconian nature of the anti-*samogon* campaign, it made almost no impact on the scale of the activity.[29]

In 1925 the government restored the state monopoly on the production and sale of alcohol. The selling of *samogon* remained illegal. By this time, Stalin had become leader of the USSR, Lenin having died in 1924. It is difficult to judge how important the change of leadership was to the shift in direction of alcohol policy: Would Lenin have made the same decision? Certainly nowhere is Stalin cited as having strong prohibitionist views like those of Lenin, although Stalin himself legitimized his decision on the basis that Lenin had approved the state sale of alcohol as a temporary measure.[30]

As early as 1922 a front-page *Pravda* article had hinted at the policy change, asking rhetorically, "Would it not be better to return to the state sale of vodka if we are not able to struggle against moonshine?"[31] The other factor to consider is the failure of the anti-*samogon* blitz campaign of 1923–24 to reduce its production. If people were going to drink alcohol regardless of its legality, logically it was better that the revenue went to the state rather than private pockets. As one top Bolshevik official put it, "The selling of *samogon* had taken on such a scale that it in the end required the sale of vodka."[32]

Communists Divided

Despite the official Soviet policy reversal with respect to alcohol, a brief antialcohol campaign took place in 1928–29. This campaign reflected the split within the regime as to what the Soviet approach to alcohol should be, which itself was merely part of a broader division as to how socialism in Russian should be built.[33] The Right Opposition—which included the economist Nikolay Bukharin, a leading opponent of state alcohol sales—held that the transition to a Soviet industrial economy should be undertaken gradually through a continuation of the New Economic Policy. Although Stalin initially advocated this view, once he became leader of the USSR he soon switched to the contrary view, which sought to implement rapid industrialization and a centrally planned economy in the shortest possible time.

As state sales of alcoholic beverages rose (accounting for 12 percent of state revenue by 1927–28), finance officials pressed for production to be increased still further. Initial projections by the State Planning Committee, Gosplan, envisaged an increase of almost 80 percent over the period 1927–31.[34] However, such plans faced fierce opposition from certain elements of the Soviet ruling elite. The renewed state retailing of alcohol had dismayed some party members on ideological grounds: they considered its sale exploitative and attempted to mobilize against the policy from within. Sovnarkom (the Council of People's Commissars, the forerunner of the Council of Ministers) passed legislation in March 1927 outlawing alcohol sales in cafés, theaters, and restaurants and encouraged the establishment of local antialcohol cells. This led to the formation of the Society for the Struggle with Alcoholism (OBSA) in February 1928.[35] A public statement by the OBSA of its aims suggested a tacit opposition to the policy of funding economic development by

alcohol revenues: ". . . to assist Soviet power in the rapid elimination of alcoholism: (i) by the development of the culture of daily life and of healthy rec-
reation, *allowing state incomes to be found from less harmful sources*; (ii) by
inculcating a consciousness of the personal and social harmfulness of alcoholism and weaning working people off alcoholism in their daily lives"
(italics mine).[36]

Many of the OBSA's founding members were prominent members of the
Soviet elite, not least Bukharin, who as editor of *Pravda* was able to lead a
major antialcohol campaign in the press during 1928–29.[37] By January 1929
more than two hundred branches of the Society had been formed, with the
All-Union Council of Anti-Alcohol Societies set up to coordinate their
activities. Activities included demonstrations against drunkenness, such as
children marching with banners to campaign against drunk parents, and
persuading local authorities to take measures such as restricting times and
places of alcohol sales.[38]

The OBSA lobbied against encouraging consumption of vodka on economic grounds, arguing that reducing consumption would boost state
income by increasing economic productivity and reducing illness, absenteeism, and crime. The widespread publicity the organization's efforts received
attests to the broad support it had within the party. Gosplan chair Gleb
Krzhizhanovskiy announced a bold plan at the Fifth Congress of the Sovi-
ets in May 1929 to reduce urban per capita alcohol consumption by 70 percent
by the end of the first Five Year Plan. This did not sit well with the Commissariat of Finance's planned increases in alcohol production, and ultimately
the power struggle was won by the pro-alcohol side. Krzhizhanovskiy was
removed from Gosplan and the Central Committee reversed his decision to
aim for a decrease in consumption. Bukharin was removed from his post as
editor of *Pravda* in April 1929 and expelled from the Politburo just a few
months later.[39] The Anti-Alcohol Societies were wound down and merged
with other societies that had a more general (and less politically controversial) focus on healthy living.[40] But the most decisive moment in Stalinist
alcohol policy came a year later, in 1930, when Stalin explicitly instructed
Molotov to expand vodka production to the greatest extent possible for the
sake of the defense of the country—to finance a major expansion of the Soviet army: "Where can we find the money? It is necessary, in my opinion, to
increase (*as much as possible*) vodka production. We need to get rid of a false
sense of shame and directly and openly move towards the *greatest possible*

expansion of vodka production for the sake of a real and serious defence of our country. Consequently, this matter has to be taken into account *immediately*. The relevant raw materials for vodka production should be formally included in the national budget for 1930/1. Bear in mind that a serious development of civil engineering will also require a lot of money, for which again we will have to turn to vodka."[41]

From here on in, the very notion that an alcohol problem existed in the Soviet Union (in any interpretation of the term) was swiftly removed—through the means of silence. The theme vanished from the press.[42] The topic of alcoholism was simply not mentioned in official Soviet discourse for about the next twenty years, until after Stalin's death.[43]

Chapter 2

Soviet Policy Doublethink

Doublethink means the power of holding two contradictory beliefs in one's mind simultaneously, and accepting both of them. . . . The essential act of the Party is to use conscious deception while retaining the firmness of purpose that goes with complete honesty. To tell deliberate lies while genuinely believing in them, to forget any fact that has become inconvenient, and then, when it becomes necessary again, to draw it back from oblivion for just so long as it is needed, to deny the existence of objective reality and all the while to take account of the reality which one denies—all this is indispensably necessary."[1]

The "Party" described in this quote is not the Communist Party of the Soviet Union. It is the government of Oceania in George Orwell's dystopian novel, *Nineteen Eighty-Four*. But as with all great satire, Orwell's fictional doublethink is a shrewd reflection of the reality that inspired it. Soviet sociologist Vladimir Shlapentokh observed that "the Soviet political elite operates with two types of standards—ideal and practical." While official Soviet discourse would portray the average Soviet citizen as already close to the ideal, when Soviet officials left the realm of ideology and propaganda and concerned themselves with addressing practical problems, they would shift from the model of the ideal Soviet citizen to a more realistic conception.[2]

A nice illustration of this doublethink at the bureaucratic level is provided by V. V. Shabalin's research into how Communist Party ethics committees in the 1920s classified drunken gatherings by party officials. While official Soviet ideology at this time regarded alcohol consumption as an unethical capitalist "survival" and de facto crime against Soviet society, drunken incidents inside the party bureaucracy were so common that the ethics committees were forced to take a more practical approach: "It could be said that alcohol consumption was an integral part of the way of life of responsible officials of that period [the 1920s]. Drunkenness was so widespread that the control committees which ensured compliance with party ethics developed an official classification for its limits. If responsible officials gathered to drink a couple of litres of beer, this was characterised as a *pyanka* or *vypivka*. If they drank a lot and to senselessness, this was a *popoyka* or even a '*popoyka* leading to diminished responsibility.'"[3]

The Soviet authorities' attitude toward alcohol throughout most of the postwar period was characterized by classic doublethink. One the one hand, official discourse denied that alcohol use was a problem. On the other hand, the leadership acknowledged that it was a problem, and periodically developed policies to address it. Despite the hugely differing political climates under the Soviet leaders Nikita Khrushchev, Leonid Brezhnev, Yuri Andropov, and Konstantin Chernenko, the short-lived measures adopted during their reigns were remarkably similar.

First, the denials. Although the topic of alcohol abuse began to be discussed publicly again soon after Stalin's death, up until the late 1970s the overriding discourse remained firmly politically correct. That is to say, the Marxist notion that alcohol abuse was a "survival of capitalism" and would eventually die out naturally under communism remained predominant. Although the "survivals" theory was briefly critiqued during the Khrushchev thaw (Khrushchev himself explicitly denied it in relation to drunkenness in 1958, asserting that "excessive drinking today is explicable only by poor education"), it was not until the 1970s that it came to be regarded as discredited.[4] The author of an English-language study of Soviet drinking complained in 1971 that "Soviet journalists and pamphleteers are content to denounce these phenomena [heavy drinking occasions] as 'survivals of the past.'"[5]

The party line was that alcoholism was higher in capitalist countries than in the USSR. This assertion was supported by inaccurate and out-of-date data. One anti-alcoholism brochure published in 1954 used incorrectly cited data from 1928.[6] The second edition of the *Bolshaya Sovetskaya Entsiklopediya* (*Big Soviet Encyclopaedia*), published in 1950, used data from 1928 to 1932 to assert that "consumption of alcoholic beverages is significantly lower in the USSR than any other country."[7] The official position of the Soviet government in the 1970s was that the prevalence of alcoholism in the USSR was "3 to 4 times as low as in capitalistic countries," a line that was repeated in the Soviet mass media and numerous scientific publications.[8]

To maintain this pretense in the face of ever-increasing alcohol production and sale, the Soviet government resorted to gradually eliminating alcohol-related statistics from the public domain. The statistical yearbook *Narodnoye khozyaistvo SSSR* (*The Soviet Economy*) ceased reporting vodka output in 1963, although some of the Union's constituent republics continued to report data in their own yearbooks into the 1970s.[9] The way the Soviet authorities had manipulated the statistics to conceal the true level of alcohol consumption was analyzed in a seminal *samizdat*[10] essay of the late 1970s, A. Krasikov's "Commodity Number One."[11] Krasikov showed that the missing beverage figures had been subsumed under the column "Other foodstuffs," which in 1963 suddenly leapt tenfold—the approximate value of the missing alcohol figures. The description of what "Other foodstuffs" included (previously listed as coffee, spices, vitamins, mushrooms, etc.) had also conveniently vanished in the same year.[12] Krasikov concluded, "Not in vain has the subject of alcohol completely vanished from the press and is steadily fading even from statistics."[13]

Censorship also took place in the academic sphere. In 1966, Boris Segal conducted a survey among the male workers at the Moscow Dynamo factory, which found that 37 percent of the sample population could be characterized as excessive drinkers or alcoholics. This unwelcome finding was deleted by the censors from the published version of Segal's work.[14] The extreme political sensitivity of suggesting that alcohol abuse was a problem in the USSR is illustrated by the following story related by one respondent, a public health scholar:

I taught classes in public health in 1982; it was under Brezhnev, a very tense situation. There was a class on alcohol abuse, a chapter in the textbook with statistics on alcohol abuse in France, the UK and other countries, but nothing about the USSR or Russia—*nothing*. And one of my students asked me a question: "What's going on, you see so many drunk people on the streets, do you have some statistics?" But after that—not on my initiative—this person was reported by the Young Communist League as someone who was asking inappropriate questions. This information was absolutely classified—it was a big dirty secret of the Soviet system.

Yet at the same time that the Soviet authorities were claiming that alcohol use was not problematic, the fact that antialcohol policies were periodically pursued throughout the postwar era shows that alcohol use was de facto regarded as a problem by the state. Official discourse on alcohol during these decades thus took on an inherently contradictory nature: as the historian Misha Levine put it, "the warning of danger and, in the same breath, assuring the public that there was nothing to worry about."[15]

Under the rule of Nikita Khrushchev (1953–64), the Soviet government passed a decree entitled "On strengthening the struggle against drunkenness and bringing order to the spirits trade" (1958).[16] The decree pronounced that antialcohol activity should not be regarded as a short-term campaign, but rather "everyday work for the eradication of one of the most tenacious and harmful survivals of the capitalist past." Despite the fine rhetoric, this "everyday work" boiled down to a series of restrictions on the sale of strong alcoholic beverages. Vodka could no longer be sold in stores selling foodstuffs, in cafés or canteens, or in any places of trade or public consumption (with the exception of restaurants) located at stations, airports, and their surrounding areas. A large number of kiosks and stalls that sold vodka on draft were closed, and vodka could not be sold before 10 a.m. Vodka and cognac sales in restaurants were subject to a 50 percent surcharge and restricted to 100 mL per customer. At the same time, it was planned over the next seven years to significantly increase the output of not only soft drinks but also beer and wine. The result of the prohibition of vodka consumption in traditional on-trade outlets was that drinking spilled out into the streets. Meanwhile, while wine and beer sales did indeed increase as envisioned by the decree (wine sales increased fourfold over the 1960s), the instruction to decrease vodka production was apparently ignored, since its sale actually increased by 60 percent over the 1960s.[17] The productive and revenue-raising arms of the state, it seems, had little interest in obeying the antialcohol directives of the Soviet leadership.

The next attempt at an antialcohol campaign after the 1958 effort under Khrushchev came in May 1972, when the Soviet government passed a decree entitled "On measures to strengthen the fight against drunkenness and alcoholism."[18] Once again the decree stipulated a significant reduction in the production of strong alcoholic beverages, with increased production of wine and beer to compensate. And once again, the measures were not introduced with any great conviction: vodka production actually increased, and there is little evidence that the USSR's long-serving leader Leonid Brezhnev (general secretary 1964–82, and himself a very heavy drinker) took them seriously.[19] The planned changes in the structure of consumption of alcoholic beverages did not happen, because ultimately the government was unwilling either to sacrifice its budgetary income from vodka or to make the necessary investment in its own production facilities to supply weak alcoholic beverages in place of vodka.[20]

The *nomenklatura*—the ruling class under the communist regime—contained a significant number of heavy drinkers for whom alcohol was in "virtually unlimited supply."[21] One Soviet author's review of antialcohol policy during the 1960s complained about officials' "liberal" attitudes toward heavy drinking.[22] Under both Khrushchev and Brezhnev, prohibition was never regarded as a real option. Rather, so-called cultured drinking was the main ideal driving alcohol policy, with Eduard Babayan—a department head of the USSR Ministry of Health and chief narcologist of the USSR—for years its main exponent.[23] Connor claimed in 1971 that "articles in the press often make a distinction between beer and wine on the one hand and stronger drink on the other—thereby, in the minds of critics, encouraging the use of the former."[24] (This distinction is arguably still reflected in contemporary Russian social attitudes toward beer, which tend to regard it as something akin to a soft drink.) Moreover, alcohol revenues continued to provide a substantial contribution to the state budget: in 1979 they accounted for 29 percent of all taxes paid by the Soviet population, and 9 percent of total state revenue.[25]

During the 1970s there was a notable decline in the accepted use of the "survivals" theory—the notion that social deviances such as alcohol abuse were merely a relic of capitalism and would die out of their own accord as the USSR progressed toward socialism.[26] It is instructive to compare the entries on "alcoholism" in the second and third editions of the *Bol'shaya Sovetskaya Entsiklopediya* (*Big Soviet Encyclopaedia*), published in 1950 and 1970, respectively.[27] The clear theme that ran through the 1950 entry was that alcoholism was a product of capitalist exploitation: "Alcoholic drinks have existed since time immemorial in the form of wines, mead and beer. However, only with the development of capitalism has alcoholism become a social scourge for the exploited masses. Two elements have particularly contributed to the growth of alcoholism under capitalism: the creation of harsh, inhumane living conditions, from which many seek a temporary 'escape' in an alcoholic haze; and the development of the mass production of vodka in large factories, sold at low prices."[28]

The 1950 entry proceeded to support its thesis by using out-of-date statistics to suggest that per capita alcohol consumption in the USSR was a fraction of that in capitalist countries.[29] In the 1970 entry on alcoholism, by contrast, the narrative that alcohol abuse was a product of capitalism was entirely absent. The statement "In Soviet society alcoholism is considered an evil" is as close as the entry came to suggesting that drinking was anti-Soviet behavior, and in discussing the measures enacted by Soviet institutions to tackle alcohol abuse it de facto acknowledged that the phenomenon was as much a problem for Soviet society as it was for its capitalist counterparts.[30]

The law-and-order paradigm had a dominant influence on how alcohol was problematized in the USSR in the postwar period. The militia (Soviet police) played a major role in the conceptualization of alcohol problems, publishing articles that emphasized the adverse effects of alcohol on public order and workplace discipline.[31] This dominance of the militia construction of alcohol problems was reflected in treatment facilities for alcoholics. In the mid-sixties the system of LTPs (*lechebno-trudovoy profilaktoriy*) was established. These were medical-correctional institutions for the compulsory treatment of alcoholism run by the Ministry of Internal Affairs (MVD). They often resembled prisons, with forced labor making up the main form of "treatment."

The 1985–88 Antialcohol Campaign

It is hard to think of a world leader whose reputation differs so much between domestic and foreign audiences as Mikhail Gorbachev. Lauded in the West for bringing democracy to the USSR and helping to end the Cold War (he was awarded the Nobel Peace Prize in 1990), he is typically regarded in Russia as a weak leader who unleashed a series of reforms without fully comprehending their consequences, then stood feebly by as the USSR disintegrated around him. But even had he not presided over the breakup of a global superpower, Gorbachev's dismal historical reputation among Russians was still more or less assured. For he also oversaw the most concerted attempt at prohibition in the USSR since the 1920s—a deeply unpopular antialcohol campaign that is still remembered with scorn by many Russians to this day.

Gorbachev became leader of the USSR in March 1985, and just two months later the government launched its antialcohol campaign. Vodka prices were doubled in two steps, so that by August 1986 a regular half-liter bottle cost 10 rubles, which was around a day's pay for the average worker. Sharp decreases in alcohol production were ordered, and sales were successfully cut from 8.4 liters of pure alcohol per capita in 1984 to 7.1 liters in 1985, 4.4 liters in 1986, and 3.3 liters in 1987. Vodka could be bought in only a limited number of shops and within limited hours. Those who were children at the time recall being forced to stand in line for several hours to reserve a parent's place in the queue while they went about their daily business. These measures were accompanied by aggressive local-level campaigns against drunkenness in the workplace and in public places, which in some cases took on the character of witch hunts.[32] Popular resentment against the shortage of vodka was neatly captured in an oft-cited Soviet joke from the time: *One man became so fed up of standing in a queue for hours on end to buy a bottle of vodka that he set off for the Kremlin to shoot Gorbachev. Returning several hours later, the man admitted defeat: the queue to kill Gorbachev was even longer than the queue to buy vodka.*

There are differing opinions about what the formal goals of the Gorbachev campaign actually were.[33] While the general aim was undoubtedly to decrease the level of alcohol consumption, the end target of the reductions was unclear—was the final goal total sobriety or simply a lower level of consumption? There are contradictory insider accounts on this point. Nikolay Ryzhkov, who was one of the leading opponents of the campaign within the government, claimed that there was a secret list of planned reductions in production of alcoholic beverages by year, and that ultimately production was to be reduced "practically to zero."[34] Gorbachev, however, maintained that it was "a myth" that the campaign represented a dry law, and claimed that such an option "was not even considered, because it was clearly unrealistic."[35]

How can we explain the dramatic policy shift, from the sense of resignation throughout the postwar period that little could be done to influence alcohol consumption and that prohibition had already been shown to be ineffective, to the launching of a radical prohibition campaign in 1985? The long-term enabling factor was an ideological shift in the way that alcohol consumption was problematized, which made reducing that consumption more of a priority for the political leadership. But the real catalyst for change was a contingent factor: power shifts between the various political actors involved allowed a small number of temperance advocates to gain control over alcohol policy, albeit for only a very short period.

Let us first consider the shift in the problematization of alcohol that took place in the 1970s and 1980s, which led to increasing concern being paid to consumption by the political leadership. Official Soviet data showed a steady rise in alcohol consumption throughout the postwar era, from 4.6 liters per capita in 1960 to 10.45 liters in 1984.[36] Such data became publicly available again under Gorbachev, after an absence from published Soviet statistics of some two decades.[37] True consumption was undoubtedly even higher if one takes account of home brewing: Treml has estimated figures of 9.8 liters for 1960 and 14.25 liters for 1984.[38] At the same time, the decline of the "survivals" theory had enabled a broadening of academic research on alcohol beyond the traditional militia paradigm. From the late 1970s research began to emerge by economists, sociologists, and medical experts, explicitly drawing attention to high levels of alcoholism and alcohol-related problems. An alarmist 1984 paper entitled "The Truth about Alcoholism in the USSR," which was widely publicized in the West, prompted the USSR's chief narcologist to give an official rebuttal and claim that alcoholism was actually on the decline.[39] Economics-based research attempted to calculate aggregate economic losses due to alcohol, undermining the old fiscal argument about the beneficial state income provided by vodka sales. It should be noted that this development demands further explanation in itself. How did this new critical research in the USSR come about? Who authorized and funded it, and why? This question has not yet been satisfactorily addressed by the academic literature. But whatever the explanation, it is clear that by the early 1980s alcohol use was increasingly being interpreted as an economic problem rather than just a law-and-order one.

The two historians who have produced the most in-depth studies of the Gorbachev campaign, Stephen White and Misha Levine, have concluded that the Politburo defined the alcohol problem in terms of its effect on both economic productivity and public order. Economic productivity (particularly catching up and overtaking the major capitalist economies) had become the major concern of the Communist Party at this time. As Levine put it, "The race and global rivalry with the USA was a real obsession and deeply motivated everything the Party did."[40] Leninist theory maintained that communist economies should enjoy higher productivity through technical superiority, but by the 1980s it became clear that the USSR was not catching up and that something had to change. This led to the idea that technical superiority demanded a new Soviet personality, which included sobriety. Thus, for the Soviet leadership the alcohol issue was above all a problem of economic efficiency.[41] This economic concern is evident in the Central Committee's resolution of 7 May 1985 entitled "On measures to overcome drunkenness and alcoholism." The resolution claimed that "great economic and moral harm" had been caused by alcohol use, and decreed that yearly decreases in alcohol production were essential for "the economic and social development of the Soviet Union." It further urged the members of all workplaces to create "a climate of intolerance of drunkenness, to any violation of labour discipline and order."[42]

As the reference to "moral harm" suggests, crime and public order still accounted for a significant part of the way the alcohol problem was framed in the USSR at the time of the campaign. The Central Committee resolution condemned drunkenness as "immoral, antisocial behaviour,"[43] and an aggressive clampdown on public drunkenness became a particular focus of the campaign.[44] As with the productivity considerations, the concern over discipline, morality, and public order predated Gorbachev. The problematization of alcohol in the early 1980s can be seen as linked to the aim of restoring "social discipline" established under Andropov and continued under Chernenko.[45] This took the form of a number of related campaigns. One of the main elements was a vigorous anticorruption drive, which included a purge of close associates of Brezhnev who were regarded as "corrupt" by the new personnel.[46] A second major element of the post-Brezhnev social discipline drive was an attempt to strengthen workplace discipline and law and order more generally. This included a crackdown on absenteeism at work (in 1983 there was a series of police raids on shops and public baths to catch workers absent without leave) and on drunkenness at the workplace and in public places.[47]

By the time Gorbachev came to power in 1985, alcohol consumption was conceived as more problematic by Soviet authorities than it had been in previous decades. Heavy consumption was increasingly regarded as having economic costs and holding back productivity. It is thus perhaps not surprising that a new antialcohol reform was already being prepared some years prior to 1985, although not with any great sense of urgency. A commission on the struggle against alcohol abuse had been established under Brezhnev, but it was not particularly active.[48]

What this new problematization of alcohol does not explain is why the reform was passed shortly after Gorbachev became general secretary, and why it took the extreme form that it did. For this, we need to look at the institutional factors and personalities that brought about the 1985 campaign. Perhaps the most important factor was a personnel change that brought about a power shift between the two different tendencies in alcohol policy: the sobriety tendency was able to triumph over the cultured drinking tendency.[49] The crucial change was the promotion of Yegor Ligachev—a teetotaler and longtime antialcohol activist—to the Politburo in 1985. Ligachev himself played down his personal role in the campaign in his memoirs, emphasizing that the decision to "declare war on drunkenness" was a collective one and that he did not even formally play a role in drafting the decree that launched the campaign.[50] However, historians generally agree that it was Ligachev together with Mikhail Solomentsev (chair of the party Control Committee and thus responsible for issues of discipline) who formed the main driving force behind the campaign.[51]

Gorbachev himself did not play a major role in the development and implementation of the policy, but his support for the principle of the reform was crucial.[52] Once promoted to the Politburo, Ligachev quickly established himself as Gorbachev's right-hand man.[53] Gorbachev, reasonably sympathetic to the goals of his close comrade's favored project, granted him a free hand in implementing it. Gorbachev later stated in his memoirs that the situation with regard to alcohol in the USSR had become "catastrophic," particularly the annual losses to the economy due to drunkenness. However, he insisted that the plan had been to reduce alcohol sales gradually, and blamed Ligachev and Solomentsev's excessive zeal for them going beyond the plan "to the point of absurdity." Gorbachev expressed regret that he did not intervene at this point, noting that "many serious people" had drawn his attention to the excesses of the campaign in private conversations. However, he stated that his heavy workload in other areas and "excessive reticence" prevented him from doing so.[54]

Almost all of the major government ministries, not to mention senior sections of the Communist Party, were at best lukewarm—and at worst wholeheartedly opposed—to even a moderate antialcohol campaign. Even though the leadership accepted in principle that reducing alcohol consumption would benefit the economy as a whole, a dry law de facto conflicted with almost all Soviet state interests at a departmental level.[55] Some in the Politburo were to claim after the antialcohol campaign that they had had reservations about it but did not voice their opposition at the time. Others who refused to sign the resolution were either forced into retirement (in the case of finance minister Vasiliy Garbuzov) or threatened with not only dismissal but expulsion from the Communist Party (in the case of the deputy director of the state planning agency Gosplan).[56] "The question for which we still have no answer," mused political scientist Jerry Hough in 1979, "is the outcome if the General Secretary favours one course of action and a Politburo majority favours another."[57] The evidence of the resolution of May 1985 suggests that it was possible for the general secretary to force through a measure in the face of resistance from his colleagues, in spite of the principle of collective leadership within the Politburo.

The Undoing of the Campaign

Although all of the major Soviet ministries were opposed to the antialcohol campaign under Gorbachev, they were unable to prevent its passage due to Gorbachev's personal support for the measure. They did succeed, however, in obstructing some measures from being implemented as planned, and in bringing about the eventual abandonment of the campaign. In short, the campaign was sabotaged from within by powerful sections of the state itself.[58]

The Ministry of Finance (Minfin) suffered particularly heavily from the campaign since the state sale of alcoholic beverages provided a significant share of its total tax revenues (around 12–13 percent in 1982, a figure that had not varied greatly since the late 1920s).[59] The economist Nikolay Shmelev, a vocal advocate of *perestroika*, warned in a *Noviy mir* essay that the sacrifice of vodka revenues was putting the financial stability of the USSR at risk: "But by giving away its revenue to the bootlegger, the government in the last two years has sharply increased its budgetary imbalance and incurred a deficit which is today being covered in a most dangerous and unhealthy way, by the printing press."[60]

The impact on government finances was one of the main reasons for the eventual abandonment of the antialcohol campaign. In 1991 Gorbachev himself acknowledged that the lost taxation revenue from the antialcohol campaign contributed to his government's budget deficit.[61]

Although there were no privately owned alcohol companies at the time of the Gorbachev campaign, that is not to say that alcohol trade interests did not exist. They did, but they were located within the state rather than outside it, notably within the Department for Trade (Mintorg). While the usual profit motive that exists within capitalist systems may have been absent, the state's own institutions of alcohol production and sale nevertheless fiercely defended their territory.[62] There was widespread resistance at central, regional, and local levels to implementing the decreed cuts in production. Mintorg was reprimanded by the Central Committee's Committee of Party Control for failing to reduce the hours for sale of vodka, and actually increasing distribution of alcohol to some union republics in 1986. The USSR Gosplan (State Planning Committee) stubbornly planned an increase in total alcohol sales for 1987, and figures for the first half of 1987 showed that even in those areas where Gosplan had planned reductions (for example, vodka sales), the reductions were not fulfilled.[63] The "industry" complained that it faced several barriers to implementation. The fact that there was significantly less revenue to be made from nonalcoholic beverages acted as a serious disincentive for the government industries concerned to switch production, as it would be almost impossible for them to hit their plan targets and collect bonuses. Mintorg played its part in convincing the Politburo to abandon the campaign through the so-called Terekh memorandum of the summer of 1988. Named after the minister of trade, Kondrat Terekh, the memorandum consisted of a dossier of evidence on the negative results of the antialcohol restrictions, including trade and fiscal losses, illegal production, the increasingly intolerable situation with regard to queuing, and the use of nonconsumable alcohol (e.g., aftershave) by the population.[64]

The campaign had no official end; rather, it faded away through a succession of quiet policy reversals. In July 1987, the criminal liability for personal *samogon* use was canceled, and in January 1988 the state sales of alcoholic beverages once again began to increase. In the winter of 1988 the Moscow authorities bowed to public discontent about the unavailability of vodka by increasing the number of outlets and hours of trading. Finally, in October 1988 the Communist Party passed a resolution ordering Soviet authorities to put an end to the situation of mass queuing for alcohol. Although the resolution officially stated that the campaign should continue through different means, de facto it signaled the end of the campaign.[65]

By the time the Soviet Union collapsed in 1991, alcohol policy had returned to a state of normality for the Russian population. Vodka was once again freely available and consumption returned to pre-1985 levels, albeit with illegal alcohol and *samogon* taking a greater share than before.[66] However, with the dramatic new economic and political circumstances of the post-Soviet era, a new volatile period in alcohol policy lay ahead.

Chapter 3

The Parasites Feed

State Capture under Yeltsin

In 1994, the chair of the Russian Foundation for Invalids of the War in Afghanistan (RFIVA), Mikhail Likhodey, was assassinated by a bomb outside his apartment. Three years later, mourners gathered at Moscow's Kotlyakovskoye cemetery on the anniversary of Likhodey's death for a memorial service. Another bomb went off, claiming fourteen victims. The RFIVA's new president, Sergey Trakhirov, was among them. Altogether the RFIVA suffered thirty-four killings and sixty-two woundings in such violent incidents.[1] In 1997, the president of the Russian Ice Hockey Federation, Valentin Sych, was ambushed by a group of assassins while traveling by car, and shot dead instantly. His wife and driver narrowly escaped with their lives. The first deputy president of the National Sports Federation (NSF), Boris Fyodorov, narrowly escaped an assassination attempt.[2]

What was behind this spate of extreme violence against the leaders of ostensibly benign charitable and nonprofit organizations? The answer, of course, was vodka. Several such organizations—including the three mentioned above—had succeeded in the mid-1990s in extracting customs privileges from the weak Russian state. This gave them the right to import alcohol and cigarettes without paying excise duty. The scope for superprofits was enormous—one estimate valued the RFIVA's excise privileges at $200 million.[3] Inevitably, the *mafiya* groupings that dominated the Russian economy at this time were soon fighting over the spoils.

Political scientists have described the arbitrary privileges extracted from the weak Russian state during the 1990s as "state capture."[4] Excise privileges were just one form of state capture. Others included the asset stripping of state companies, the state's de facto loss of control over its functions of tax collection and law and order, and the infiltration of the state by the *mafiya*. State capture was to have a profound effect on the alcohol situation in 1990s Russia, and the attempts to reverse it have shaped alcohol policy for much of the post-Soviet period. Yet ironically, in the period immediately following the fall of the USSR, it was the state itself that seemed determined to surrender control over the alcohol market.

The State's Third Hunger Strike, 1991–92

Two significant "hunger strikes" took place in the USSR when the state voluntarily deprived itself of its enormous alcohol revenues: the 1914–25 prohibition and the Gorbachev prohibition of 1985–88. The third in this series of hunger strikes was the dramatic liberalization of the alcohol market as part of Yeltsin's market reforms. At first, the conceptual grouping of prohibition with alcohol market liberalization may seem contradictory: the former policy dramatically restricted alcohol's availability, while the latter flooded the market with it. However, in one important respect—the historical dependence of the Russian state on alcohol revenues—the two policies are conceptually analogous. Both the Soviet-era prohibitions and the Yeltsin-era market liberalization dramatically reduced income to the state budget to the extent of contributing to fiscal crises, with the result that the state was compelled to reverse the policies (or more accurately in the case of the third, post-Soviet hunger strike, *attempt* to reverse it). While the reversal of a prohibition is relatively straightforward, trying to reestablish state control over a liberalized, semicriminal alcohol market proved a mammoth task. It is this attempt to regain control over the lucrative alcohol market that has defined alcohol policy throughout the entire post-Soviet period.

The most obvious way in which the state surrendered control over the alcohol market was the abolition of the state's monopoly on the production and trade of alcohol. This was brought to an end by presidential decree in June 1992. But there was another policy that, through unintended consequences, encouraged the development of a black market that was beyond the state's reach. Ironically, rather than liberalization per se, it was the continued state regulation of vodka prices in the context of price liberalization for most other consumer goods. Some of the damage had already been done in the final year of the Soviet regime. In April 1991, the Soviet prime minister Valentin Pavlov brought in price reforms that allowed 30 percent of goods to be sold at market prices, while a further 55 percent of goods were subject to dramatic price increases (60 percent on average). The price of lower-grade vodka, however, was frozen at its previous level. The net result was that the real price of vodka (i.e., relative to the consumer price index) fell by 52 percent in 1991.[5] The Soviet Union was officially dissolved on 26 December 1991. The rapid transition to the free market under Yeltsin saw extensive price liberalization come into effect on 2 January 1992, in accordance with the presidential and government decrees "On measures for price liberalization" passed in December 1991. Prices were freed for almost all goods except those considered "essential public goods," such as bread, milk, salt, baby food, and medicines. It is a measure of the perceived political importance of alcohol that vodka and for-consumption ethyl alcohol were also included on the list of essential public goods. Vodka therefore retained a stable, state-designated price until April 1992, when the prices of essential public goods were also freed (although regional governments still had the right to limit vodka prices, and many did so). As the price of vodka was kept artificially low while prices for other consumer goods were rising, its real price fell dramatically—by 44.4 percent between January and May 1992.[6] The result of the massive fall in the real price of vodka in 1991–92 was that the legal supply could not match demand: vodka disappeared from the shelves, and illegal alcohol filled the vacuum, bringing months of enrichment for *mafiya* structures.[7] Indeed, in this early period, private sales of alcohol commanded higher prices than state ones, partly because the market-clearing price was significantly above the state-regulated price, and partly because the latter incorporated convenience factors such as more extensive times and places of sale.[8]

It is important to remember that Russia's market liberalization was enacted in a rapid, ad hoc fashion. One of the most urgent tasks in the eyes of the new political elite was to ensure that the Communists could not return to power, which in the early years of post-Soviet Russia seemed a very real possibility.[9] A rapid move away from the command economy, liberalizing and privatizing with the greatest possible urgency, was a matter of protecting against the return of communism. As Fituni has summarized the situation: "A logical programme of change never existed in the minds of reformers; nor were the goals of reform clearly defined, the necessary stages determined, or the results foreseen. . . . The legality of reformers' actions or behaviours was often sacrificed for the sake of what they believed to be political necessity."[10]

The liberalization of the alcohol market was therefore not alcohol policy in the sense of a policy adopted specifically for alcohol, but rather part of an all-encompassing fundamental economic reform that itself had as much to do with political expediency as achieving long-term economic goals. The resultant effects on the alcohol situation, while unintended and unexpected, were nevertheless dramatic. According to the State Statistics Committee, by the end of the 1990s vodka accounted for 80 percent of alcohol consumption in contrast to 49 percent in 1984, while the proportion of wine decreased from 40 percent to 7 percent over the same period.[11] This was partly a consequence of the antialcohol campaign of 1985–88, where the destruction of large areas of vineyards resulted in a fivefold decrease in grape production. In the Kuban, for example, wine production stood at not more than six million dal in 1998, down from twenty-two million dal in the mid-1980s.[12] But even more significant was the fact that Russia was flooded with cheap vodka in the 1990s. This was the result of three main factors. The first two have been discussed above: the state's fixing of an artificially low price for vodka in 1991–92, followed by market liberalization and the dismantling of the state's alcohol monopoly. The third factor was the state's de facto loss of control over its basic functions of law enforcement and taxation, which led to the widespread avoidance of excise duty.

Excise Privileges and the Excise Black Hole

The weakness and fragmentation of the state are central to understanding the dominance of the *mafiya* and shadow economies in Russia in the 1990s. With the loss of the Communist Party bureaucracy—the strong central authority that had held the Soviet state together—there was little incentive for individual state agencies to continue to serve the government when competing paymasters emerged. The state thus lost its monopoly over the legitimate forms of coercion (notably taxation and law enforcement) that are the cornerstones of modern nation-states. The old organized crime structures that had ruled the Soviet underworld were able to adapt and flourish in the new world of chaos and lack of central authority.[13] The "near paralysis of state authorities" led to the situation where *mafiya* structures were better able to provide the functions required by business (security, contract enforcement, and guarantee of property rights) than the state itself. Money that would traditionally be paid in taxation was instead paid to *mafiya* groups in exchange for the services that the state was incapable of providing.[14] Organized crime was also able to expand its influence within the state, establishing marriages of convenience between the *mafiya*, on the one hand, and politicians and bureaucrats, on the other.[15] In the sphere of security a kind of de facto privatization took place that blurred the lines between the state and the new private sector. An explosion of new private security agencies absorbed former officers from the KGB and its successor the FSB, as well as other so-called power ministries such as the Ministry of Internal Affairs (MVD) and the Army Intelligence Department. Although they were officially no longer in the service of the state, their informal connections meant that they often enjoyed access to the information systems and operative resources of the state organs. Still others were allowed to act as private security consultants for businesses while still in active service with the FSB.[16]

The inability of the state to fulfill its basic tax collection functions led to a dramatic decline in federal tax revenues. The eventual result was a massive default on government debt in August 1998 and resultant financial crisis.[17] Alexandr Nemtsov calculated that in 1993 the federal government received less than 20 percent of what it officially should have collected in excise duties on alcohol. Officials stated that during this early period, "the state budget has never, in all its history, received such a small portion of the sales of alcoholic beverages."[18] The effect of this excise black hole was to suppress alcohol prices. The Russian Ministry for the Economy calculated that, in the summer of 1994, a liter of imported vodka in Moscow cost less than 40 percent of what it should have cost, taking into account all relevant costs and overheads—an enormous difference that can be accounted for only by widespread nonpayment of excise duty.[19] This dominance of the illegal market was typical of many spheres of the Russian economy in the 1990s, not just the alcohol sector. First deputy interior minister Pavel Maslov put the size of Russia's shadow economy in 1997 at 750 trillion rubles per year (1997 prices), equivalent to 45 percent of the country's overall turnover.[20]

As if the widespread avoidance of excise duty was not creating enough problems for the exchequer, the state's income was further reduced by special privileges granted to several organizations that allowed them to import goods without paying customs duties. It is a measure of the degree of state capture in Russia at this time that such vital revenues were surrendered to private interests in this way—and that the privileges took so long to reverse. The phenomenon began in late 1993, when a presidential decree granted the NSF exemption from customs payments on goods imported for international sports tournaments. An executive order of May 1994 extended the exemption to all goods purchased by the federation. Vodka quickly became the good of choice imported by the federation, mainly because of the superprofits it generated—despite the fact that the NSF sold it substantially below the average market price in Russia. The excise privileges were soon extended to other charitable organizations, which also took advantage of the enormous profits to be made by importing vodka. Even the Moscow patriarchate cashed in through its Department of External Relations, dealing mainly in the import of duty-free cigarettes but also vodka. The scope for superprofits was much less in the beer market due to higher production costs per gram of pure alcohol, but nevertheless even some beer importers made use of charitable foundations' customs privileges to avoid excise duty.[21] The effects of these excise privileges were twofold: first, the cost to the federal budget in lost excise revenues was enormous (4 trillion rubles in 1994); and second, domestic alcohol producers that did not benefit from the privileges were rendered uncompetitive.[22]

Inevitably, the super-revenues that excise privileges opened up to the charitable foundations meant that the *mafiya* were quick to follow. Some *mafiya* groups posed as qualified charities and foundations, and they ultimately took control of the customs privileges owned by the genuine foundations too. In these early post-Soviet years, *mafiya* networks were not only deeply integrated in the emerging Russian market economy,[23] they also bought themselves well-connected "roofs" (*kryshi*—which also means "protection" in this context), through either the law enforcement agencies or politicians and government officials.[24] In short, the *mafiya* effectively infiltrated both state and civil society organizations. Sports clubs, churches, and other organizations with a status that provided tax or export-import privileges were a particular target.[25]

The stripping of the federal budget's excise revenue did not go unopposed: the Ministry of Finance soon proposed a decree reversing the privileges. But this just signaled the start of the battle as the NSF and other organizations fought to preserve their lucrative new cash cows. The bulk of the privileges were eventually brought to an end in 1996. The foundations and the *mafiya* were not the only ones who benefited. It also provided a means for companies involved in importing alcohol to avoid excise duty: they could simply pay a foundation or charity a fee to import the alcohol on their behalf, the fee being a fraction of the duty avoided. Although hard spirits and cigarettes were the most profitable items to import, some beer distributors also took advantage of the arrangement. This was at a time when domestic production of beer was still stilted, and the novelty of imported foreign beer provided a lucrative niche market, especially in Moscow.[26] Thus, the impact of state capture in the form of customs privileges reached far beyond the official beneficiaries. It transformed the entire structure of the alcohol market. Legally operating firms were forced to resort to informal gray practices just to remain competitive. Ultimately the government was forced to spend $9 billion just to bring the excise privileges for charitable foundations to an end, by the state buying off the remaining contracts the foundations had in place.[27] One can only guess at the total loss to the state from excise privileges in the first half of the 1990s. And as related at the start of this chapter, greater still was the human cost in terms of lives and bloodshed, as *mafiya* groups battled for control of the proceeds.

The North Ossetian Problem

The small Caucasian republic of North Ossetia is perhaps best known to Westerners for the Beslan hostage crisis, where in September 2004 Islamist insurgents from the nearby war-torn republic of Chechnya seized control of a school. Over 330 civilians were killed, the majority of them children—thanks in part to a heavy-handed operation to end the siege by Russian security forces. But several years before the Chechen war for independence spilled over into North Ossetia, this small Caucasian corner of the Russian Federation became the unlikely hub of illicit vodka production in the country.

Even before the 1985 antialcohol campaign, North Ossetia had gained itself a stranglehold in the Soviet alcohol market. As much as one-third of the alcohol allotted to the Ministry of Agriculture for supplying the whole of Russia found its way (often by means of corrupt officials) to North Ossetia, resulting in the rapid emergence of a local alcohol industry that employed an incredible one-third of the republic's adult population.[28] Although these plants were shut down during the Gorbachev campaign, they were never destroyed, and simply reopened for business a year or two after the campaign had passed. In the early post-Soviet years, North Ossetia produced around 40 percent of vodka consumed in Russia, most of it illegal. Alexandr Nemtsov described it as "the main, if not the only source of wealth in the republic."[29] Although market reforms took away North Ossetia's state quota supply of ethyl alcohol, the republic's convenient location near the borders of Ukraine and Georgia aided black market production. Cheap alcohol was transported into North Ossetia from Ukraine and listed as transit alcohol destined for Georgia—thereby avoiding the payment of Russian customs and excise duties. The alcohol was transferred to North Ossetia's vast network of alcohol factories, while the paperwork listed that it had continued its journey to Georgia.[30]

The North Ossetian black market for vodka was squeezed first by the introduction of new customs duties on transit alcohol. The supply of cheap alcohol was further squeezed following the standoff at the Roki Tunnel on the border between Russia and Georgia in July 1997. The director of the Federal Border Service, General Andrey Nikolayev, ordered Georgian alcohol transporters not to cross the border (and unilaterally moved the border posts in the process), while customs officers began to demand the correct duty be paid on the alcohol. The vast sums of money at stake resulted in a standoff, with everyone refusing to pay the duty, while more alcohol tankers continued to arrive. The Georgian president and Foreign Ministry protested against the action, apparently motivated as much by the financial threat to the Georgian authorities through their *mafiya* connections as the integrity of the border. Yeltsin relented and ordered Nikolayev to return the border to its former place, resulting in the latter's resignation in December 1997. Nevertheless, despite being a defeat on paper, the Roki Tunnel standoff did lead to a subsequent decline in illegal alcohol flows from Russia to Georgia.[31]

Monopoly Pipe Dreams

It did not take the federal government long to regret surrendering control over the alcohol market in the haste of economic reforms. Just one year after abolishing the state monopoly, the government was attempting to restore it. On 11 June 1993 President Yeltsin passed Decree No. 918 "On the restoration of the state monopoly on the production, storage, wholesale and retail sales of alcoholic goods,"[32] with prime minister Viktor Chernomyrdin signing a corresponding government resolution on 22 April 1994.[33] Despite the ambitious-sounding title, this did not represent the reintroduction of a genuine state monopoly on alcohol production, but rather an attempt to bring some degree of order to the alcohol market by introduced a licensing and quota system. The corresponding government resolution for translating the decree into law was similarly delayed, eventually being issued on 26 September 1994.[34] But even after the resolution had been passed it was barely implemented and had very little effect on the chaotic and criminalized alcohol market.[35] Despite this situation, the State Inspectorate for the Guarantee of the State Monopoly on Alcoholic Products had been formed in August 1993 from the remnants of the old Soviet alcohol inspectorate, and continued to operate for several years under the pretense of reestablishing some form of state monopoly. An unintentionally amusing exchange between a journalist and the head of the agency (by now renamed a federal service) in 1996 demonstrates the absurdity of the gap between official discourse and reality:

Journalist: So has a state monopoly on the production of alcohol actually been re-established or not?
Alla Vdovenko: It has been in the process of being re-established since 1994. It's a complex and very long process. Work on its re-establishment has taken place, is taking place and, I am absolutely sure, will continue to take place.[36]

In an attempt to succeed where the 1993 legislation had failed, the Russian parliament passed a new law in 1995, "On State Regulation of the Production and Sale of Ethyl Alcohol and Alcoholic Products."[37] Once again, the law asserted the establishment of a state monopoly on the production and sale of alcoholic products. This amounted to making producers

and sellers of alcoholic products subject to licensing, and mandatory declaration of the volume of beverages produced and sold. Although this could
hardly be called a monopoly, the law took further steps to ensure that the
alcohol industry was at least brought closer to home. It included protectionist provisions that sharply limited the import of alcoholic products into Russia (no more than 20 percent of all alcohol sales could be imports, and no
less than 80 percent of those imports had to be wine). It was prohibited to
use foreign investment to create organizations to import or sell alcoholic
beverages stronger than 12 percent alcohol by volume (abv). President Yeltsin had originally vetoed the law due to these protectionist provisions, which
conflicted with the country's obligations to the European Union, but parliament overturned the veto.[38]

The government's attempts to regain its lost revenues continued to
dominate alcohol policy in the mid-1990s. At the same time that the 1995
legislative package "On State Regulation . . ." was passing through parliament, the government established an interdepartmental commission for
consideration of alcohol issues, under the leadership of first deputy minister
for the economy, Yakov Urinson. Representatives of the so-called *siloviki*
(security services officials) were among its members. The commission was
tasked with finding ways to increase income to the state budget from the
production and sale of alcoholic products, which had fallen to an unprece-
dentedly low level, a fraction of the share received even during the height of
the Gorbachev antialcohol campaign.[39] One of the most important policy
developments was that beginning 1 January 1997 all alcoholic products had
to be marked with labels indicating that excise duty had been paid on them.
It was as a direct result of this that the Duma passed a law in December 1996 depriving beer of the status of an alcoholic beverage,[40] thus avoiding the need for beer to be marked with excise stamps.

Despite the government's frantic efforts to regain its lost alcohol revenues,
the constant flow of legislative measures brought little success. According to
one estimate, by the end of the 1990s the monetary losses to the state in the
alcohol market (i.e., from unpaid taxes and duties) amounted to approximately 30–35 billion rubles annually. This was comparable to around
10 percent of federal budget revenues in 1997.[41] Thus, even toward the end
of the 1990s, state capture remained a significant feature of the alcohol
market. While some forms of state capture had been eliminated (e.g., the
extraction of excise privileges by certain groups), other forms—notably the

breakdown of the state's monopoly on taxation and law enforcement, and rent extraction from state-owned producers—were still strong. But in the battle for control of Russia's alcohol market, the pendulum was about to swing back toward the state, under the leadership of a hitherto little-known security services official turned politician: Vladimir Vladimirovich Putin.

Chapter 4

Regaining State Control under Putin

The iconic vodka brand Stolichnaya is perhaps the most globally recognized symbol of Russian alcohol. In the postwar Soviet period, bottles with the distinctive red-and-white label featuring a drawing of Moscow's famous Hotel Moskva (*stolichnaya* means "capital city") hit Western shop shelves. Stolichnaya vodka thus became one of only a handful of Soviet brands known to Westerners.

Before the fall of the USSR, Stolichnaya vodka had been distributed abroad by the state-owned monopolist vodka exporter Soyuzplodoimport. But in 1991 Soyuzplodoimport was privatized into a joint-stock company of the same name. Little information is available on the privatization of Soyuzplodoimport, but Putin's government later judged that there had been discrepancies in the privatization process that rendered it illegal and a case of corporate theft. What we do know is that entrepreneur Yury Shefler and some associates worked their way into the newly privatized vodka exporter by buying up a blocking stake in one of its major shareholders—Rosvestalko, a Kaliningrad-based vodka producer. By 1997, Shefler had attained the post of president of Soyuzplodoimport.

What happened next was an act of corporate raiding[1] outrageous in its audacity. In 1997, Shefler created a rival vodka exporter of which he was president, with an almost identical name—Soyuzplodimport (i.e., minus the third "o"), abbreviated to SPI for convenience. A few months later Shefler sold the trademarks of Soyuzplodoimport's forty-three leading brands of vodka—including the world-famous Stolichnaya and Moskovs-kaya brands—to his own SPI company for the nominal sum of $300,000.[2]

In 2000, newly elected president Vladimir Putin resolved that the state should reclaim what he regarded as its "captured" alcohol assets, by any means necessary. The Stolichnaya brand possessed not only high commercial value but also enormous symbolic value as the vodka that for decades had represented the might of the USSR in the international alcohol market. In May 2000 masked police stormed SPI's Moscow headquarters and ransacked offices, confiscating documents and computers. SPI's CEO Alexey Oliynik claimed, "These storm troopers openly said they were assigned to destabilise our business rather than find any proof of our guilt."[3]

The state's recapture of its old alcohol assets was carried out with little regard for legal due process. The Russian government simply unilaterally declared that it was taking back the disputed vodka brands, on the grounds that SPI had obtained them illegally in the first place. In October 2000, prosecutor general Vladimir Ustinov wrote to prime minister Mikhail Kasyanov, requiring that SPI's brands be returned to the state "in accordance with the instructions of the President of the Russian Federation." "In this case, the state may restore its rights independently, without a court decision," stated Ustinov's letter. Accordingly, Kasyanov's cabinet issued a decree "to restore and protect the exclusive rights of the Russian Federation" to vodka brands.[4]

In 2001, the government created a new state-owned federal enterprise to contest the rights to all disputed vodka brands and manage them once obtained. It was given a rather familiar name—Soyuzplodoimport. At the end of the year, the Supreme Arbitration Court ruled that the privatization of the original Soyuzplodoimport had been illegal. Accordingly, forty vodka brands, including Stolichnaya, Moskovskaya, and Russkaya, were registered to the Ministry of Agriculture, which duly handed them over to the new state-owned Soyuzplodoimport.[5] SPI's CEO related that the company continued to contest the decision in the courts, apparently obtaining several favorable decisions, but "the Prosecutor General's Office overturns them all."[6]

The next step was for the state to go after SPI, and then after Shefler himself. In February 2002 Russian customs officers impounded $10 million worth of SPI vodka due to be exported to the United States. SPI duly switched its production from Kaliningrad to the Latvijas Balzams distillery in Riga, Latvia. The Russian government asked Western distributors to boycott SPI, on the grounds that the disputed vodka brands now belonged to the Russian state.[7] The Russian Prosecutor General's Office issued a warrant for Shefler in July 2002, on the grounds that he had allegedly threatened to kill Vladimir Loginov, the former deputy agriculture minister, who had been appointed director-general of the newly created Soyuzplodoimport. Shefler fled to Europe, moving his company SPI with him, which he based in Luxemburg. Russia continued its pursuit of Shefler, having an extradition request for the businessman refused by the UK in 2010.

The Stolichnaya case is instructive as it provides a perfect example of how the state capture of the 1990s was displaced by business capture in the 2000s.[8] Business capture is an eclectic concept that encompasses such trends as the state taking back control of strategically important industries, "authorized" corporate raids, rent-seeking behavior by officials and *siloviki*, and the use of the state's administrative resources to give preferential treatment to businesses owned by those who are "one of us."[9] Although as a concept "business capture" contains inherent tensions,[10] the underlying notion is that now it was the state calling the shots, rather than external vested interests.[11]

Vladimir Putin became president of the Russian Federation in May 2000, having served as acting president since Yeltsin's shocking resignation on New Year's Eve 1999. One of Putin's priorities was to restore the integrity of the federal government, clawing back control from the hands of the asset strippers, oligarchs, and powerful regional governors who had dominated under Yeltsin. There was a determined effort under Putin's first presidency to curtail the power of the so-called oligarchs and repatriate the resources of strategically important industries back to the federal state. In his 2000 electoral campaign Putin had promised that "there [would] be no oligarchs of this kind of a class," which drew parallels with Stalin's policy of "liquidating the kulaks as a class" in the late 1920s.[12] In the same month that SPI's offices were raided by armed police, May 2000, the offices of Vladimir Gusinsky's

Media-Most empire were also raided. Media-Most owned the NTV television channel, which had aired critical coverage of Putin. Gusinsky was forced under threat of prosecution for embezzlement to sign ownership of Media-Most over to the state-owned energy company Gazprom, from which it had taken out a loan that was under dispute. Gusinsky subsequently fled to Europe while on bail.[13] Other oligarchs met similar fates. The most powerful of all the Yeltsin-era oligarchs, Boris Berezovsky, fled to the UK in November 2000 and was subsequently granted political asylum. Widely regarded as part of "the Family" (Yeltsin's inner circle), Berezovsky had been one of Putin's backers to succeed Yeltsin as president, and had even founded a political party (Unity) to support him. But as the Putin administration moved against the oligarchs, opening tax investigations into their dealings, Berezovsky first went into open opposition against Putin, then fled, conducting his opposition activities from the safety of London.[14] Berezovsky died under mysterious circumstances at his Berkshire home in 2013.[15]

But regaining state control over the alcohol industry necessitated more than the ad hoc pursuit of individual oligarchs. A systemic means of managing the recovered alcohol assets was required. Thus, in the same week that he was sworn in as president, Putin signed a decree creating a state holding company for alcohol production.[16] Rosspirtprom was created as a federal state unitary enterprise, later being transformed into a state-owned joint stock company on 16 January 2009. It was to bring together all government shareholdings in alcohol companies under a single state-owned holding company, with alcohol enterprises that were already wholly state-owned being made into subsidiaries of Rosspirtprom.

Ironically, given the essentially "Putinite" nature of Rosspirtprom, the idea of a state holding company for alcohol had already been circulating for a couple of years prior to Putin's accession to the presidency. The first attempt to set up such a structure had been made in 1998 by deputy PM Gennady Kulik; Boris Yeltsin had signed a decree on the need to establish such an enterprise. Kulik lost his job when Yevgeny Primakov's government was sacked in May 1999. But this was not the only reason why the project was not realized; the idea also faced strong opposition from certain quarters within the government. The Ministry of State Property, the Ministry of Agriculture and Food, and the Ministry of Taxes and Assessments were at the same time pushing proposals directly opposed to the concept of Rosspirtprom: that the remaining state-owned alcohol companies should be privatized.

Leonid Kholod, head of the government staff's agriculture department, asserted: "We are not in favour of this idea. It runs contrary to the industry's general policy of privatisation."[17]

Under Putin, of course, any such ideological commitments to privatization soon evaporated. Nevertheless, when Rosspirtprom was established it was not clear just how far its role would extend. Was the idea just to bring order to enterprises in which the state already owned a stake (or was in the process of repatriating), or would it be tasked with bringing an even larger market share under state control—possibly even reconstructing the old state monopoly? Its functions were not spelled out anywhere when its creation was announced.[18] While Rosspirtprom certainly developed monopolist ambitions once it had established its position in the market, whether this was Putin's original intention is unclear.

What *is* clear is that Rosspirtprom was designed to pursue political aims as well as business ones. The Russian press often ironically referred to the new state holding company as the "Ministry of Alcohol." Rosspirtprom has also been described as a "second Gazprom"—the vodka equivalent of Russia's giant state-owned energy conglomerate. Gazprom's economic and geopolitical importance for the Russian state can hardly be overemphasized: its income accounted for an enormous 7 percent of Russian gross domestic product (GDP) in 2007, and it supplied over half of the gas imported by EU countries.[19] For Putin, Gazprom was to be his "prime personal project" right from the start of his presidency.[20] Under Yeltsin, Gazprom had operated less like one of the world's largest energy companies, and more like a bank for oligarchs—it loaned billions of dollars that the oligarchs seemed to have little intention of repaying.[21] Upon becoming president in 2000, Putin quickly moved to replace Gazprom's management with his own people, including future president Dmitry Medvedev as company chair.[22] Similarly, Rosspirtprom was intended to reassert federal control over alcohol assets and to put an end to the capture of them by private interests. While vodka did not have quite the same economic importance as gas, its potential contribution to the Russian economy and federal budget revenues was more than sufficient incentive for Putin to wish to bring it back under centralized state control. There was also a political dimension: like gas, affordable supplies of vodka were seen as essential to the maintenance of public opinion. As the journal *Ekspert* put it: "Vodka may not be gas or oil, but it too is a strategically important product. So important that to control its production it was necessary to create an alcohol equivalent of Gazprom."[23]

An even more overtly political goal was Rosspirtprom's role in Putin's centralization drive and the establishment of the Kremlin's "power vertical" over the then largely autonomous regional governors.[24] The journalist Yulia Latynina regarded the creation of Rosspirtprom as "a cornerstone of Putin's centralisation policy, because to implement centralisation the governors had to have their control over state budget cashflows removed, and vodka sales generated no less than half of those cashflows."[25] Nikolay Petrov, in an academic paper analyzing regional vodka markets, concurred that the establishment of Rosspirtprom was "a serious blow to the financial positions of governors. This was actually the first of Putin's powerful centralising steps, less noticeable than the creation of federal regions, but very important." Vodka revenues had become "almost the main pillar" of regional budgets and were used to finance gubernatorial and parliamentary campaigns. That said, the scale and significance of vodka revenues varied greatly from region to region. It is interesting to note that the ethnic and autonomous republics were among the highest regional earners from vodka, although there were also significant variations within this: Bashkortostan's alcohol industry revenues provided around 12 percent of the regional budget in 1998 thanks to its regional state monopoly, while neighboring Tatarstan raised almost no revenues from alcohol.[26] In a nod to the link between federal political authority (the "power vertical") and federal control of the alcohol market, one journalist wittily labeled Rosspirtprom "Putin's vertical in the alcohol business."[27]

The Struggle for Control

While it was simple enough to create Rosspirtprom on paper as a legal entity, establishing it as a functioning state holding company was a long and sometimes violent struggle. As soon as the decree establishing Rosspirtprom was signed, regional authorities began bankrupting factories that produced alcoholic beverages in order to take them out of commission as state property. Within four months, twelve major factories had been bankrupted, eluding federal control.[28] Rosspirtprom was forced to cut deals to bring the factories under its control, such as handing board positions to vested interests. Sometimes, most notably in the case of Moscow's famous Kristall distillery, state-sponsored violence was used in order for Rosspirtprom to gain control. A controlling 51 percent stake in Kristall was held by the Moscow city government, headed by the then-powerful mayor Yury Luzhkov. In August 2000 the factory was stormed by the Federal Tax Police, heavily armed and wearing balaclavas, who had been sent to gather evidence of tax evasion. As with so many instances of business capture by the federal state in the 2000s, "tax evasion" was a pretext for disposing of the company's leadership while the state awarded itself ownership of the enterprise. But in the case of Kristall, legal niceties soon gave way to a physical struggle for control, and a month-long armed standoff ensued. The federal authorities' approved new director, Aleksandr Romanov, occupied Kristall's central offices with his own small army. Deposed director Yury Yermilov was admitted to a hospital, but he declared his chief accountant Vladimir Svirsky as his successor, and Svirsky and his own armed troops held the rest of the factory, all while the vodka production lines continued to operate. A Moscow court initially ruled Romanov's appointment as illegal, then a few weeks later dramatically reversed its decision and upheld Romanov's appointment. One can only speculate as to the political wrangling that took place between the Moscow city government and the federal government behind the scenes to bring about this judicial *volte face*. But the upshot was that Romanov was sufficiently empowered to take the whole plant unopposed by Svirsky's forces, and federal control over Kristall was established.[29]

By early 2001, Rosspirtprom controlled 130 vodka and spirits producers. It broke the resistance of directors who were holding out against it, calling annual shareholders' meetings and replacing the directors with its own representatives.[30] There were also human casualties in the struggle for control. In July 2000, the general director of the Smolensk vodka factory Bacchus was killed on his way to Moscow. Hours earlier, Rosspirtprom had telephoned him in Smolensk to check up on him, as they had been informed—only a little prematurely—that he had been killed.[31] In May 2002, Viktor Alexeyev, manager of Rosspirtprom's eighteen core distilleries, was found dead in his apartment with five stab wounds. The day after Alexeyev's murder, Pyotr Minkov, the co-owner of a spirits retail outlet in Moscow, was killed by a shot to the head at the entrance to his apartment building. Minkov had formerly worked for the economic crime department of the MVD.[32] Sergey Zivenko claimed that when he was general director of Rosspirtprom, attempts were made on his life, and that the price of removing him from his job was $10 million.[33] The establishment of federal control over the state's alcohol assets was eventually achieved, but it had not been an easy fight.

Monopolist Ambitions

It seems evident that once Rosspirtprom's control over its assets had been established, its management harbored ambitions to turn it into a monopolist alcohol producer. This was rarely explicitly stated, but was commonly understood by insiders. Much of Rosspirtprom's policy activity in the mid-2000s was de facto directed at awarding itself the status of alcohol monopolist,[34] a point that was emphasized by one respondent, a former Rosspirtprom employee:

> ALB[35]: What were the aims of Rosspirtprom at this time [mid-2000s]?
>
> Respondent: To become a monopolist in the market. At least, there was no official aim, because the company did not have a system of management, therefore there was no official aim. But all the activity we conducted was directed at becoming a monopolist.

Rosspirtprom's plans to unilaterally establish itself as an ethyl alcohol monopolist actually reached quite advanced stages, to the point where it had even drafted a bill to establish the monopoly system and found a friendly deputy in the State Duma to sponsor it. However, even at this advanced stage the monopoly project was ill thought out and verging on fantasy, according to the ex-Rosspirtprom official:

> I wrote a draft bill, I wrote it and cried—well, laughed and cried—because I could see it was complete lunacy. I submitted it, suggested amendments which some deputy in the Duma had to lobby for—amendments favorable to Rosspirtprom. In particular, the amendments provided for the creation of a structure which would have controlled all the operations with ethyl alcohol in the country, i.e. centralized purchase and sale of ethyl alcohol across the entire country. From my point of view it was complete lunacy. I spoke to my manager about it—how could I write amendments to this law if it's complete nonsense?

Rosspirtprom director Pyotr Myasoyedov gave some public indication of Rosspirtprom's monopolist ambitions in 2005, when he stated that it was necessary to introduce a state monopoly on the wholesaling of spirits. However, he also warned that other reforms were necessary before that could take place, notably the creation of a unified federal agency to oversee the alcohol beverage industry—in other words, the regulator that was to be founded in 2009 by the name of Rosalkogolregulirovaniye (RAR).[36] This gives an early indication of how RAR grew out of the Rosspirtprom project, something that is discussed more fully in chapter 6.

Valery Draganov, then head of the State Duma Committee for Economic Policy and Entrepreneurship, remarked in 2005 that the soon-to-be-introduced Unified State Automatic Information System (EGAIS) represented the "partial" introduction of a state monopoly.[37] This was something of an exaggeration: EGAIS was ultimately only a centralized monitoring system for recording the volume of alcohol manufactured by private companies. However, the line of thought—that EGAIS was the first step toward a state monopoly—is revealing. Certainly 2004–6 was when the talk of reintroducing a state monopoly on alcohol was at its height in government circles. A curious advocate of a state monopoly appears to have been general prosecutor Vladimir Ustinov. In June 2004, according to one leaked letter, Ustinov wrote to Putin urging him to consider introducing a state monopoly for the sake of the federal budget. "Alcohol production has always been an important source of income for the state budget," began Ustinov's letter. But, he continued, the illegal market was depriving the state of this income source. Only 20 percent of productive capacity was being used to make legal alcohol; illegal alcohol accounted for 40–50 percent of total production. "The budget is losing out on billions of roubles every year," emphasized Ustinov. His letter concluded: "I would ask you to instruct the Government of the Russian Federation to do the necessary economic calculations of the potential government expenditure for deciding the issue of introducing a state monopoly on the manufacture and distribution of ethyl alcohol, alcohol and alcohol-containing products, and on a temporary moratorium on the import of ethyl alcohol."

The letter was forwarded to prime minister Mikhail Fradkov, with the simple handwritten instruction (apparently written by Putin): "Please consider. Needs resolving."[38] To what extent the calculations and logistics of introducing a state monopoly were seriously assessed by the government we do not know. But we do know that the Agriculture Ministry was also calling for a state monopoly, and in July 2005 Putin himself spoke publicly in favor of such a monopoly.[39] Soon afterward, in October 2005, the idea was debated in the State Duma, in response (it would appear) to Putin's pronouncement.[40] However, Putin then performed a *volte face*: in August 2006 he opposed draft amendments to the law on the state regulation of alcohol production that would introduce a state monopoly on alcohol in Russia, on the grounds that it would violate wider Russian law and "not comply with the principles of a market economy." A few months later, in early 2007, Putin came out conclusively against a state monopoly: "There is talk in some quarters now of introducing a state monopoly on alcohol. The issue is not one of a monopoly, however, but of poor-quality products. There are a number of different approaches we could take."[41]

What changed Putin's mind? In 2006, the compulsory EGAIS, which records the amount of ethyl alcohol both produced and used as a raw ingredient by distillers, was rolled out throughout the alcohol industry. The system did not operate properly, causing alcohol production to grind to a halt and severe shortages at retail sale. These shortages apparently led to a highly publicized epidemic of alcohol poisonings as consumers turned to surrogates. The poisonings epidemic in turn produced a flurry of public discourse about the necessity of reintroducing a state monopoly on alcohol. Duma speaker and United Russia chair Boris Gryzlov went as far as to state, "It's not enough to ensure a state monopoly on the production and circulation of pure alcohol. I think it's also time to raise the issue of a state monopoly on the sale of products that contain alcohol."[42] *The Times* of London even suggested that the Russian government, aided by the state-controlled media, had deliberately exaggerated the scale of the poisoning epidemic to create a pretext for the introduction of a state monopoly.[43] But ironically, it seems that the very crisis that at the time seemed likely to bring a state monopoly closer actually turned the ruling elite against the idea. The EGAIS disaster made it clear that the logistics of centrally managing alcohol production would be hugely complex, and the cost of mistakes would be high. If a mere federal monitoring system could cause such chaos, what kind of catastrophe could the introduction of a genuine state monopoly bring about? The stakes were not just financial but also political, as the Russian political elite saw maintaining a steady flow of affordable vodka as crucial to re-taining the support of popular opinion. Faced with such high risks, it is understandable that a state monopoly was regarded as a utopian ideal best left alone.

"Where's All the Money Going?"

Once Rosspirtprom managed to gain control over its assets it seemed to have everything in its favor to become a profitable and dominant market player. Even without monopoly status, in 2000 it controlled 30 percent of the vodka and spirits-producing industry, and 50 percent of the ethyl alcohol–producing industry.[44] This included some of the country's most valuable vodka plants, most notably the prestigious Moscow Kristall distillery. However, a decade later its market share had fallen dramatically. In 2010 Rosspirtprom was Russia's second-largest vodka producer, but now controlled only around 10 percent of the market. Nevertheless, its management proclaimed ambi-tious plans to occupy up to 40 percent of the Russian vodka market by 2015, which would represent an enormous feat of expansion for any company, let alone one that had lost two-thirds of its market share over the previous decade.[45]

In 2008, the Accounting Chamber of the Russian Federation published the results of an investigation it had carried out into Rosspirtprom's man-agement of its federal assets. The report was scathing of Rosspirtprom's per-formance, estimating that in 2006 alone the federal budget was deprived of 5 million rubles' worth of share dividends due to Rosspirtprom's poor per-formance. By July 2006, Rosspirtprom had amassed overdue tax debts to budgets of all levels of government of around 3.8 billion rubles, and it sim-ply did not have the means to pay them. It was at this point that one of the regular rounds of relicensing was due to take place within the industry. Given that federal law states that a company cannot be issued with a license if it has tax debts, this represented a serious threat to the survival of many of Rosspirtprom's companies. Rosspirtprom managed to save itself by getting its parent ministry, the Ministry of Agriculture, to agree to a one-off rise in its debt limit in 2006, and securing a 5 million ruble loan from the state-owned bank VTB. But despite the bailout, Rosspirtprom's track record of unprofitability and defaulting on tax payments continued. One respondent, a prominent alcohol industry journalist, in 2012 described Rosspirtprom's state of affairs as follows:

> Rosspirtprom is a strange state company which has a number of pure alcohol factories and vodka factories. . . . It doesn't pay taxes because it's unprofitable, and what's the point of having a state company if it doesn't pay taxes on profits, not having any profits it can't pay taxes on them. . . . And in addition we know that—at any rate a year ago [i.e., 2011] this was the case—Rosspirtprom was holding back payment of a very large sum in excise duty to the Tax Service. They couldn't pay the excise because they had no money, but they continued to operate. So it makes you wonder why these enterprises continue to operate, who needs them and where all the money's going."

Where *was* all the money going? How could Rosspirtprom be the country's second-largest vodka producer, and yet at the same time be so massively unprofitable and riddled by debt? How was it that this sustained period of business capture by the Russian state had not led to a profitable state company contributing healthy tax revenues to the federal budget? Part of the answer is due to poor management. The substandard management of state-owned industries is an issue that Putin raised early on in his first term as president, stating in his 2002 federal address: "The management of state-owned assets is another important issue. . . . Of almost 10,000 wholly state-owned enterprises, only a handful are operating in a truly efficient manner. . . . I should also remind you that we still do not know the exact size of the state sector. An inventory of state-owned assets, which has been discussed many times, remains unfinished."[46]

Lack of effective controls over its component companies was a problem the Accounting Chamber highlighted in the findings of its investigation into Rosspirtprom. The report stated that the federal enterprise's representatives "have in a number of cases not been adequately provided with effective control over all aspects of production and financial performance, the consequence of which was the creation of preconditions to reduce [the companies'] financial results, in some cases driving them to bankruptcy."[47]

Management systems among Rosspirtprom's central command appear to have functioned little better. The respondent who worked at Rosspirtprom in the mid-2000s was at pains to emphasize just how bad the management standards at the federal enterprise were:

Respondent: I never once saw the director general in person. I never saw him, I didn't know what this guy looked like, this leader. But I was constantly making decisions for him, you understand? . . . Communications were completely out of sync: the standard of management at the time in the company was 'Soviet' in the bad sense of the word. The level of management was disgusting, the lack of communication, for example . . . I communicated with about twenty different managers in the management structure, and there was only one truly competent manager, a man who did not simply sit in his place, but who understood business processes and tried to develop the business.

ALB: So the rest of the people were KGB types?[48]

Respondent: No not KGB; bureaucrats in the worst sense of the word—that is, *gosudarstvennoye boloto* [government swamp]. . . . "Stagnation" is totally the word I would associate with this company.

Poor management can provide only part of the explanation for where Rosspirtprom's would-be profits were going, however. It would appear that an equally significant factor was as follows: rather than combating the asset stripping of state-owned alcohol companies, the existence of Rosspirtprom has actually facilitated it. To understand how and why this took place, the next chapter examines one of the most important trends shaping contemporary state alcohol policy: the informal influence of businessmen with close ties to the governing elite.

Chapter 5

The Judo Gang

Informal Networks and Perceptions of Power

Vladimir Putin's lifelong passion for judo is well known. He took up the sport as a teenager, became a black belt just a few years later, and was awarded the rare eighth dan in 2012. He has authored several books on the subject, and as president has sparred for the TV cameras on several occasions. Putin even credits judo with putting him on the right track as a teenager, stating that if it were not for the sport, "I'm not sure how my life would have turned out. It was sports that dragged me off the streets."[1] What is less well known is the role that judo plays as an informal locus of power for Putin's inner circle of closest associates.

The concept of *sistema* is essential to understanding how politics and policymaking operate under Putin. Literally meaning "system," *sistema* refers to the informal, network-based system of governance that interacts with formal state institutions to shape the functioning of the entire state and political machinery in Russia.[2] *Sistema* provides a conceptual framework for understanding why the alcohol market is becoming concentrated in the hands of a few privileged individuals with close ties to the political elite (*svoi*—those who are "one of us"), and how administrative resources and state alcohol policy are being manipulated to bring this about. Although all businesses are formally equal before Russian law, in practice, some businesses are "more equal than others" in that they enjoy the protection of some part of the state and benefit from its administrative resources, while unwanted rivals are targeted by selective application of the law.[3] The alcohol regulator RAR is arguably an example of this: it has been accused of operating as an instrument to clear the alcohol market for *sistema* interests.[4]

The brothers Boris and Arkady Rotenberg are childhood friends and former judo partners of Vladimir Putin. They became billionaire businessmen in the 2000s following Putin's accession to the presidency. The Rotenbergs have made the bulk of their fortune through their business Stroygazmontazh Corporation (SGM Group), which specializes in building gas pipelines for the state-controlled gas monopoly, Gazprom. Formed in 2008 from five pipeline construction companies procured by the brothers, SGM is a relatively recent Rotenberg concern. One of their main business interests prior to this was the banking sector. SMP Bank (which stands for the North Sea Route bank) was established in April 2001 with each of the brothers owning 36.83 percent of capital; their MBTS Bank (the International Bank of Trade Cooperation) was purchased in 2002, with Arkady and Boris each owning a 29.07 percent share.[5] The Rotenbergs have remained in regular social contact with Putin since their childhood sporting days. One report claimed in 2012 that Putin gathered an intimate group of friends every couple of weeks for a late-evening game of ice hockey. Arkady Rotenberg was said to be a regular, along with Gennady Timchenko, a friend and apparent business associate of Putin's from his Saint Petersburg career in the 1990s, whose Gunvor oil trading company has enjoyed a meteoric rise over the past decade similar to that of the Rotenberg empire.[6]

It is a widely reported "open secret" that Putin's inner circle informally assembles around his favorite sport of judo. In 1998, when Putin was still relatively unknown in political terms (he was made head of the FSB that year), he and Arkady Rotenberg formed the Yawara-Neva Judo Club in Saint Petersburg. Gennady Timchenko was also a cofounder. Rotenberg became Yawara-Neva's general director, while Putin was its honorary president. Another member of Putin's circle, Viktor Zubkov, was made a member of the board of trustees and chair of the club's audit commission soon after, in 1999. Zubkov is best known for serving as prime minister during the final months of Putin's second presidency (September 2007–May 2008), before becoming first deputy prime minister during Putin's tenure as prime minister between his second and third presidencies (2008–12). However, he was also a long-term board member of Rosspirtprom, and his role as chair of the Government Commission for Regulating the Alcohol Market will be discussed in chapter 13. Another interesting Yawara-Neva cofounder is Vasily Shestakov, yet another judo partner from Putin's youth who dramatically reinvented his career. In 1999 Shestakov transformed from a judo trainer in Saint Petersburg to a political operator, helping create the Unity political party to provide Putin with an official base of support. Unity merged with two other parties to form the ruling party United Russia in 2001, while Shestakov later became a Duma deputy for the puppet opposition party A Just Russia.[7]

The centrality of the "judo gang" to Putin's informal locus of power was laid bare by the U.S. government's sanctions of March 2014 against key members of the Putin regime. Sixteen government officials and four private individuals were targeted by the sanctions for "acting for or on behalf of or materially assisting, sponsoring, or providing financial, material, or technological support for, or goods or services to or in support of, a senior official of the Government of the Russian Federation"—a thinly veiled reference to Putin.[8] Three of the four private individuals were members of the judo gang: Boris and Arkady Rotenberg, and Gennady Timchenko.

While the Rotenbergs did not hold a formal position in Rosspirtprom, their interests were closely intertwined with it from its foundation. Through their commercial structures they owned shares in the two most highly valued Rosspirtprom companies: the prestigious Moscow Kristall distillery and OAO Bryanskspirtprom. Most Rosspirtprom alcohol plants were turned into Rotenberg clients, keeping their accounts with the Rotenberg-owned banks SMP and MBTS.[9] Representatives of Rotenberg structures served on the boards of directors of nine Rosspirtprom-owned plants in 2011.[10] Perhaps most illustrious was the rise of Igor Aleshin, who in 2006 moved from SMP Bank to become deputy director general of Kristall, then its CEO the following year. In 2008 Aleshin was appointed deputy—and then in 2009 head—of Rosspirtprom. Even former Rosspirtprom director general and subsequent RAR head Igor Chuyan has ties to the Rotenberg empire: in 2005 he was appointed to the board of directors of the Chistiy Kristall trading house (the distributor for Kristall), the same year that Arkady Rotenberg acquired a share in the company.[11]

The ties between the Rotenberg empire and Rosspirtprom—capital, services, and cadres—are numerous and strong enough for their unofficial linkage to be regarded as highly significant. Is it possible—as one respondent suggested—that the Rotenbergs were involved in the foundation of Rosspirtprom from the very beginning? Although most of the Rotenbergs' current billions have been made from gas pipelines, which generate revenues that dwarf those offered by alcohol production, it is worth remembering that this part of their business empire was built up much later, from 2008 onward. The Rotenbergs in 2000 were not particularly wealthy by their current standards. It is thus plausible that the idea of a de facto "public-private partnership"[12] to dominate the alcohol market would have been a lucrative proposition for the Rotenbergs at the time. The choice for the first director general of Rosspirtprom, Sergey Zivenko, adds further weight to this theory. Small-time businessman Zivenko became acquainted with Arkady Rotenberg in 1999, although how exactly is not clear. In the same year they formally entered into business together, registering two firms with offices on Moscow's prestigious Noviy Arbat. One of the firms was called ZIROT (a combination of the first letters of the two founders' surnames) and dealt in wholesale trade, including alcohol.[13] One is forced to wonder how a virtual unknown like Zivenko could have gotten anywhere near the government's radar to be considered as a possible head of Rosspirtprom, were it not for his Rotenberg connections.

Another interesting piece of evidence that hints at possible Rotenberg involvement in the foundation of Rosspirtprom is the account of Andrey Illarionov, Putin's then economic adviser. Illarionov related some years later that Putin kept his economics inner circle in the dark about the project. When Illarionov found out secondhand about the decree establishing Rosspirtprom, he phoned minister of finance Alexey Kudrin to ask if he knew anything about it. Kudrin replied that he did not. German Gref, the minister for economic development and trade, was also in the dark. "Prior to this, all issues that had anything to do with the economy, almost on a daily basis, to the smallest detail, Putin had discussed with the participation of the three of us," related Illarionov. "I soon realised that for Putin, there are two distinctly separate groups of people—let's call them the 'economics group' versus the 'business people.' With the one group—Kudrin, Gref and me—Putin discussed general economic issues; while with the help of the other, he established control over property and financial flows."[14]

The other billionaire who is sometimes cited as part of the Putin-affiliated network in the vodka industry—albeit to a lesser extent than the Rotenbergs—is Vasily Anisimov. Anisimov carved out his business in the 1990s as a metals trader, buying up metals at state-subsidized prices and selling them for massive profits on the world market. Like the Rotenbergs, Anisimov enjoyed a massive leap in wealth under Putin's presidency: Forbes estimated his wealth at $350 million in 2004, but by the end of Putin's second term in 2008 it had reached $4 billion.[15] Anisimov's proximity to Putin is less clear than in the case of the Rotenbergs, but those respondents who mentioned him all described him as either a "friend" of Putin or part of Putin's "group." Certainly Anisimov and Arkady Rotenberg are friends—a fact they have both publicly acknowledged—and they are said to have neighboring houses in Akulinino, an exclusive residential area of suburban Moscow that is home to mansions thought to be owned by high-ranking officials.[16] A symbolic recognition of Anisimov as part of Putin's unofficial circle came in March 2010, when he was made president of the Russian Judo Federation, and thus joined the Rotenbergs, Gennady Timchenko, Viktor Zubkov, and Putin himself as part of the judo gang.

Putin in a Bottle

In late 2003, a new brand of vodka hit Russian shelves. Literally meaning "little Putin," Putinka vodka was deliberately intended to capitalize on the popularity and perceived strength of the Russian president. The brand did not disappoint, enjoying almost immediate success. In 2004 Putinka shot into the top three best-selling vodkas in Russia, and by 2005 had claimed the number one spot.[17] Clever marketing indeed; but what is barely known even inside Russia is that the story of this highly symbolic vodka brand illustrates the mysterious hidden ties between Anisimov, the Rotenbergs, and state vodka interests. Who exactly owned the Putinka brand has always been shrouded in mystery, but in 2014 an investigation by one of Russia's leading alcohol industry journalists revealed that the rights to Putinka had been acquired by a company called Real-Invest—which appeared to be owned (through convoluted ownership structures) by the Rotenberg empire. However, even the previous owner of the trademark, a company called PromImpeks, had links with Rotenberg structures, and some high-level market participants have speculated that the Rotenbergs could have been behind the Putinka brand from the very start.[18]

For many years Putinka was produced by Moscow's Kristall distillery—which, of course, was itself owned in part by Arkady Rotenberg. In 2009 Vasily Anisimov acquired a large stake in Kristall as well as several other former Rosspirtprom-owned distilleries, which were in effect unofficially privatized into his hands (see next section). He also founded his own vodka distribution company—the East European Distribution Company (VEDK)—in the same year, which immediately became the exclusive distributor for Rosspirtprom vodkas and, later, for Putinka.[19]

Anisimov is notoriously cagey about discussing his alcohol assets. In 2015 he insisted that he no longer had any involvement in VEDK, although a company insider cited by the Russian business daily *RBK* flatly contradicted this. Nevertheless, it seems almost certain that by January 2016 Anisimov had sold VEDK—or perhaps more accurately, offloaded it to die in someone else's name. VEDK had already parted ways with Rosspirtprom's brands at the end of 2013,[20] and on 1 January 2016 it also lost the distribution rights to Putinka. VEDK survived for literally only a matter of weeks after this: on 15 March 2016 it filed notification to the tax service of its own liquidation.[21]

What would become of the once-mighty Putinka? The brand was fast becoming a shadow of its former self. In the spring of 2015 it had been the fourth best-selling vodka in the country, but by the spring of 2016 had tumbled to fifteenth place.[22] Yet it seems that Anisimov was not prepared to give up on Putinka just yet. In 2016 it emerged that a little-known company called Alkomir had concluded an agreement with the equally mysterious Real-Invest to use the Putinka brand. Alkomir, it turned out, was owned by the Coalco group—Anisimov's famous investment company.[23] To put it more simply, it appeared that Anisimov had licensed the rights to the Putinka brand from his friend Arkady Rotenberg.

But who was to distribute Putinka, now that Anisimov's VEDK was no more? Here a new player enters the scene, but one no less shrouded in mystery and intrigue. In 2015, a hitherto little-known vodka distribution company called Status Group exploded onto the market. At the start of 2015, Status Group had around 5 percent of the market by sales volume. By the end of the year this had rocketed to over 18 percent—an astonishing increase of over 250 percent in less than twelve months.[24] Like VEDK before it, Status Group was granted exclusive distribution rights for state-owned brands of vodka.[25] But who was the end beneficiary of Status Group's spectacular growth? Unsurprisingly for the secretive Russian vodka market, this detail remained undisclosed—a fact that did not escape the suspicious eye of Valentina Matviyenko, the chair of Russia's upper house of parliament. At a special hearing on the state of the alcohol market in November 2015, Matviyenko voiced concern about how Status Group had managed to achieve such rapid growth in the market. "How is it that our number one exclusive distributor, registered offshore, is growing at such a great rate of knots? What is this, some kind of miracle?"[26]

Status Group, it seemed, had effortlessly taken the place once occupied by VEDK, distributing state-owned vodka brands and the liquid symbol of presidential power, Putinka. Suspicious competitors pointed out that the similarities did not end there. Former VEDK managers could now be found working in key positions at Status Group.[27] Could it be that Anisimov himself was the end beneficiary of this new market leader? Anisimov himself has denied having any involvement in Status Group, but this has done little to quell the rumors.[28]

The growing concentration of industry in the hands of billionaire friends of Putin is far from limited to the alcohol market. It is part of a much wider trend that has taken place in Russia's strategic national industries, and derives from Putin's preferred methods of governance. Putin's preference when filling important posts is to use *svoi* (those who are "one of us"), whom he already has personal experience of dealing with and therefore trusts.[29] The fact that *svoi* tend to be part of the same informal networks helps ensure loyalty. Appointees fulfill their prescribed role in return for their "reward" (being given a profitable or prestigious position); because they are tied into the network, the rewards that have been bestowed on them can be just as easily taken away. It is notable that the Rotenberg brothers have been given prominent places in models of classification of Putin's elites. In Evgeniy Gontmakher's "Planets" model they appear in the first circle of planets closest to Putin (along with—interestingly—Father Tikhon Shevkunov, whose role in shaping a new antialcohol discourse will be discussed in chapter 11). They also feature in the "Kremlin towers" model of Vladimir Pribylovskiy.[30]

Sociologist Alena Ledeneva has emphasized that the operation of formal hierarchies in Russia can be fully understood only if the workings of informal *sistema* networks are integrated into the analysis.[31] This applies equally to the specific case of alcohol policy formation. The workings of state institutions connected with alcohol, such as Rosspirtprom and RAR, make only partial sense if the informal network dimension of the judo gang and its wider circle is not considered.

State-Approved State Capture

Rosspirtprom was apparently set up to enable the state to regain control over its alcohol assets and put an end to the asset stripping that saw state property being siphoned off into private hands for a fraction of its market value. But a closer look suggests that the asset stripping has continued, only now the assets are being stripped by "approved" members of Putin's *sistema.*

One of Rosspirtprom's earliest accused asset strippers was its first director general, Arkady Rotenberg's business partner Sergey Zivenko. In July 2002 prime minister Mikhail Kasyanov signed a resolution removing Zivenko from his post as director general of Rosspirtprom.[32] Just three weeks earlier, the Accounting Chamber of the Russian Federation had begun an investigation into Rosspirtprom's activities, the results of which were published in 2003. While the report carefully avoided explicitly accusing Zivenko of asset stripping, it noted that he had authorized the sale of shares held by Rosspirtprom at significantly below their market value. "The actions of Rosspirtprom director general S.V. Zivenko caused significant damage to the rights and legal interests of Rosspirtprom, as well as to the interests of the state as protected by current legislation," concluded the report, before cryptically recommending that an "information letter on violations of the law" be sent to the prosecutor general of the Russian Federation, "so that the perpetrators may be brought to justice."[33] Prosecutors did indeed open a case against Zivenko for abuse of authority (including alleged asset stripping) that year,[34] but in the end the case was dropped. Zivenko fell on his feet, setting up in the alcohol market in his own right and quickly establishing himself as a significant player in the market. However, property rights in Russia are transient in nature; as easily taken away as they are illicitly obtained, they are guaranteed only for as long as one remains located within the *sistema* networks. Some years after he left Rosspirtprom, it appears that Zivenko and Rotenberg had a falling out. The reason is not known; one insider respondent explained simply (as if no more explanation were required), "Zivenko says Rotenberg fucked him, and Rotenberg says Zivenko fucked him." Soon after this conversation, as if like clockwork, the alcohol market regulator RAR took away the license from Zivenko's one remaining vodka plant.[35]

"A clear example of how bankruptcy is becoming an instrument of privatisation" is how the national newspaper *Vedomosti* described the bankruptcy of one Rosspirtprom plant.[36] In 2006, the Rosspirtprom-owned, Krasnoyarsk-based vodka factory Yarich took out bank credit to the tune of 10 million rubles, with its property as the guarantee. The debt was then sold on through a succession of alcohol companies, eventually coming into the possession of the trading house SDS-Alko in April 2009, which then took out a successful court action to demand the repayment of the debt. When Yarich was unable to repay, SDS-Alko took out a court action for the bankruptcy of Yarich. A few months later a new company, OOO Krasnoyarsk Vodka Factory, began operating at the Yarich site, owned not by Rosspirtprom but by SDS. Thus, the former Rosspirtprom asset had effectively been privatized into SDS's control.[37]

This form of unofficial privatization is how the oligarch Vasily Anisimov acquired his vodka assets. As described in chapter 4, in 2006 Rosspirtprom took out a loan of some 5 billion rubles from the state-owned bank VTB to repay its tax debts (for comparison, the authorized capital stock of Rosspirtprom was around 9 billion rubles). Rosspirtprom repaid the debt not in cash but in factories. Between October 2009 and April 2010 the Moscow Arbitration Court issued several decisions on the transfer of state assets for repayment of Rosspirtprom's debt to VTB, as well as the recovery of interest and fines totaling over 1.7 billion rubles. Kremlin officials at the time gave assurances that the shares VTB received would be kept in trust for five years, and that up to 2015 it would not be able to resell them to anyone except Rosspirtprom. After this period, the state would have a preferential right to buy the companies. However, by June 2010 Vasily Anisimov had bought an 86 percent stake in the Kristall distillery from VTB, as well as a controlling stake in ten other distilleries.[38]

Thus, although the formation of Rosspirtprom represented a form of business capture by the state, in practice state capture has continued in the form of the most lucrative alcohol production facilities being unofficially privatized into the hands of certain individuals. As paradoxical as it may sound, this is best described as state-approved state capture. Like the dominance of *sistema* networks in certain key Russian industries, this form of state-sponsored asset stripping is not unique to the alcohol sphere. A parallel trend has been observed in the state-owned Russian energy giant Gazprom. Since 2001 Gazprom was chaired by Alexey Miller, who had served under Putin in the Committee for External Relations in the Saint Petersburg Mayoral Office from 1991 to 1996. Between the years 2003 and 2007, according to a study by two leading Russian oppositionists, 6.4 percent of Gazprom's shares (equivalent to around $20 billion) disappeared from its balance sheet, and the loss cannot be accounted for.[39] A number of Gazprom's assets have been sold to friends of Putin at reduced prices. For example, the gas industry insurance association Sogaz was sold off in an opaque manner, and a large share of it ended up owned (either directly or indirectly via subsidiary companies) by Rossiya Bank. Rossiya Bank management estimates suggest that the purchase of Sogaz cost it around $120 million, whereas the real value of the company is in the area of $1.5–2 billion—a value that has been helped by the fact that after purchase it began insuring some major state-owned companies, just as Rosspirtprom's companies began using the Rotenbergs' banks.[40] Rossiya Bank through its structures also bought the TV channels NTV and TNT from Gazprom for $166 million; just two years later they were valued at $7.5 billion. The largest shareholder in Rossiya Bank is Yury Kovalchuk, another friend of Putin's from his Saint Petersburg days. Kovalchuk was the fourth private individual placed on the U.S. sanctions list in 2014, alongside the Rotenbergs and Gennady Timchencko. Moreover, a single organization was also subject to the sanctions: Rossiya Bank itself. The sanctions named Rossiya Bank as "the personal bank for senior officials of the Russian Federation" and described Kovalchuk as one of Putin's "cashiers."[41]

Oppositionists Boris Nemtsov and Vladimir Milov calculated in 2008 that "over the last few years as a result of machinations to bleed Gazprom of assets, the corporation has lost control of assets to a value exceeding $60 billion."[42] The Rotenbergs themselves have also been major beneficiaries of the sale of Gazprom assets. In 2008 Gazprom sold them several of its subsidiary companies, in particular the ones that supply and construct pipelines. It then began placing large orders with these same companies. The Rotenberg firm

StroyGazMontazh won nineteen such tenders with Gazprom in 2009 alone, in some cases being the only bidder.[43] Such is the nature of *sistema* that the benefits of being "close to Putin" are commonly seen as not only financial. Such individuals are also perceived as having influence in policymaking decisions.

The Policymaking "Black Box" and Perceptions of Power

Ledeneva describes *sistema* as "an open secret that represents shared, not yet articulated, perceptions of power and the system of government in Russia."[44] The word "perceptions" is important here. Kryshtanovskaya and White have referred to the "black box" of Russian policymaking, in which decisions are made outside official policymaking structures by opaque informal groupings.[45] The nontransparent nature of Russian policymaking means that even those who are close to the policymaking process are often unaware of how a particular decision was made and by whom. Gleb Pavlovsky, who worked as a Kremlin adviser between 1996 and 2011 and was regarded as one of Putin's key political technologists, claimed that even he could "hardly claim to understand the real mechanisms of power in today's Russia."[46] Policy actors and observers tend to compensate for the "black box" by constructing their own explanatory frameworks of how decisions were likely to have been made, based on "open secrets" about the informal ties and private interests of key individuals. Thus, *sistema* is partly composed of (and functions on the basis of) shared subjective perceptions of "how things are" and who is influencing what. One example of this is official appointments under Putin's administration. Ledeneva noted that observers tended to interpret such appointments as being made on the basis of informal network affiliation (e.g., Petersburgers, *siloviki*) even when such a network principle was not in fact in operation.[47]

My fieldwork interviews revealed two striking findings in respect to perceptions of the power of informal networks in alcohol policymaking. The first finding was that the policy "black box" was a dominant feature of respondents' accounts. Even individuals who could be considered insiders typically did not know how a particular decision had been reached, or who was responsible for it. One beer industry executive, whose very job it was to find out who was making policy decisions and try and influence them accordingly, expressed their frustration at just how difficult it was to find out this information: "Excise duty on beer was increased by 200 percent in 2010, and according to our information it was Putin's idea; maybe the Rotenberg brothers told him this brilliant idea, I don't know. . . . So you never know who may approach, for example, the prime minister [i.e., Putin at this time] and whisper into his ear some brilliant new idea. This is a very nontransparent, nondemocratic process—sometimes it's really hard to get any information."

The second striking finding, also indicated by the quote above, was that informal networks—and in particular the Rotenbergs—were widely regarded as influential actors in alcohol policy. It is difficult to know whether and to what extent the Rotenbergs intervene in policy decisions, and indeed respondents noted that they could only guess at this. But the prevailing assumption among most policy stakeholders—from public health activists to beer and vodka industry participants—is that alcohol policy is directed in the Rotenbergs' interests and that they are at least able to exert influence should they wish to do so. The following statement from a public health respondent represents a typical view held by respondents of all types: "I can only guess, and my guess is that they [the Rotenbergs] have a large influence because they say that Chuyan is connected to them, and Zvagelskiy. . . . And if that's right, if they control Chuyan and Zvagelskiy and talk to Putin that means that they completely control alcohol policy in Russia. I mean, not 100 percent control because there is of course the Ministry of Health, there is beer lobbying, there is wine lobbying, there is public health pressure including the Church . . . but still, they have huge influence."

In fact, a majority of my respondents noted that a powerful section of the vodka industry was controlled by personal friends of Vladimir Putin, and these individuals were thereby perceived to have influence on state alcohol policy. Of the sixteen respondents who could reasonably be expected to be aware of them, nine respondents mentioned (without prompting) the Rotenberg brothers in the context of influence on state alcohol policy, while four mentioned Vasily Anisimov. One additional respondent did not mention any individuals by name but referred to "Putin's friends." Altogether, eleven of sixteen respondents made some kind of reference to the influence on alcohol policy of businessmen who are personal friends of Putin.

The informal network dimension provided by Putin's *sistema* is thus central to a full understanding of alcohol policy in contemporary Russia. Numerous examples are given throughout this book—the eventual form taken by Medvedev's antialcohol initiative, excise duty policy, and the activity of legislators in the State Duma. The activities of the federal alcohol market regulator RAR need to be understood not only in the context of increasing federal control in the alcohol market but also that of creating administrative resources to operate for the benefit of *sistema* interests. It is to the creation of this new regulatory beast that we now turn.

Chapter 6

An All-Powerful Regulator

On 25 November 2015, an extraordinary showdown took place in the Federation Council, Russia's upper chamber of parliament. Valentina Matviyenko, the Federation Council's charismatic chair and former governor of Saint Petersburg, delivered a humiliating dressing down to a senior state official, accusing his agency of incompetence and possible corruption. The agency in question was the country's federal alcohol regulator, and the target of Matviyenko's wrath was Igor Chuyan, the former Rosspirtprom director general who had headed the regulator since its formation in 2009. "Don't you feel responsible for the critical state of the alcohol market?" thundered Matviyenko. "Aren't you tired of this post?" Matviyenko proceeded to instruct the Anticorruption Committee to investigate Chuyan for his alleged informal connections with the alcohol business. While Chuyan squirmed in the gallery, Matviyenko told him: "There's a lot of rumours about your affiliation with the alcohol business. . . . It's possible that it's just rumours, it's possible that your enemies are slandering you. . . . As Rosalkogolregulirovaniye has gathered for itself practically all functions, but still regulates badly, the possibility of corrupt factors must be examined, so that either these rumours can be publicly refuted and the subject of them exonerated, or they can be confirmed and the appropriate conclusions drawn."[1]

The Federal Agency for Regulating the Alcohol Market—Rosalkogol-regulirovaniye, commonly abbreviated as RAR—was created by presidential decree on 31 December 2008.[2] This represented a major innovation in federal alcohol policy. For the first time in the post-Soviet period, the various aspects of regulating the alcohol market—which had previously been carried out by as many as seven government departments and agencies—were brought together under one "meta-regulator." How can we explain the creation of a brand new agency: who lobbied for its formation, and why were they successful? And even more important, why has the agency become mired in allegations of poor performance and corruption?

As ever with decisions that are made within the "black box" of federal policy formation, the question of how RAR came to be formed is not an easy one to answer. However, the evidence from industry media reports from the 2000s, combined with the testimony of respondents, suggests that there were two parallel sources of pressure to establish a unitary authority to regulate the alcohol industry. The first source of pressure was Rosspirtprom and the informal *sistema* interests described in the previous chapter. The second was the domestic alcohol industry[3] in general. It may seem ironic that the wider industry was in favor of such an agency given the anti–free market beast that RAR was to become, but this irony is only apparent with the benefit of hindsight. In fact, alcohol producers had been proposing such an authority since 2003, the idea being that it would provide a single point of contact for producers and simplify their bureaucratic interactions with the state. In addition, legal producers hoped that a unitary authority would be better able to combat the substantial illegal market that eroded their revenue.

Among those respondents who felt able to answer the question, there was general agreement that Rosspirtprom under Igor Chuyan was the main lobbyist for the formation of RAR. Most admitted that they could not know for sure as the process was nontransparent, but this was the almost universal perception. Some also mentioned that the Rotenbergs through their vested interests in Rosspirtprom were likely to have lobbied, which again illustrates the common perception that the Rotenbergs have a strong influence on alcohol policy. The following response from a public health activist respondent was rather typical:

In Russian we say *zapasnaya zadnitsa*, which means a "spare arse." So when you are in some position in the government that you can open some jobs, and you know that you might be fired quite soon, you create some kind of job for yourself, or sometimes for your relatives or people you owe some favor to. So I think RAR was exactly that.... The person who was appointed the head of it, Chuyan, was the main lobbyist for setting it up. And he had a good case because alcohol is a problem, and if alcohol is a problem the typical reaction in the Russian government is that you need to set up a separate agency that will be responsible for solving this problem. . . . Chuyan lobbied the senior government basically, and I'm sure the Rotenberg brothers and other people around Putin were very much in favor of it because they hoped it would help to get more control over illegal production which is the main competitor of their vodka.

This account appears to present us with a puzzle, however. If the industry at large—plus influential *sistema* forces—were in favor of the creation of an alcohol market regulator, why did it take so long for one to be formed? Perhaps the most plausible explanation is provided by political science models of bureaucratic self-interest. It has been observed that the leaders of a bureaucracy will typically lobby for policies that expand its functions, as this will normally provide it with a larger budget and increased power and prestige.[4] Since policy space is limited, different departments and agencies compete with one another to ensure that policies maximize their own interests, and to protect their policy territory from encroachment by other bureaucratic departments.[5] Unsurprisingly, none of the ministries and authorities that then shared the functions of regulating the alcohol market wanted to give up their power over an industry that had an estimated $20 billion a year turnover in 2006.[6]

It took an industry-wide crisis to provide the catalyst for change. That crisis arose in 2006 as a result of the botched implementation of a new centralized monitoring system for alcohol. Law No. 102 on the Regulation of Ethyl Alcohol was signed by President Putin on 21 July 2005 and took effect 1 January 2006. The main provisions included the introduction of new excise stamps (which had to be affixed on the territory of the Russian Federation) and the introduction of EGAIS (the Unified State Automatic Information System), which records the amount of ethyl alcohol used and produced, including its volume and concentration. All production facilities were required to obtain the necessary electronic recording equipment to feed into EGAIS, which would allow records to be automatically collected and sent to the centralized information system. Alcohol producers and importers were required to submit data to EGAIS starting 1 January 2006, with wholesalers required to do so starting 1 July 2006.

The failure of EGAIS to operate properly first paralyzed distilleries, while imported wines and spirits with old excise stamps were withdrawn some time later. In the first eight months of operation alone, the overall losses to the industry were estimated at $230 million. It also led to a shortage of alcohol on the shelves and a reported spate of alcohol poisonings as people resorted to black market alcohol and substitutes. That the operation of EGAIS was bound in federal law meant that it was impossible to suspend the system while the problems surrounding its operation were resolved, and the crisis deepened still further when wholesalers were drawn into EGAIS chaos in July 2006.[7]

The Union of Alcohol Market Participants (SUAR) proposed the establishment of a unified government body to oversee the activity of the alcohol industry in August 2006. The union stated that the "crisis" that had arisen in the Russian alcohol market stemmed from poor coordination among government agencies. The establishment of a state body with the working title of the Federal Agency for Management of the Alcohol Market was discussed in August 2006 at a meeting in the Ministry of Agriculture devoted to the crisis in the alcohol market.[8] Toward the end of that year, the State Duma Committee on Economic Policy published a list of proposed measures, which included the creation of a single federal authority for regulating the alcohol market.[9]

First deputy prime minister Viktor Zubkov took control of the creation of the service.[10] Zubkov, it will be recalled, was a board member of Rosspirtprom and connected to the Rotenbergs through the Yawara-Neva Judo Club. Zubkov's comments in 2008, when the decree on the formation of RAR was being drafted, revealed much about his priorities for the new body. He was particularly concerned that revenue from excise taxes had decreased in 2008 and that the illegal market was continuing to blossom. His only reference to public health concerns was that "the health of citizens is being threatened by counterfeit products," with no mention of the scale of alcohol consumption as a whole. It was already being planned at this stage that the new agency would set minimum prices for wholesale and retail sale of vodka, based on the minimum for which a company could produce an entirely legal bottle of excise-paid vodka (then considered to be 80 rubles at retail sale). It was planned that RAR would inherit the regulatory functions then carried out by the Ministry of Finance, Ministry of Agriculture, and Ministry for Economic Development, but not those of the Federal Tax Service.[11]

Why did the other departments concerned not oppose having their powers taken away? Perhaps just as important as the government's desire to create a new unified authority, the crisis situation served to weaken the opposition from other bureaucratic departments to surrendering their powers to a new authority. The political scientist James Wilson noted that a bureaucracy may not necessarily defend its turf if it is a difficult area that opens it up to criticism,[12] and it appears that the EGAIS crisis turned federal alcohol policy into exactly this kind of hot potato. Deputy agriculture minister Igor Rudenya's statement at the August 2006 crisis meeting that the ministry would not oppose a new federal agency surprised many at the time, but it offered a way for the ministry to rid itself of responsibility for resolving the crisis and protect itself from potential future criticism.[13] It was a convenient solution for all concerned, including the government itself. Nevertheless, there was still opposition from individual departments over the transfer of some of their functions. It has been claimed that the Ministry of Finance came out against transferring responsibility for issuing excise stamps to the new body, on the basis that the function is inextricably linked to excise tax and should not be taken from the Federal Tax Service, although interestingly the latter itself did not object to the transfer of part of its functions.[14] The Ministry of Agriculture also opposed the transfer of some of its functions. Minister of agriculture Alexey Gordeyev's relations with Zubkov were reportedly strained. When the formation of RAR was being finalized in early 2009, Gordeyev was transferred out to the provinces by President Medvedev, becoming governor of the Voronezh region (effectively a demotion).[15] Deputy agriculture minister Nikolay Arkhipov had hoped to become the head of RAR, and for a long time was considered almost an official contender for the chair by insiders.[16] Significantly, however, it was the Rosspirtprom chair, Igor Chuyan, who was appointed head of RAR.

The RAR-Rosspirtprom Tandem

RAR's aims as officially stated are both vague and broadly defined. According to the presidential decree of 31 December 2008 that established RAR on paper, its role is "to develop and implement public policy and legal regulation in the sphere of production and sale of ethyl alcohol and alcoholic products," as well as "control, surveillance and provision of services" in this area.[17] It is thus important to note that RAR functions both as a policymaking body (responsible for developing alcohol policy for the Russian Federation and drafting new federal laws) and as a regulator: licensing alcohol production, issuing excise stamps, and operating EGAIS. This runs counter to the general principle of "separation of powers" within government: that a single institution should not have the power to both develop policy and to carry out enforcement in the same area.

A government resolution of 24 February 2009 instructed RAR to develop, by October 2009, proposed changes to federal legislation "to optimise the exercise of state powers in the sphere of production and sale of ethyl alcohol and alcoholic products."[18] To what ends the state's powers needed to be "optimised" the resolution did not specify. One public health respondent expressed their frustration at the vagueness of RAR's goals: "In RAR's official functions [*polozheniye*], there is nothing written about reducing consumption—it regulates, and that's it. It's not even written to what aim it regulates! It just regulates!"

Although RAR's official aims are ambiguous, there was widespread agreement among respondents together with experts quoted in the Russian media that, based on its performance so far, it would appear to have an "unofficial task": to clear the alcohol market of small companies, leaving just a handful of major players. The consolidation of the alcohol market was a clear statistical trend in the years immediately following RAR's foundation. The number of alcohol distilleries in Russia fell from 747 on 1 April 2010 to 675 on 1 January 2011. Of these, 35 had legal applications filed to annul their licenses, and a further 243 had their licenses suspended.[19] RAR revoked 62 licenses in 2009, 120 in 2010, and 156 in 2011.[20]

Was RAR formed with the deliberate aim of wresting alcohol companies out of private control and into the hands of the state and/or *sistema* networks? Or is this phenomenon an unintended consequence of the creation of a unitary authority with such extensive powers over a highly lucrative sector of the economy? It is certainly no secret that certain individuals at the heart of federal alcohol policymaking have stated their desire to dramatically reduce the number of firms operating in the Russian alcohol market. Viktor Zvagelskiy, the United Russia Duma deputy and former Rosspirtprom executive, boasted in a television appearance early in 2011 that RAR had closed

70 percent of alcohol factories in the country.[21] The chairman of the State Duma's Expert Committee on Alcohol Production and Sale, Leonid Vigdorovich, also publicly stated that the number of players on the alcohol market should be reduced.[22]

It is notable that RAR and Rosspirtprom share strong network ties. The transfer of personnel from Rosspirtprom to RAR indicates the informal closeness of the two bodies. RAR's chief executive Igor Chuyan served as director general of Rosspirtprom from June 2006 until his appointment as head of RAR in January 2009. Prior to this he had worked for Rosspirtprom in various roles since 2002. Two of Chuyan's six deputies at RAR also followed him directly from Rosspirtprom. Perhaps most significant, Chuyan served on Rosspirtprom's board of directors while continuing to head RAR. Needless to say, the head of a federal regulatory authority serving on the board of a company whose activities his authority is supposed to regulate was a clear conflict of interest. It will be recalled that first deputy prime minister Viktor Zubkov—who oversaw the creation of RAR—was also a longtime member of Rosspirtprom's board of directors. Zubkov only stood down in 2011 following president Dmitry Medvedev's instruction that government ministers could no longer serve on the boards of directors of state-owned companies.

Market analysts have accused RAR of acting to artificially consolidate the alcohol market, to the benefit of Rosspirtprom and companies belonging to other privileged individuals in the *sistema* network. Vadim Drobiz, perhaps the most famous Russian alcohol market analyst, has usefully conceptualized this relationship as a "public-private partnership": "The present market clearing is carried out in the interests of the public-private partnership, the managing company of which is Rosspirtprom. The partnership currently controls about 6–7 percent of the market for vodka, but wants to raise its stake to 30 percent. This can only be achieved if a significant proportion of manufacturers leave the market."[23]

Following its creation, RAR acquired an impressive range of powers for exerting control over the alcohol market in Russia. Its wide-ranging powers have enabled it to seemingly employ a tactic best described as over-regulation and under-enforcement: RAR establishes requirements that are almost impossible for any producer to meet, and uses violation of them to suspend the production of targeted companies, while quietly ignoring violations by favored companies. RAR has faced criticism from many market participants for making unnecessarily burdensome administrative demands and establishing licensing requirements that are almost impossible for all but the largest producers to meet. It tightened the requirements for production storage facilities, requiring companies to own warehouses of at least one thousand square meters—a size not owned by most producers, and expensive to obtain (one commentator estimated the cost to be at least $1 million). The scale of paperwork demanded by RAR (some companies claim sending documentation weighing up to 30 kilograms) provides the agency with a potential hold over producers, because in principle a few typos could be sufficient to deny a company a license.[24] One respondent, a vodka producer, related that RAR required warehouses to be an impossibly low temperature—16 degrees Celsius—which could be achieved only by purchasing prohibitively expensive equipment. The respondent believed that this was a pretext used by RAR to close down unfavored companies.

A second tactic that RAR has used in its apparent bid to reduce the number of players in the market is to deprive companies of a license on legally ambiguous pretexts. Two Russian lawyers, Elena Ovcharova and Nataliya Travkina, conducted a review of cases where alcohol producers whose licenses had been revoked appealed to arbitration courts, and found that RAR repeatedly exceeded its powers by trying to impose licensing requirements that had no basis in law. The analysis found that in most cases, the courts overturned RAR's decision to revoke the license.[25] Ovcharova and Travkina found that RAR officials exercised considerable personal discretion in whether to grant a license to a particular company, concluding that alcohol licensing laws "are being implemented on the basis of unlimited administrative discretion bordering on tyranny." A special investigation by the newspaper *Novaya gazeta* put the point more bluntly: "[RAR] is not an authority—it's a farce. In no other area is there anything like it: in charge of everything and everyone, and not answerable for anything."[26]

Part of the problem is that the law itself is vague. At a special RIA Novosti press conference on the alcohol industry, Ovcharova complained that the poor drafting of the law gave RAR a sense of supreme power: "For some reason we don't get concise answers from RAR. Why? Because they think that they're the only ones—there's only the government above them, and they feel that their powers are unlimited. Why do they feel that their powers are unlimited? Because the law isn't fully spelled out [*ne v polnye mere opredelyen*]."[27]

Ovcharova added that law-abiding companies had been driven to bankruptcy during the recent round of relicensing, while others had to make substantial investments to meet the "not even requirements, but whims [*kaprizi*] of RAR staff." In some cases, even if a case did go to court, the court's decision mattered little for the future of the company. Even when the courts overturn RAR's refusal to issue a license, the time taken to bring the case to court, plus delays by RAR in acting on the court's judgment and issuing the license[28] can be enough to put a producer out of business. The system for compensating firms for losses caused by the unlawful decisions of public authorities does not work in practice. Companies receive only nominal legal costs, which do not come anywhere close to covering the losses from halting production for several months.[29] One insider told me that while some companies whose licenses were taken away went to the arbitration courts to try to have the decision overturned, others did not bother, because they did not feel that they could succeed in a conflict with RAR even with a judicial decision in their favor.

The futility of trying to appeal against RAR's decisions in court was also described by a vodka producer respondent. However, according to this respondent, one way to convince RAR to reverse its refusal to issue a license was to pay a sufficiently large bribe:

Respondent: My company hasn't been able to get a license for eighteen months. I can't get a license for a warehouse of 200 quadratic meters. I just can't. I've already submitted an application at least ten times, they refused me; they said what was wrong, I corrected it. Now I have an *ideal* warehouse—it's already impossible to say that I don't. But all the same they refuse me. They think up whatever you like. And they understand that if I take them to court I'll win. But if I win the case then they'll close me down on other grounds. They'll find something that I haven't done "just so."

ALB: What do you think they wanted from you, a bribe?

Respondent: Yes, if I were able to give a big bribe that would resolve the matter. But I don't have such large sums of money.

ALB: How did you know that they wanted a bribe?

Respondent: We know all of this because we always have our acquaintances around us, our friends who in such a situation give money and get what they need. Therefore I know who I'd need to approach if I had the money. I can't come to RAR and give [the bribe] to any of its staff, they wouldn't take it from me. I know who I need to go to. There are people who are *posredniki* [middlemen]. So I can give them the money and the bureaucrat can take it from them. Everyone knows who they are.

Another informal practice that RAR has been accused of employing is forcing retailers and wholesalers to buy from its preferred companies. Two respondents—one a brewing executive, one an industry journalist— claimed they had received reports of such incidents from their colleagues in the industry. Of course, it is impossible to verify such claims, as the journalist themself conceded—it has become a kind of general complaint within the industry, but with no one prepared to name any names: "It's not provable, because the prosecutor will not have anything to do with it as there's no evidence. But just because I often talk with all the market participants, I hear such complaints from them. As a rule these complaints are also anonymous. They simply do not indicate who is complaining about it, because everybody has to work in this market; everyone still wants to make money in it somehow."

RAR has been accused of being complicit in hostile takeovers, or *reiderstvo* (raiding),[30] in the alcohol industry. While the full scale of *reiderstvo* is hard to establish, it was a widespread phenomenon in the Russian economy in the 2000s: one senior Russian politician estimated in 2008 that at least 10 percent of enterprises were engaged in fighting off corporate raids.[31] Moreover, *reiderstvo* is not only typically accomplished by the corrupt use of the state bureaucracy's administrative resources but also often actually instigated by corrupt officials.[32] A vodka producer claimed that RAR finds a pretext to deprive a targeted company of its license, which enables *sistema* interests to mount a hostile takeover: "In practice, RAR has become an instrument for restructuring the market. Basically it simply takes what these people [*svoi*] need, those who want to take it for themselves, and simply closes the firm down. It has absolutely all the levers necessary. They turn up and pick fault; pick fault with whatever they like—and take away your license."

One brewing executive respondent related a similar process while explaining why the brewers fear being regulated by RAR: "The same happened with a lot of vodka distilleries in Russia. Many distilleries got their licenses suspended, then obviously they went bankrupt because they could not produce vodka; and then some companies related to Rotenberg or somebody else acquired these assets at quite a low price. And then obviously the distilleries were magically granted this long-needed license."

The founder of the Saint Petersburg–based distillery VinRus claimed that in the spring of 2009 he was approached by some mysterious individuals with a proposal for him to give them a 51 percent share in his company. Sensing that the individuals were corporate raiders, the owner refused. Between April and December of that year, RAR carried out at least five separate checks on the company, and in December eventually closed it down due to a torn label. The owner related: "Previously such issues were dealt with in due course: I called the tax office, the inspectors came and changed the defective label. But here the torn label was grounds to close me down."[33]

An apparent attempt at *reiderstvo* bankrupted the North Ossetian plant Istok, once the largest alcohol producer in Russia and second largest in Europe. The factory made the lion's share of its profits from champagne, usually selling out its stocks at New Year's and collecting the revenue in the spring. For the intervening period Istok would take out credit from Sberbank—Russia's largest bank, which is partially state owned—an arrangement that continued for ten years. But in 2009 a succession of bureaucratic obstacles drove Istok deep into debt: Sberbank refused it credit for the first time; the excise stamps it needed to sell its finished products were withheld. The management and workers of the plant blamed its closure on the machinations of raiders.[34] Istok was eventually declared bankrupt in April 2012 and Rosspirtprom announced its interest in buying it up (although in the end no deal was done and the plant remained inoperative).

RAR versus the Federal Antimonopoly Service

RAR's main protagonist within the state has turned out to be the Federal Antimonopoly Service (FAS). The two state bodies have regularly traded blows over RAR's regulatory activities and their effect on competition in the alcohol market. When RAR posted a draft order on its website relating to the containers in which alcohol could be stored, FAS issued a press release warning that the agency risked violating competition law by creating barriers to entry in the industry.[35] When FAS backed the alcohol distribution company Vinograf in its dispute with RAR over obtaining a license, RAR challenged FAS in the Moscow Arbitration Court.[36] FAS has nevertheless continued to investigate RAR on the grounds of suspected violations of competition law. One of FAS's complaints was that RAR was relying on regulations that applied to the Federal Tax Service while its own regulations were still being drawn up and awaiting approval. "This is a common practice and something FAS can hardly be ignorant of," retorted RAR.[37]

In June 2011 FAS head Igor Artemev took the ongoing struggle with RAR a stage further, directly appealing to the Russian government to revise RAR's powers. Artemev expressed concerns that RAR was exceeding its powers by overstating the requirements for the issuance of licenses, and requested that the Government Commission on Regulating the Alcohol Market look into the issue, something that the commission's chairman, Viktor Zubkov, indicated it would do. FAS stated that it had received "a large number of complaints against Rosalkogolregulirovaniye related to its placing administrative barriers in the issuing of permits and the lack of an adequate regulatory framework."[38] According to FAS, RAR still did not have in place administrative regulations that gave it the authority to regulate the market.

If—as many in the industry believe—RAR is deliberately working to restrict competition in the Russian alcohol market, it has enjoyed considerable success. When RAR was established at the start of 2009, there were 317 companies producing alcoholic beverages in Russia (excluding beer). By January 2016, the figure was just 189.[39] But rival vodka producers are not the only threat to Rosspirtprom and *sistema*-controlled alcohol companies. For in the 2000s, a new beverage emerged to rival vodka's popularity, especially among the younger generation of consumers. Beer was taking the Russian alcohol market by storm.

Chapter 7

Beer

The New Pretender on the Russian Alcohol Market

Which alcoholic drink do you most associate with Russia? It would be surprising to find someone who answered anything other than vodka. And it would seem stranger still if someone answered beer. Our strong cultural association of vodka with Russia is entirely justified by historical consumption patterns. Russia's traditional drinking style belongs to the "North European pattern," where strong alcohol—typically vodka—is consumed in periodic binges.[1] Beer was never a particularly popular beverage in the USSR, where supply dictated consumption. There was some slight growth in consumption in the postwar decades—in 1961 average per capita beer consumption was 12 liters, which gradually rose to a peak of 24 liters on the eve of the antialcohol campaign in 1985.[2] But this was still only a tiny fraction of consumption levels in traditional beer-drinking countries such as Germany and the United Kingdom. For comparison, per capita beer consumption was over 140 liters in Germany in 1985, and around 110 liters in the UK.[3]

The fall of the Soviet Union did not bring about any real change in beer consumption—indeed, it actually declined slightly over the first half of the

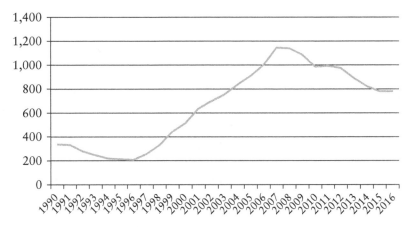

Figure 7.1 Beer production in Russia (million deciliters), 1990–2016 (Rosstat). Data source: *Rossiyskiy statisticheskiy yezhegodnik* **(Russian Statistical Yearbook) (Moscow: Rosstat).**

1990s. But from 1996 onward, a dramatic growth in beer consumption took place that transformed Russia into one of the world's largest beer markets. From a per capita figure of 15 liters in 1996, consumption spiraled to 80 liters in 2007, a level similar to the EU average. By 2010, this average level of consumption combined with its large population size made Russia the third-largest beer market in the world, with 6 percent of global beer consumption and production.[4] Beer can be regarded as an urban beverage: its consumption in major cities is almost double the Russian average. This may be due to the poverty of rural areas of Russia: one gram of alcohol in beer is 2.5 times more expensive than a gram of alcohol in vodka, with *samogon* and counterfeit vodka naturally being even cheaper.[5]

Interestingly, trade plays hardly any role in the Russian beer market, with the vast majority of beer consumed being produced domestically.[6] Thus, the boom in beer consumption between 1996 and 2007 was mirrored by a massive expansion in domestic production (see fig. 7.1). Although the Russian beer market initially depended on imports in the early post-Soviet years, the 1998 default encouraged the development of domestic beer production by making imported beer uncompetitive. Thus, according to Russian state statistics, imports of beer between January and November 1999 decreased by 64.8 percent compared with the same period in 1998. The 1996 declassification of beer as an alcoholic product may also have helped the growth of the domestic beer industry, by creating a gap in prices for domestic and imported beers.[7]

Despite the overwhelmingly domestic production, the Russian beer market retains an international character through the ownership of the main producers. The dominant Russian beer producer, Baltika (which had 34.7 percent of the market in 2015), is owned by Carlsberg. The rest of the market is dominated by three other international firms: ABInbev, Heineken, and Efes Rus, which all have market shares in the teens. The largest Russian-owned brewers, Ochakovo and Moscow Brewing Company, each had only around 3 percent of the market.[8] Much of the beer produced by the multinationals is sold in the form of local brands specific to the Russian market. Indeed, it is interesting to note that, although in the early Yeltsin era imported beer was being marketed as a trendy Western product,[9] by the mid-2000s it was overwhelmingly being marketed as a traditional Russian product.[10]

Koen Deconinck and Johan Swinnen produced an in-depth analysis of beer's dramatic growth in popularity in Russia in 1996. They found that, although price effects seem to have played some role in suppressing demand for beer before that date (the price of beer doubled relative to that of vodka between 1992 and 1995), the role of price after 1996 was ambiguous. The authors cite other factors that combined to form a perfect storm that fueled the dramatic growth. First, while the advertising of vodka was heavily restricted by law in 1995, beer advertising remained much less so until the late 2000s. Although full bans on alcohol advertising do not tend to affect overall consumption, the few studies that have been conducted suggest that partial advertising bans may have an effect in terms of switching *between* types of alcoholic beverages.[11] Beer advertising was a huge market in Russia (in 2005 it was the second-most-advertised product on Russian television[12]), and thus its advertising advantage over vodka may have played a role in encouraging Russian consumers to move to beer. Changing consumer preferences brought about by advertising are likely to have been multiplied by the "network effect" in beverage consumption. Put simply, the fact that alcoholic beverages are usually consumed in social settings means that once a beverage has reached a "critical mass" of popularity it becomes established as the standard drink to consume in social contexts.[13] In addition to the factors proposed by Deconinck and Swinnen, it should be added that the increased availability of beer over vodka played a factor. A presidential decree in April 1997[14] prohibited the sale of alcohol stronger than 12 percent abv from "small retail outlets not having a shop floor"—that is, the hut-like kiosks that were ubiquitous in Russian towns and cities. This made beer much more readily available for purchase compared with vodka. The net result was that the proportion of people drinking beer increased from 23 percent in 1995 to 57 percent in 2003, consistent with the hypothesis of network effects causing a new beverage to snowball in popularity.[15]

Multinational Beer versus Russian Vodka

References to the beer lobby and vodka lobby are ubiquitous in narratives of Russian alcohol policy, among actors of all types: public health activists, journalists, and industry analysts, as well as brewers and vodka producers themselves. This ubiquity applies equally to statements made as part of public discourse, and the confidential and in-depth accounts provided by my respondents during fieldwork interviews.

Lobbyists are rent-seeking agents who seek to extract privileges from the government. But because lobbyists' rent seeking is in essence akin to "favor seeking," for it to be politically feasible it needs to be disguised or represented as somehow in the "public interest."[16] For example, placing a minimum price on alcohol may produce a transfer of resources away from consumers to alcohol companies (it is in effect a government-enforced cartel keeping alcohol prices artificially high), but can be presented as a public health measure.

The concepts of the beer lobby and vodka lobby, it seems, are central to all observers' explanatory frameworks of alcohol policy formation. But who these mysterious lobbies are composed of and how exactly they bring their influence to bear on policy formation is rarely explicitly stated. Part of the reason why the concept of lobbies is so widely used in the first place is because its vagueness is useful. Because the "black box" of the policymaking process is so opaque, the notion of lobbies is used as a default explanatory factor to fill the gaps when the precise manner in which a policy was decided is unknown. Thus, the machinations of lobbies are in part subjective projections that form part of observers' explanatory frameworks, making sense of events that would otherwise be unexplained. That is not to say that these lobbies do not have a real existence—far from it—only that as *concepts* they contain a subjective element.

While the concepts of the beer and vodka lobbies are partly subjective, they do have real characteristics that we can compare and contrast. In fact, the two lobbies are very different in nature, reflecting the divergent characteristics

Table 7.1 Characterization of beer and vodka lobbies in Russia

	Beer lobby	Vodka lobby
Ownership	Transnational	Domestic
Market consolidation	Consolidated	Nonconsolidated
Transparency of ownership	Clear capital structures	Unclear capital structures
Lobbying practices	Formal lobbyists (government relations departments)	Informal (suspected) lobbyists
Connections to political elites	Lacks elite ties	Reliant on elite ties
Proximity to the state	External to the state	Integrated within the state

of their respective industries—a point that was emphasized by several respondents. It is these differences that are central to understanding the shift in the balance of power between the two lobbies (to the benefit of vodka) that took place over the 2000s. The differences are summarized in table 7.1.

The beer market in Russia is largely dominated by four multinational producers (Carlsberg, ABInbev, Heineken, and Efes) operating through domestic companies and brands. The structure of the vodka industry stands in stark contrast to this. Although some relatively large players do exist, such as Roustam Tariko's Roust (which produces the premium vodka Russian Standard, a brand that has enjoyed breakthrough success in Western markets), the Russian vodka market is nowhere near as consolidated as that of the brewers. The number of vodka producers remains large, despite the trend toward market consolidation of recent years, and they are predominantly domestically owned. Furthermore, the industry's structures of capital are best described as "shadowy" (*tenevoy*)—it is not always clear who owns what, and chains of ownership are complicated by opaque holding companies and shell companies.

The divergent characteristics of the beer and vodka industries reflect strongly on their lobbying structures and practices. Almost the entire Russian beer industry is represented by one producers' association, the Union of Russian Brewers. In theory this provides the brewers with a strong lobbying foundation, as they can argue as one unified sector. Individual beer companies' lobbying activity is formalized through their government relations departments (commonly known as GR in Russia). However, in practice the brewers'

GR departments are weak, according to one respondent, a lobbying expert: "Unfortunately they [beer companies' GR departments] are not very numerous, and they're not sufficiently well-financed. I don't know why that's the case, it's a mystery to me, because from 2003 the position of brewers has been getting worse compared with other sectors of the alcohol market, and in theory their shareholders . . . should put more finances into GR. I'm not talking about any kind of corruption, I'm talking about civilized lobbying. But it's hardly happening at all, and the GR departments in the beer industry look very weak."

The same respondent contrasted the weakness of the beer companies' GR activities with the success of their counterparts in the tobacco lobby. The two industries are comparable in that they both sell excisable goods that have a negative effect on people's health, but the beer industry, claimed the respondent, was losing the lobbying battle compared with tobacco—"and most of all it's because tobacco companies pay a lot more attention to GR." The respondent suggested that the American-dominated ownership structure of the tobacco industry may be responsible for this: aggressive lobbying is a more familiar part of American business culture than for the Europeans who own the brewing industry.

A public health respondent echoed the sentiment that the beer lobby is poor tactically: "The beer industry is just a transnational lobby. They're well-structured but they're not very strong strategically. For example, I told them many times, 'You should push for vodka tax increases,' but it took them a few years to do this, to realize it, because they were just thinking of defending themselves. But the stronger way for them is to work against vodka, because they're substitute goods."

At a formal level, the vodka industry has few official lobbyists. Unlike the brewers, vodka companies do not tend to have GR departments that consult with government representatives and engage with the media. Indeed, if only official organizational structures were taken into account, one would be hard pressed to identify more than a handful of vodka lobbyists. The essence of the contemporary Russian vodka lobby is rooted in the industry's ever-closer integration with the state. At the formal level this consists of the federal project to consolidate state vodka holdings in Rosspirtprom. But there are also informal dimensions: *sistema* networks with private vodka interests such as the Rotenbergs, as well as state actors perceived to be acting as insider vodka lobbyists—a prominent example being the State Duma deputy Viktor Zvagelskiy, whose case is examined in a separate chapter. Thus, in a

2012 interview Russian lobbying expert Pavel Tolstykh suggested that the vodka lobby's strength derived not from formal lobbying networks as commonly understood, but rather from the vodka industry's ever-closer integration with the state: "What is the secret of [the vodka lobby's] success? I think the explanation lies in the closer ties of this industry with the government— not through lobbying channels, but due to the fact that officials directly control a substantial part of the business."[17]

A public health respondent made a similar point when asked which lobby groups are the most effective in influencing government alcohol policy: "Well of course the vodka industry [is the most influential]. Basically it's so institutionalized that the old vodka industry lobbyists got marginalized. They don't even need lobbyists and public speakers."

This point is illustrated by the various industry organizations representing vodka distillers that disappeared without a trace in the late 2000s: the Union of Alcohol Market Participants, the National Alcohol Association, and the North-West Alliance of Alcohol Business Participants. Indeed, it appears that the only remaining active industry organization representing domestic vodka producers[18] is the Union of Alcohol Producers (SPAP). SPAP is closely tied to the state-sponsored vodka industry: Rosspirtprom and companies affiliated to it are members of the union. It is not easy to obtain professional information on its chair, Dmitry Dobrov, but we know from media citations that as well as heading SPAP, he worked as a communications chief at Rosspirtprom between at least 2006 and 2010, and possibly even longer.

The beer industry, by contrast, lacks elite contacts within the state, or as one expert tellingly put it, is "unusually unreliant" on them.[19] For one respondent with a background in the vodka industry, the very concept of lobbying meant having elite contacts within the state itself. Since the brewing industry does not have such contacts, the concept of a beer lobby made no sense to this respondent: "I can understand who we're thinking of when we talk about the vodka lobby: we know what the media have written that in the authorities there are people who represent the interests of vodka companies. At present there is not a single person in the authorities who has been connected with the brewing business; therefore if we talk about the beer lobby, what is it, who do we mean?"

Lobbying expert Pavel Tolstykh has also suggested that the corporate, multinational character of the beer industry handicaps its ability to match the vodka lobby in the use of informal payments to influence policy:

The second reason for the success of the vodka producers lies in their greater mobility: such structures find it easier to "get hold of ready money" and promptly send it to address specific issues. I think an analysis of the Russian spirits market, with rare exceptions, cannot be considered without a serious corruption component. For beer producers, such lobbying on the principle of the nineties is generally not available: there is a rigid system of control at different levels and stages (financial control, management control, control by the board of directors, monitoring by the compliance office etc.), which makes the procedure for withdrawal of significant funds practically impossible.[20]

Is it really the case that the brewing lobby operates without facilitating payments? Other respondents expressed their suspicions that the industry did make such payments where necessary, although they acknowledged they could not prove it. One public health respondent alleged that both vodka and beer lobbies pay for positive coverage of their arguments in media outlets, including respected broadsheet newspapers:

ALB: So they actually have contracts? "You give us this much money, we give you this much coverage"?

Respondent: Yes. And especially on bills, on tax proposals, things like that. They develop proposals. . . . It's very different, a whole spectrum of GR, corruption, media work, PR, things like that.

The practice of paid-for material presented as ordinary news, known as *dzhinsa* or *zakazukha*, is a relatively widespread phenomenon in the Russian media.[21] Although it is almost impossible to prove individual instances of the practice, its prevalence means that we should expect use of it as a lobbying tool by Russian policy stakeholders.

The Beer Backlash

The major alcohol control law of 2011 contained many provisions, but it is best known as the law that reclassified beer as an alcoholic product in Russia. To fully appreciate how the passage of the 2011 law represented a shift in the balance of power between beer and vodka lobbies, it is necessary to understand how beer became decategorized as alcohol in the first place, and how the subsequent backlash against beer came about.

As related in chapter 3, in the mid-1990s the government launched a legislative offensive aimed at recouping the substantial losses to the treasury from illegal alcohol sales and excise tax avoidance. One of the most important resulting changes was that starting 1 January 1997, all alcoholic products had to be marked with labels indicating that excise duty had been paid on them. It was in response to this that the Duma passed a law in December 1996 depriving beer of the status of an alcoholic beverage,[22] thus avoiding the need for beer to be marked with excise stamps.

There were numerous legislative attempts to reclassify beer as an alcoholic beverage in the years immediately following the change, none of which were successful. The Russian Public Chamber's 2009 report *Alcohol Abuse in the Russian Federation* detailed these attempts and suggested that on each occasion they were successfully undermined by beer lobbyists. In September 1998, for example, the State Duma passed an amendment reclassifying beer as alcohol and increasing the tax burden on brewers, but it was rejected by the upper chamber of parliament, the Federation Council, allegedly in return for continued investment programs by Western beer companies. A further attempt to reclassify beer in June 1999 was also defeated. A similarly unsuccessful attempt was made in December 2000 when, to counter the threat, the heads of the five largest breweries in Saint Petersburg allegedly sent a letter to President Putin, requesting the dismissal of chief medical officer Gennady Onishchenko from office. Although Onishchenko survived, he was apparently forced to retract his proposals under "serious pressure" from the then minister of health, Shevchenko.[23] Such an audacious attempt by business to try to influence the position of a government official may now seem incredible, but, whether true or not, it reflected the perceived strength of the beer lobby at the turn of the century.

Thus, in the early 2000s, it seemed that a strong, united beer lobby reigned supreme over an almost nonexistent vodka lobby. Beer enjoyed a significant legislative advantage over vodka that had been acquired in stages throughout the 1990s—mainly through increased restrictions on strong drinks not being applied to beer. Vodka had been banned from television advertising in 1995, and banned from sale in kiosks in 1997, but beer remained free of these restrictions. Beer had been declassified as an alcoholic beverage in December 1996, thus exempting it from the requirement to affix excise stamps to its bottles, and the numerous attempts to reclassify it had been unsuccessful. In terms of the respective strength of their lobbies, it also seemed that the beer industry had everything in its favor. But just a decade later, beer's legislative advantage had been significantly (although not entirely) diminished. There was general agreement among respondents that by the late 2000s, the vodka lobby had displaced the beer lobby in terms of influence. How can this be explained?

It is interesting to note that the legislative clampdown on beer (the Western import) occurred simultaneously with Russia's political rejection of building closer relations with the West. While the connection is too vague to claim as a causal link, it is nevertheless highly symbolic. Broadly speaking, there were two major landmarks in the decline of the beer lobby's influence: the provocative advertising campaign for Klinskoye beer (early 2000s), and the foundation of the new alcohol regulator RAR (2009). The former created a sociopolitical backlash against what appeared to be the targeting of minors by beer companies, while the latter created an apparent ally of the state-sponsored vodka industry at the level of the federal bureaucracy. But there was also a third event that may have had a more significant effect than one might expect at first glance: the Baltika brewing company's change of president in 2004. Let us examine these factors in turn.

Even at the peak of beer's popularity in 2007, consumption of it was not particularly high in comparative terms, and it did not overtake vodka in terms of amount of alcohol consumed by the population. In terms of recorded consumption alone, in 2010 spirits accounted for 51 percent of pure alcohol consumed, compared with beer's 38 percent,[24] but the large unrecorded vodka market means the true ratio was more likely 60–70 percent for spirits and 20–30 percent for beer. But the rapid growth in beer's consumption—and the manner in which it was being consumed—made it particularly noticeable and led to its consumption being problematized. Beer consumption was more visible than that of other beverages because it was often consumed in the manner of a soft drink in public places, a point made by a brewing executive respondent: "The fact is that beer consumption in Russia is very visible. If you walk along the street and through parks in the summer, everywhere people are drinking beer. They buy it at kiosks, which are everywhere; while waiting for a bus someone will buy a beer from a kiosk next to the bus stop. . . . People don't drink other types of alcohol in this way, on the street."

A related factor is that beer consumption is more associated in the public mind with underage drinkers than other types of beverages, which provokes negative social reactions. The problem the brewers encountered in the early 2000s was that they were perceived as actively targeting underage drinkers. This was particularly overt in the case of an advertising campaign for one brand, SUN InBev's Klinskoye, in the early 2000s. Several respondents believed that the notorious Klinskoye advertising campaign was directly responsible for the Duma passing legislation significantly tightening beer advertising in 2004. One brewing executive, for example, believed that a provision of the advertising law that was applied exclusively to beer—the ban on depicting people or animals in its advertisements—was due to the Klinskoye campaign, with its youthful actors and aggressively "teenage" style. Beer advertising had also become tiresomely pervasive on television at this time. It was estimated to account for around 10 percent of the entire Russian television advertising market in 2003.[25] According to TNS-Gallup, the quantity of television advertising for beer was second only to that for mobile telephones in 2005.[26]

A package of amendments to the law "On Advertising" was duly passed by the Duma in August 2004, adding several restrictions relating specifically to the advertising of beer. Beginning 1 January 2005 it was forbidden to use images of people or animals, or cartoons, in beer advertisements, and beer could not be advertised on television or on the radio from 7 a.m. to 10 p.m. local time. Beer advertisements could not be carried on the first or last page of newspapers or magazine covers. Advertisers were required to devote 10 percent of the advertising space or time to warnings of the harm caused by beer, and advertisements could not imply that the consumption of beer "plays an important role in achieving public, athletic or personal success" or claim that beer "improves physical or psychological well-being or quenches thirst."[27] The sociopolitical backlash against beer was beginning.

"Beer Alcoholism"

Another sign of the increasing problematization of beer in the 2000s was the emergence of the concept of "beer alcoholism." The term is often associated with chief medical officer Gennady Onishchenko (1996–2013), and while it is not clear whether Onishchenko himself coined the term, his regular use of it as a senior government official certainly contributed to its entry into standard media and bureaucratic discourse. The host of the TV debate show

Open Studio introduced an episode dedicated to discussing beer consumption by observing that "Chief Medical Officer Gennady Onishchenko says that 'beer alcoholism' is killing Russia." A panelist on the show, the chief doctor of a narcological hospital, pointed out that medical classifications of alcoholism do not distinguish between the type of drink consumed. As he rightly put it, "beer alcoholism" is "just a kind of slang."[28] Nevertheless, the concept of beer alcoholism has become an integral part of Russian discourse on alcohol; I have even observed academic papers given on the subject at scientific conferences. Other myths about the effects of drinking beer abound in the Russian media, for example, its hormonal effects. Professor Alexandr Nemtsov related with frustration, "Here [in Russia], we are endlessly told that due to beer men grow female breasts, and all sorts of other nonsense."

One brewing executive respondent went as far as to describe the spread of the notion of "beer alcoholism" as part of an "organized campaign" against the brewing industry: "The beer industry since the mid-2000s has been facing an organized public campaign against beer. Both public health officials and the media are engaged, and probably this campaign is nurtured by local spirits producers. And the idea was to instill the idea of 'beer alcoholism' in the media. I remember the person who first mentioned this term was Gennady Onishchenko around 2002–3, and it really became some kind of word of mouth."

The idea that Onishchenko was actively working at the bidding of domestic vodka interests, as this respondent seemed to suggest, is somewhat far-fetched: Onishchenko was a devout teetotaler. But he was also firmly loyal to the governing elite. I witnessed Onishchenko unashamedly urge all delegates at the second congress of the Church-Public Council for Protection Against the Alcohol Threat in February 2012 to vote for Putin in the upcoming presidential elections, as it was essential for the future of the country. It was perhaps less politically sensitive for Onishchenko to criticize the beer industry than the domestic vodka industry, with its informal ties to the governing elite. Certainly, Onishchenko demonstrated his loyalty to Russia's governing elite with some highly symbolic policies: his conveniently timed bans on the import of certain products were frequently a source of mirth in the Western media. The list of Onishchenko bans that coincided with crises in Russia's diplomatic relations with the countries concerned included Georgian and Moldovan wines, Ukrainian chocolate, Lithuanian dairy products, and Belarussian vegetables. It is also worth noting that Onishchenko had personal conflicts with the brewing industry, which may have contributed to his negative attitude toward beer. According to the testimony of one public health respondent, Onishchenko once privately claimed that the beer industry "threatened to kill him." Given that the beer industry reportedly tried to get Onishchenko sacked from the government in 2000, there was understandably no love lost between the two parties.

A Brewer in the Judo Gang

As vodka became increasingly affiliated with the state through the 2000s, both formally (in the form of Rosspirtprom) and informally (through *sistema* networks incorporating Putin's friends, such as the Rotenbergs and Anisimov), the lobbying power of vodka interests increased as well. It is thus even more intriguing to learn that Russia's largest brewer, Baltika, had—but lost—a well-placed *sistema* member of its own.

Taymuraz Bolloyev headed up Baltika between 1991 and 2004. From its establishment as a state enterprise in the dying days of the Soviet Union, through privatization in 1992, and major regional expansion from 1997 onward, Baltika's corporate structure changed dramatically. Bolloyev had many job titles: director, then director general, and finally president. But he was always indisputably the man in charge. His signature was even featured on the labels of Baltika's beers. In 1993, Baltic Beverages Holding (BBH), a Scandinavian holding company formed specifically to invest in the countries of the former Soviet Union, became Baltika's major shareholder and investor. Baltika is famously based in Saint Petersburg. If Bolloyev's account is to be believed, a major role in facilitating the BBH investment deal—so crucial to Baltika's subsequent success—was played by the chair of the Saint Petersburg city government's Committee for Foreign Liaison. Fluent in German and well versed in European culture, he persuaded the Scandinavians that their investment would be safe and offered them his word as a guarantee. That official was Vladimir Putin.[29]

As well as their mutual connection to Saint Petersburg, Bolloyev and Putin shared a love of sport, particularly ice hockey and judo. And so it was that Russia's leading brewer became part of Putin's judo gang. Bolloyev was a member of Yawara-Neva's board of trustees from its foundation in 1998—and indeed, he still serves as the chair of the board of trustees to this day.

Baltika pumped sponsorship money into Yawara-Neva from its very foundation, paying to reconstruct and equip the club's judo halls.[30] In 2003 it jointly organized with Yawara-Neva the Russian President's Cup[31]—an annual international judo tournament established in 2000, the first year of Putin's presidency.

Little is known of the reasons why Baltika and Bolloyev parted company in 2004: both parties have kept quiet on the issue. Officially at least, it was Bolloyev who chose to move on. However, reading between the lines, it may be that Baltika's Scandinavian owners, BBH, chose to replace Bolloyev with one of their own men. Bolloyev had led Baltika from its humble beginnings as a Soviet enterprise, before BBH came on board. By contrast, his replacement as president at Baltika, Anton Artemiyev, was a BBH man, having served as one of its executive vice presidents since 2000. But whatever the ins and outs of what happened behind the scenes, the upshot was that the brewers had lost their one sure connection to Putin's informal networks, just at the time when vodka's informal connections were in the ascendancy. While Bolloyev's proximity to Putin was nowhere close to that of the Rotenbergs, his presence in the judo gang may have been sufficient to provide a degree of protection for the brewers, and a counterweight to vodka interests. With Bolloyev gone from Baltika, no longer would Putin be regarded as the Saint Petersburg brewery's "godfather."[32] The brewers were now well and truly outsiders.

Thus, by the mid-2000s, clouds were already on the horizon for the brewers. Beer's rapid growth in popularity was starting to bring about a sociopolitical backlash, and it had lost ground to vodka interests in the struggle for informal policy influence. But things were about to get even worse for the beer industry. In December 2007, a former senior manager at Rosspirtprom was elected to the State Duma as a deputy for United Russia, the "party of power" that dominates contemporary Russian politics. Quickly carving out a role for himself as a prominent talking head on state alcohol policy, Viktor Fridrikhovich Zvagelskiy was soon to prove a thorn in the brewers' side.

Chapter 8

The Brewers' Nemesis in the Duma

In the late 2000s, the name of Viktor Fridrikhovich Zvagelskiy became ubiquitous in Russian alcohol policy. Whenever there was a televised debate or discussion on alcohol issues, Zvagelskiy was almost always present. Zvagelskiy entered the State Duma at the December 2007 parliamentary elections, having been listed at number eleven (out of eighty) on the ruling party United Russia's regional list for the city of Moscow. He was reelected as a United Russia deputy at the parliamentary elections of December 2011.

Nearly all respondents mentioned Zvagelskiy as an important actor in Russian alcohol policy formation. Alcohol policy was unofficially Zvagelskiy's exclusive preserve in the Duma, although how he gained this monopoly is unclear, as a public health activist respondent related:

Respondent: I tried to work with the vice-chair of the Health Committee from the ruling party, Gerasemenko, but he couldn't do anything, because in United Russia they say that alcohol is Zvagelskiy. And there is no other way to work with the parliament on alcohol, because opposition parties don't have the chance to push anything through.

ALB: So how has it happened that only Zvagelskiy in United Russia deals with alcohol issues?

Respondent: That is not clear. But it is so. Perhaps there are no other active leaders, perhaps there is an agreement with Zvagelskiy. It's a decision of the United Russia leadership.

What *is* known is that, according to the Central Election Commission, Zvagelskiy was one of the main sponsors of United Russia's regional election fund in Moscow at this time.[1] Commenting on the effectiveness of Zvagelskiy's influence on alcohol policy in the Duma, lobbying expert Pavel Tolstykh suggested that Zvagelskiy's financial support of United Russia played an important role: "This funding, it is not difficult to guess, buys off the support of the majority faction in such cases."[2]

Zvagelskiy entered the State Duma straight from Rosspirtprom, where he had served two years as deputy CEO under Igor Chuyan. But in addition, there were persistent reports in the Russian media that Zvagelskiy himself had private interests in vodka production. One such report stated that according to the Unified State Register of Legal Entities (EGRYuL), in March 2004 Zvagelskiy established a cooperative called Artel "Yat," which was transformed into the joint stock company Vodka Artel "Yat" one year later. *Novaya gazeta* reported that when Zvagelskiy ran for the Duma in 2007, he listed Vodka Artel "Yat" as one of his sources of income. As is typical of the opaque vodka market, the capital structure was rather convoluted. EGRYuL's 2007 data listed half of Yat's authorized capital as being owned by the Red Star plant—the founders of which were Yat's director Leonid Vigdorovich and Viktor Zvagelskiy.[3]

Zvagelskiy always strongly denied being a founder or owner of Vodka Artel "Yat," even calling into question the legality of the company's operations to distance himself from it:

I am engaged with alcohol in the State Duma because I am well-versed in these matters. I was a hired manager in a managing company, rather than in Vodka Artel "Yat"; a deputy director general, not the founder or owner. Now, I understand that the words of a Duma deputy—that he is neither a co-owner or founder, that he never handed over control of all the shares or any part of them, that he has no affiliation with it—may not be believed. And although it sounds ugly, I know perfectly well what the current owners of the company which is attributed to me are doing, and I sincerely wish that this company would quickly close. In my impression, they do not operate entirely legally.[4]

However, Zvagelskiy's strenuous denials made little impression on other participants in the alcohol policy sphere. Regardless of whether Zvagelskiy really did have private interests in vodka production, my respondents tended to regard it as an open secret that was beyond doubt. One respondent, also a vodka producer, summed up the prevailing attitude:

Respondent: Zvagelskiy's always been involved in vodka, he produces it. "Yat" is his vodka.

ALB: Although he says it's not his.

Respondent: Let him say that. Everyone knows it is. He needs to say that because he can't have a business while he's a Duma deputy. In fact, people don't leave business when they become deputies, obviously they officially sign the business over to someone else. In particular there's the vodka Kazyonka, it's also his vodka. He's always been in alcohol, so of course when he went into politics he stuck with what was close to him. And so it's quite easy for him, he operates in the interests of his own [*svoi*] and certain given interests.

Whoever the true owner is, Yat's Kazyonka vodka is no stranger to controversy. Kazyonka became embroiled in an advertising scandal when the brand was launched in 2009. The advertising of strong alcohol on posters and billboards, it will be recalled, has been subject to a complete ban since the 1990s. In 2008, before Kazyonka vodka was launched, the streets of Moscow were flooded with billboards declaring *Kazyonka. Coming soon. The movie.* Movie industry insiders claimed to know nothing of a film with such a title; nevertheless, it was listed on the Ministry of Culture's website as having been granted a distribution certificate. The company that had commissioned the "film," TK Holding, was registered to the same address as Vodka Artel "Yat," in the name of an erstwhile director of the latter. Unsurprisingly, no film by the name of *Kazyonka* materialized, and Kazyonka vodka launched in 2009 with a font and color scheme identical to that of the "film" poster.[5] The Federal Antimonopoly Service (FAS) expressed its determination to fine the founders of Kazyonka, although it succeeded only in fining the advertising agencies that displayed the billboards.[6]

In July 2010, Zvagelskiy threatened to take the national daily newspaper *Novaya gazeta* to court for claiming in an article that he was one of the founders of Vodka Artel "Yat." *Novaya gazeta* not only refused to withdraw the claims but also published and ridiculed Zvagelskiy's threat to sue. It could hardly retract the information, stated the newspaper, when the deputy's name, "typed into any Internet search engine, immediately gives a mass of links to Viktor Fridrikhovich Zvagelskiy as one of the founders of Artel 'Yat.'"[7] However, Zvagelskiy followed through with his threat to take *Novaya gazeta* to court—and won the case.[8]

Despite Zvagelskiy's successful pursuit of *Novaya gazeta* through the courts, he was publicly branded a "vodka lobbyist" on numerous occasions by a whole range of actors. The prominent market analyst Vadim Drobiz said, "Of course, the fellow lobbies the interests of the beverage industry."[9] Independent lobbying expert Pavel Tolstykh stated in an interview with RBC Daily that "Viktor Zvagelskiy is quite evidently representing the interests of strong alcohol in the State Duma, but instead of engaging in a real 'whitening' of the market (which if the will existed on the part of the state would not be a huge problem), he reflects the interests of a particular group possessing personal interests in the alcohol industry."[10]

On several occasions the accusation that he was a vodka lobbyist was made to Zvagelskiy's face on national television. The founder of the Russian Coalition for Alcohol Control, Kirill Danishevskiy, accused Zvagelskiy of being a representative of the vodka lobby when they both appeared as panelists on the discussion show *Otkritaya Studiya*.[11] Journalist Gleb Pyanikh accused Zvagelskiy of being "a vodka king disguised as a Duma deputy" when the two came face-to-face on an NTV discussion show.[12] Perhaps most forthright was the renowned Soviet actor Nikolay Burlyaev when he faced off with Zvagelskiy on the *Poyedinok* (Duel) debate show, aired on the main state-owned TV channel *Rossiya-1*: "What amazes me is this. [You are] a person holding a responsible post in the State Duma, regulating excise duties and such tasks. . . . But you yourself are involved in the manufacture of alcohol. Why were you put in that post? Why are you, a person manufacturing and trading vodka, standing here in front of me? . . . Mr Gryzlov[13] should never have put you in that post! A person with vested interests in the alcohol industry . . . It's a governmental mistake. And perhaps it's in part thanks to you that we're heading into this abyss, because you have this in your hands. You're lobbying!"[14]

In view of the collective public "outing" of Zvagelskiy, it is perhaps unsurprising that almost all respondents, without prompting, named Zvagelskiy as a key player in state alcohol policy formation, and usually in the same breath labeled him as a vodka lobbyist. Thus, despite Zvagelskiy's best efforts to portray himself as an antialcohol campaigner and deny his links to the vodka industry, the latter was regarded as common knowledge among the whole range of policy actors and observers.

Zvagelskiy, for his part, blamed the use of *cherniy piar* (black PR)[15] by the beer industry for labeling him a vodka lobbyist: "The stories about my aspirations as a lobbyist have spread in the media only after we started to address beer. . . . Breweries have special budgets allocated for PR, they have very drawn up work with the media. And I can say with confidence that all the recent attacks on me have been inspired by the beer community, and no one else."[16]

In view of the range and number of individuals who have called Zvagelskiy a vodka lobbyist, it seems doubtful that this reputation is solely the work of black PR from the beer industry. Nevertheless, Zvagelskiy's remark is revealing in another respect: it demonstrates the open hostility between him and the brewing industry, with which he has had several very public clashes. Danishevskiy, who may reasonably be considered neutral in the war of words between the vodka and beer camps, stated on national TV, "The information campaign against beer has undoubtedly been organised by the vodka lobby, a representative of which in my opinion is Mr Zvagelskiy."[17]

What did this "information campaign" consist of? Zvagelskiy was quick to utilize the discourse of "beer alcoholism" described in the previous chapter. "Beer alcoholism is in a range of cases more dangerous than alcoholism from spirits" and "the risk of developing alcohol dependence is greater among beer drinkers than wine or spirits drinkers" were among the statements contained in the explanatory memorandum to the 2011 alcohol control bill, drafted by Zvagelskiy.[18] In public discourse, Zvagelskiy selectively cited alcohol consumption statistics to imply that beer consumption was much higher than vodka consumption in Russia, whereas in reality the opposite situation pertained. The key to such sleight of hand is to cite statistics that measure the volume of beverage, rather than grams of pure alcohol consumed. Obviously a pint of beer is hardly equivalent to a pint of vodka, but such details are easily glossed over when quoting statistics on live television. Thus, on the *Otkritaya Studiya* discussion show Zvagelskiy claimed that spirits consumption in Russia accounted for only 20 percent of total consumption—not exactly a lie if one is talking about the volume of liquid sold, but certainly misleading.[19]

Zvagelskiy has also routinely criticized the quality of Russian-produced beer, claiming that it is of inferior quality to that produced in traditional beer-brewing countries. The Duma deputy sparked a major controversy at a parliamentary hearing of 27 January 2011 (convened to consider the government's alcohol control bill) when he stated that up to 90 percent of beer produced in Russia was not in fact real beer, as it was made with concentrates. "Unfortunately, we do not drink beer," asserted Zvagelskiy. "We think that we drink beer, but this drink can be called whatever you like, for example 'beer-containing.'"

The Union of Russian Brewers strongly contested Zvagelskiy's accusations and filed a lawsuit against him. At a hearing of the Moscow Arbitration Court on 30 March 2011, the court dismissed the case against the Duma deputy. Zvagelskiy claimed victory, stating that "the quantity and quality of the evidence provided by my side convinced the court that my position was correct."[20] The Brewers' Union, meanwhile, claimed that the case had been dismissed on a technicality—that Zvagelskiy's defense had claimed that the Brewers' Union was not legally entitled to file a lawsuit, and thus the merits of Zvagelskiy's criticism of Russian beer had not been considered by the court.[21]

In sum, Zvagelskiy's presence in the legislature was a major coup for the vodka lobby, and in particular his old boss at Rosspirtprom, Igor Chuyan. With Chuyan heading up the powerful new alcohol regulator RAR, and Zvagelskiy assuming leadership over alcohol issues in the Duma, in 2009 a powerful new tandem was in place to cut the beer industry down to size.

Chapter 9

"Vodka Is Our Enemy, but Who Said We're Afraid of Enemies?"

According to Russian legend, alcohol is the reason that its people adopted Christianity. In the tenth century, several hundred years before the advent of vodka distilling, Grand Prince Vladimir "the Great" ruled Kievan Rus, the precursor of the modern Russian state. Upon receiving a delegation of Muslim Bulgars, who described the requirements of their religion—including abstinence from alcohol—Vladimir is said to have remarked, "Drinking is the joy of the Russes. We cannot exist without it." The grand prince duly adopted Orthodox Christianity as his people's religion.[1]

Yet, if Russians cannot live without alcohol, it would seem that they find it hard to live with it, too. Opinion polls have long suggested that excessive alcohol consumption is perceived as a major national problem by the Russian population. Russia's state polling agency, VTsIOM, has a long-running series of opinion polls asking about "the most important problems facing the country." Between 2006 and 2011, "alcoholism and drug addiction" was consistently either the most common answer given by Russians or a very close second (figure 9.1).

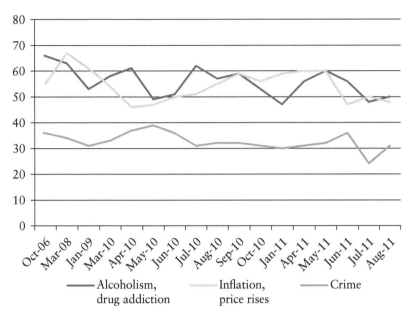

Figure 9.1 Russian public opinion on the most serious problems facing the country (VTsIOM, 2006–2011). The survey question was "Of the problems listed below, which do you consider most important for the country as a whole?" (closed question, not more than seven answers; as multiple answers were possible, summing the responses exceeds 100 percent). "Alcoholism and drug addiction" and "inflation" occupied either first or second place over the entire period. One of the responses that typically placed between third and sixth, "crime," is shown for comparison.

In similar polls, alcoholism has consistently featured as the second or third most serious problem facing the country from a broad range of social and economic issues.[2] Interestingly, this perception of the severity of the alcohol problem is also widespread among young people: in a nationwide survey of young Russians aged fifteen to twenty-nine asking about the most critical issues they faced, alcoholism was the most frequently cited answer (58 percent).[3]

Strong antialcohol sentiments consistently registered in Russian public opinion appear to present us with a paradox. How can the Russian population be opposed to excessive alcohol consumption and yet, at the same time, participate in such consumption? This chapter explores two possible explanations for the alcohol paradox. The first is that society is deeply divided, with one "drunken" half consuming alcohol in huge volumes, while

the other "sober" half suffers the consequences. The second possible explanation is that people exhibit a kind of doublethink, regarding the alcohol
consumption of society at large as undesirable or immoral, but failing to problematize their own consumption. But before we turn to society's opinions on
alcohol consumption, there is an important factual matter to settle: how much
does Russia actually drink?

So How Much Does Russia Drink?

The stereotype of Russians as heavy-drinking vodka lovers is renowned
worldwide, but to what extent is this borne out by statistical data on alcohol
consumption? This question is much more difficult to answer than one
might imagine, because there is in fact no reliable measure of per capita alcohol consumption in the Russian Federation. Data on beer consumption are
sufficiently reliable due to the illegal beer market being very small, while
wine accounts for such a small share of the structure of consumption that its
data have no real impact on overall per capita consumption statistics. Measuring vodka consumption, however, has always presented serious problems
and continues to do so today, due to the enormous scale of the illegal market.

The source for official government statistics is the Federal Service for
State Statistics, known as Rosstat. Rosstat's annual publication the *Russian
Statistical Yearbook* (*Rossiyskiy statisticheskiy yezhegodnik*) contains data on alcohol production and sale of alcoholic beverages. However, these are both
unreliable as measures of consumption. Production figures may be of interest in their own right, but they do not take account of imported alcohol and
also considerably underreport actual production due to the large scale of illegal vodka production. Likewise, data on sales do not take account of black
market sales. Estimates of the illegal alcohol market vary by author and by
year, but a typical figure is 50 percent of the spirits market.[4]

According to Rosstat sales figures, per capita consumption never rose
above ten liters during the entire post-Soviet period. Such low figures are
generally regarded as inaccurate in Russia. Indeed, the Russian government
itself does not rely on Rosstat's data in formulating alcohol policy. The government line in the run-up to the 2009 antialcohol campaign was that per
capita consumption was eighteen liters, around double that reported by reported by Rosstat.[5] Two eminent academic specialists on alcohol consump-

tion in Russia, Alexandr Nemtsov and Vladimir Treml, made separate attempts to estimate total per capita consumption (including illegal alcohol and home brewed *samogon*) through the 1980s and into the post-Soviet period. Nemtsov used a combination of fluctuations in the sale of sugar (the main ingredient of *samogon*) and medical markers of alcohol consumption, such as deaths from external causes where alcohol was found in the blood.[6] Nemtsov's and Treml's estimates are numerically very close to each other, as shown in figure 9.2. In contrast with the official state figures, these data suggest that per capita consumption never fell below twelve liters during the post-Soviet period in the years covered by the estimates (i.e., up to and including 2001), and exceeded thirteen liters for the majority of those years.

The final year of Nemtsov's estimates is 2001. This leaves a lack of reliable data on per capita consumption in the 2000s. What, then, is the source of the government's famous "18 liters" statistic from 2008–9? This estimate was produced by Rospotrebnadzor, the consumer protection agency that comes under the Ministry of Health and was headed by Gennady Onishchenko at the time. The method by which this estimate was calculated has

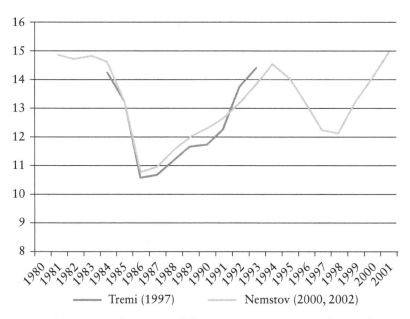

Figure 9.2 **Estimates of per capita alcohol consumption in Russia (liters of pure alcohol), 1981–2001. Both sets of data are reproduced in Nemtsov, *Alkogol'naya Istoriya Rossii*, 20.**

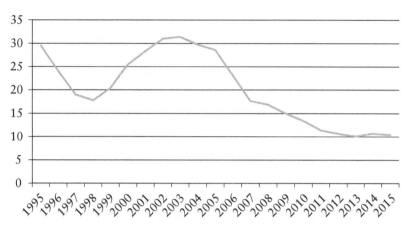

Figure 9.3 **Rate of death from accidental alcohol poisoning in Russia (per 100,000).** Data source: *Rossiyskiy statisticheskiy yezhegodnik* (Russian Statistical Yearbook) (Moscow: Rosstat).

not been made public, but a public health respondent told me that this statistic was "horrible, because it gave an estimation that one-third of beer is illegal in Russia, and there is no basis at all for that."

An indication of the *trend* of per capita alcohol consumption (as opposed to absolute figures) can be provided by both the rate of death from accidental alcohol poisoning and the rate of alcohol psychosis. These data are shown in figures 9.3 and 9.4 (data for the former are not available for the years 1991–94).

It can be seen that the two indicators suggest almost identical trends: peaks of alcohol consumption in 1995 and 2003, with a trough in 1998 (the year of the financial crisis and devaluation of the ruble) and a steady decline in consumption from 2004 onward. It is thus interesting to note that these data suggest that a large decline in per capita consumption had already taken place prior to the adoption of antialcohol measures from 2009 onward, and that the decline that took place after 2009 was simply the continuation of a long-term trend.

Possible Cleavages in Russia's Alcohol Consumption

Is it possible that the alcohol paradox in Russian public opinion is the result of a significant social cleavage in Russian alcohol consumption, with one section of the population consuming excessive amounts of alcohol, and the

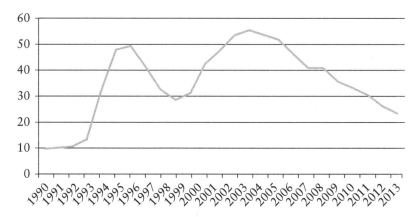

Figure 9.4 Incidence of alcohol psychosis per 100,000 in Russia. Data source: WHO European Health for All database (HFA-DB).

other section relatively little? One notable divide is gender. In general, it is difficult to obtain definitive data on gender-specific per capita consumption—even if production and sales data were reliable (which we have established they are not in Russia), such data obviously cannot be broken down by gender. Gendered consumption patterns can thus be established only by survey data. Nevertheless, such data do exist: numerous academic studies have found large differences between male and female alcohol consumption in Russia.[7] It should be noted that the phenomenon of women consuming significantly less alcohol than their male counterparts is not unique to Russia; similar ratios can be observed across a wide spectrum of European countries, including Germany, France, the United Kingdom, and Finland.[8]

But how does this gender gap in alcohol consumption translate into public attitudes toward state alcohol policy? A moderate gender divide was recorded in a VTsIOM opinion poll of August 2009, which surveyed "support for a new anti-alcohol campaign" (the poll coincided with the launch of what the media labeled President Medvedev's antialcohol campaign). Women were more inclined to support such an initiative, with 71 percent supporting it, as opposed to 57 percent support among men. Nevertheless, the gap of 14 percentage points, while significant, is not large enough to be said to constitute a major social division. Similarly, a FOM opinion poll of June 2012 revealed only a modest difference between male and female support for arguably the most effective antialcohol measure: price increases. The poll surveyed support for the upcoming increase in the minimum vodka price, which was to rise by almost one-third the following month. Twenty-six percent of men supported the measure, while female support was only slightly higher at 33 percent. Exactly half of males were opposed to the measure, with 40 percent of females also opposed. Roughly a quarter of respondents of both sexes were undecided, an interesting result in its own right. This evidence suggests that while females consume significantly less alcohol than their male counterparts, gender does not represent a major social divide in attitudes toward alcohol.

Another possible division that could account for the contrasting attitudes toward alcohol in Russian society is that between drinkers and teetotalers. Again, it is not easy to ascertain true abstention rates in a country, as we are reliant on survey data and self-reporting. It is striking that, among the available data that exist for Russia, abstention rates vary substantially. The WHO's country alcohol profiles do contain such data, although their provenance is not given. According to the data from the 2014 edition of the profiles, in 2010, 38 percent of females and 25 percent of males in Russia were abstainers (defined as aged fifteen and older and not having taken an alcoholic drink in the last twelve months). A FOM opinion poll of 2012 gave slightly lower figures, with 35 percent of women and 19 percent of men identifying as teetotalers.[9] However, the New Russia Barometer survey of 2000 produced substantially lower figures: here, only 18 percent of women and 7 percent of men reported that they never take a drink of something alcoholic.[10] Nor can the ten-year gap between the New Russia Barometer and WHO data be held responsible for the dramatically different results, because WHO data for the year 2000 also exist[11] and actually gave higher, not lower, figures: 50.6 percent for females and 29 percent for males.

The large variance in the findings of different surveys gives serious cause for concern about the reliability of survey data on abstinence in Russia. There are reasons to believe that the higher figures overestimate the true proportion of teetotalers in the country. Anecdotally, when I presented them at a Russian conference on alcohol issues, some experts expressed disbelief that such high figures could be accurate. One factor may be that in Russian society beer is often not regarded as an alcoholic beverage,[12] so some beer drinkers may be reporting themselves as nondrinkers. It may also be that some respondents do not recognize drinking in moderate doses, or as part of social rituals, as "drinking." It is interesting to note that the New Russia Barometer survey question referred to "taking a drink of something alcoholic," which has a rather milder connotation than "drinking." The question also explicitly stated "including beer," reminding respondents that beer was included in the concept of an alcoholic beverage. This more considered framing of the question may account for the lower rates of self-reported abstinence given by the New Russia Barometer as compared with other surveys.

An additional factor that may contribute to overreporting of abstention has been raised by M. F. Nikolayeva, one of the organizers of a survey of drinking habits in the Pskov region in 2011. The survey produced a result that runs contrary to most anecdotal evidence: rural areas in the region were found to have a higher proportion of teetotalers than urban areas. Nikolayeva suggested that the more conservative social attitudes of rural residents led to them deliberately underreporting their drinking to a greater extent than urban residents: "The highest proportion of 'non-drinkers' was in rural areas. It is essential to understand that a proportion of respondents most likely conceal instances of consuming alcoholic beverages: the practice of alcohol consumption outside of celebrations and rituals is considered taboo, a violation of traditional social norms. Therefore, the fact that Pskov and Velikiye Luki had higher proportions of weekly alcohol consumers according to the survey may be explained by the greater candour of urban respondents compared to their rural counterparts."[13]

While there is some limited evidence of cleavages in Russian society with respect to alcohol consumption, it does not seem sufficient to explain the alcohol paradox in Russian public opinion. The differences between male and female drinking habits appear to produce only relatively small gaps in social attitudes toward alcohol between the genders. There is some evidence that in spite of high per capita consumption, Russia may have a significant proportion of abstainers, which could suggest a social cleavage in attitudes toward drinking. However, the potential unreliability of these statistics means that much further research would be needed before we can be sure that such a cleavage exists. Moreover, the data we have do not give any indication as to what the sociological basis of such a cleavage could be. For example, Gusfield interpreted Prohibition in the United States as an attempt by one social group (temperance-orientated Protestants) to impose their cultural authority on another social group (Catholic immigrants).[14] But there seems to be no analogical divide in Russian society underlying attitudes toward alcohol. A hypothesis that would seem to have greater explanatory power is that, rather than a simple societal divide, the alcohol paradox is a manifestation of what Levada has called "Russian doublethink"—that is, contradictory normative attitudes held simultaneously at the level of individual cognition.[15] Let us assess the evidence for such an understanding of the alcohol paradox.

Double Standards and Alcohol Doublethink

In August 2009, inspired by the launch of what the media labeled the "anti-alcohol campaign," VTsIOM conducted a national opinion poll of Russians' support for such a campaign. It is revealing to compare support for the concept of a general, abstract campaign with support for specific measures. Sixty-five percent of respondents stated they would support a "new antialcohol campaign" in Russia: 71 percent of women and 57 percent of men. The specific measures that enjoyed most support were a ban on the sale of alcohol to those aged under 21 (63 percent); a ban on the advertisement of all forms of alcohol, including weak alcoholic beverages (57 percent); and propaganda for a "healthy, sober way of life" (47 percent). It is notable that none of these measures cause any real cost or inconvenience to drinkers. But when asked about the measure that could have a real effect on everyday consumption—"increasing prices on alcoholic products"—support fell to a paltry 19 percent.

This result suggests there is much more to the alcohol paradox than a simple societal cleavage between drinkers and nondrinkers; otherwise, we would expect the level of support for hard-hitting measures like price increases to be much higher. This leads us to ask whether Russian society is guilty of applying double standards to drinking behaviors. Do Russians misrecognize their own drinking as unproblematic, seeing only the problems caused by other people's drinking but not those caused by their own consumption? Sociologist Alena Ledeneva developed Bourdieu's notion of "misrecognition" of behavior while analyzing the concept of *blat*—the use of personal contacts to obtain preferential treatment in the Soviet economy.[16] She found that her respondents tended to identify provision of such favors by others as *blat* (and thus immoral or corrupt), but when they themselves were engaged in similar behavior they misrecognized it as "helping a friend"—that is, a moral, or at the very least harmless, act. As Ledeneva put it, "The system of denial is based on a contradiction between what one sees in other people as an observer and in oneself as a participant."[17]

Is it possible that large numbers of Russian people misrecognize their own drinking in a similar way—seeing the harm caused by other people's drinking but not that of their own? There are various reasons why misrecognition is particularly likely in the sphere of alcohol consumption. First, being drunk reduces one's awareness of the impact one's own behavior has on others. So, for example, an individual who is drunk is more likely to be desensitized to the noise he is creating and its impact on those around him than if he were sober. Second, on a psychological level, the Freudian defense mechanism of "denial" is often observed among those diagnosed with alcohol problems. Here, because the fact that one has an alcohol problem is too uncomfortable to accept, the individual denies that it is true or minimizes its seriousness. It is therefore possible that someone could misrecognize the problematic nature of their own alcohol consumption due to denial. Finally, it is possible to rationally hold the belief that consumption by certain groups or in a certain pattern is problematic, while one's own drinking the same quantity of alcohol is not. The obvious example here is underage drinking, but other examples could include drinking in public places as opposed to in a private setting, or drunkenness as opposed to everyday consumption at a level that does not cause drunkenness.

It is not easy to find evidence of misrecognition of problem drinking in opinion poll data. Evidence of such a phenomenon is best revealed through the use of semistructured interviews, ideally supplemented by interviews with witnesses to the drinker's behavior (e.g., family members or neighbors). This was the method Ledeneva used in her study of *blat*. Nevertheless, some tentative evidence for the hypothesis that Russians view other people's drinking as problematic but not their own is provided by an in-depth VTsIOM opinion survey that gives approval ratings for various measures passed by the major alcohol control law of July 2011.[18] It is noteworthy that 91 percent of respondents who reported drinking alcohol several times a week approved of tougher punishments for selling alcohol to minors, only a little less than the figure for those who stated they never drink (96 percent). This suggests that a high proportion of Russians see teenage drinking as a problem but do not see their own drinking as a problem. The high levels of support for antialcohol measures in the abstract, but widespread opposition to price rises, also suggest that it is "other people's drinking" that is viewed as the problem.

What the above-mentioned factors do not explain is why the alcohol paradox seems to manifest itself in Russian society much more strongly than in other Western societies. Is it simply a reflection of the vast quantities of alcohol consumed: the higher the per capita consumption, the greater the level of misrecognition? That is certainly possible. However, an additional explanation is offered by Yury Levada's concept of "Russian doublethink." Levada, a Russian sociologist, developed George Orwell's satirical concept of "doublethink" (see chapter 2) into a scientific description of the "paradox of mass consciousness" that is a legacy of Soviet society and continues to pervade Russian public opinion. The ethical demands that the Soviet regime placed on its citizens, that is, sacrifice of individual interests to the interests of the state, were largely impossible to fulfill. This led individuals to adopt "cunning" forms of behavior, persistently seeking out loopholes in the regime's normative system to justify their actions: "The cunning man . . . constantly requires self-deception for the sake of his own self-preservation (including the psychological) and for the sake of overcoming his own split personality and justifying his own cunning."[19]

Levada used corruption and bribe-taking as an example of how Russian doublethink operates at the level of individual cognition. Such means are recognized as immoral, but the fact that "everyone" uses them serves as a cunning justification for one's own use of them.[20] An individual may equally apply such logic to drinking occasions that are seen as socially necessary. For example, Boris Segal, writing in the Gorbachev era, suggested that drinking bouts played a functional role in sealing business contracts and maintaining good relations with superiors and coworkers. Furthermore, he related that numerous public holidays and private celebrations (in particular, weddings, funerals, and birthdays) all traditionally require heavy drinking as part of their social rituals.[21] The New Russia Barometer survey of 2000 listed six possible reasons why people drink, and asked respondents to what extent the reasons applied to them personally. It is interesting to note that "marks special occasions" was by far the most common reason identified by respondents: 70 percent of male respondents and 69 percent of females said that this "definitely" applied to them. The next most common reasons, "helps to relax" and "people with me are drinking,", were recorded as "definitely" by only around a third of respondents.[22] It may well be that vodka's central role in these various social rituals in Russia allows people to justify their consumption to themselves in such circumstances.

With the doublethink theory in mind, let us return to the opinion poll data on alcohol policy. Russian drinkers themselves are enthusiastic about antialcohol measures that do not cause any real personal cost or inconvenience to them, but are more likely to oppose measures that reduce the availability of beverages or increase their cost. VTsIOM's in-depth 2011 survey of public attitudes toward various antialcohol measures[23] found that a relatively high number of those who reported drinking alcohol several times a week supported banning the advertising of all alcohol from television, radio, and cinema (81 percent, as compared with 96 percent of nondrinkers). Not being able to watch commercials for alcoholic beverages is not a particularly great hardship for a drinker to bear, while the high level of support for a ban suggests that even many regular drinkers perceived the existence of alcohol problems in Russia; otherwise it is hard to explain why they would support a ban.

Opinions were more ambiguous when it came to provisions that would have a more tangible effect on drinkers. Regarding the rule that so-called weak alcoholic beverages[24] could be sold only in containers of 330 mL or less, 41 percent of regular drinkers were for and 46 percent were against, while the corresponding figures for nondrinkers were 80 percent and 12 percent, and 62 percent and 26 percent for occasional drinkers. Interestingly, the ban on the sale of beer in nonstationary outlets (i.e., kiosks and tents, a widespread form of "shop" in Russia) was supported by a majority of regular drinkers (61 percent, with 36 percent against), although this support was significantly less than among occasional drinkers (78 percent for, 19 percent against) and nondrinkers (90 percent for, 7 percent against).

There can be no doubt that, according to opinion poll data, alcohol problems are viewed as a real and serious issue by Russian society at large. However, support for concrete policy measures is more ambivalent. Part of the problem in explaining the paradox is that these polls do not tell us *why* exactly Russians view alcohol use in their country as a major social problem. Problems, after all, are simply subjective interpretations of phenomena, and alcohol use can be problematized in a variety of ways.[25] Is the Russian public, like their government, troubled by alcohol's role in population decline, or do they view it as problematic for reasons closer to home: disruption caused by drunken neighbors or alcohol-related violence on the streets, for example? Are certain social groups more concerned about alcohol problems than others, and if so, why? It is this understanding of how, exactly, ordinary Russians problematize alcohol use that is the key to understanding more fully the alcohol paradox in Russian society. More in-depth sociological studies of Russian attitudes toward alcohol use are needed in order to fully understand the apparently paradoxical attitudes toward drinking in Russian society.

Alcohol Populism: Does Public Opinion Matter?

It has been established that Russian public opinion displays ambivalent and contradictory attitudes toward alcohol consumption at the societal level. But to what extent does public opinion have any influence on state alcohol policy? One might be forgiven for assuming that the answer is "very little." Russia under Putin is often described as having a system of "managed democracy" owing to its lack of genuine electoral competition and the role of the Kremlin in regulating opposition. Since 2003, the party of power, United Russia, has enjoyed electoral dominance, while the Kremlin has created "virtual" opposition parties to weaken genuine opposition parties such as the Communist Party (KPRF).[26]

Yet there is evidence that public opinion actually plays a powerful role in the Russian political system. Daniel Treisman has used statistical analysis to show that, from Gorbachev onward, Russian leaders' ability to enact reforms has been constrained by their public approval rating.[27] According to the theory of the superelite advanced by Russian political scientist Aleksey Zudin, the monocentric system of power that has developed under Putin (as opposed to the polycentric system of power that existed under Yeltsin) is particularly dependent on stable public contentment as its underpinning. Zudin states that ever since Putin's atypically high approval rating appeared early in the second Chechen war in autumn 1999, there has been a stable relationship between the Kremlin and the public. He calls this phenomenon "Putin's majority," which brings political stability and provides the basis for the formation of a monocentric system. Whereas the basis of Yeltsin's polycentric system was an alliance between the Kremlin elite and other centers of power, such as regional elites and the oligarchs, the foundation of the monocentric system has become an unofficial "social contract" with the public, bypassing and enabling a break with the old elites of the Yeltsin period.[28] As Zudin explains, it is vital for the preservation of the Putinite regime that public contentment be maintained: "Broad public support is the main condition for the development of political monocentrism, so its preservation has become a vital political function. With the arrival of Putin, maintenance of social stability has become one of the primary policy objectives. An unstructured but strong relationship with society, the political incarnation of which is the presidential rating, is recognised as a valuable political resource."[29]

It is thus telling that Russian politicians' approaches to alcohol policy tend to mirror the alcohol doublethink in Russian public opinion. Both pro- and antialcohol policies advocated by politicians in the run-up to elections are labeled by commentators as "populist" and a cynical attempt to win votes. In accordance with the alcohol doublethink, the public perceives an "alcohol problem" and in principle are in favor of it being resolved, providing it does not impact too heavily on their own drinking. Thus, rhetoric and symbolic measures are popular, but as shown by the opinion poll data cited above, policies that impact too heavily on the consumer are not. For example, one prominent Russian alcohol market commentator claimed that the major changes to the alcohol law in July 2011 gave the authorities "the possibility before the Duma elections and then the presidential elections to use populist rhetoric about how well they are fighting alcoholism."[30] A radio broadcast in May 2010 posed the question as to whether the government's proposal to reclassify beer as an alcoholic product was "populism, or a genuine fight for the health of the nation."[31] One respondent, a government relations specialist with a major beer company, suggested that there was a fashion among Duma deputies to introduce their own antialcohol private members' bills, because it was an easy means of gaining positive media coverage—despite that their bills stood almost no chance of success:

> Respondent: We had to deal with a number of deputies' personal initiatives on alcohol regulation; there has been a plethora of them over the past years, sometimes there were simultaneously over four dozen bills pending decision in the State Duma regarding beer and alcohol regulation.
>
> ALB: Why were there so many?
>
> Respondent: I think because it's a popular topic to gain political score—fighting tobacco, fighting alcohol. All deputies who are not from the United

Russia party, or who are not representing the government's or the president's will, they of course clearly understand that their personal initiatives will not go far in the Duma, because in my experience Putin's regime has established a very strict law-making discipline, such that only draft bills coming from the government, or from the president, or from the key people in the ruling party, have a chance to become law. Others were suspended or rejected or repealed.

ALB: So a lot of the bills were from opposition politicians who knew they wouldn't be successful?

Respondent: Some of them were from opposition party politicians, some of them were from ruling party deputies but not the key ones.

ALB: So they're doing it to try and gain popularity with the public, or . . . ?

Respondent: Yes, because they could get some positive coverage in the media presenting themselves as fighters against the alcohol threat, or the tobacco threat. It could only be a win-win game for them, because if the draft bill was rejected or suspended they could say that some "notorious alcohol lobbyists" prevented this bill from passing and so on, that there is a conspiracy. So in any case they could get quite positive coverage in the media. For most of them it was the ultimate goal.

However, when it comes to concrete measures that could have a real effect on the Russian consumer's drinking patterns, the meaning of populism in alcohol policy changes. The term "populism" is especially applied to policies that keep the price of vodka low: commentators see expensive vodka as leading inevitably to popular discontent. Vladimir Putin's stated opposition to excise tax increases on both tobacco and alcohol has been described as "populist."[32] One Russian alcohol industry journalist suggested that the reason why biannual increases in excise duty on alcohol and tobacco were introduced in 2012 (in January and July, as opposed to the single annual increase in January in previous years) was so that alcohol prices would not increase too steeply before the presidential election in March 2012. It is also striking that in 2012 the annual rise in the minimum retail vodka price took place in July (i.e., safely after the presidential election), whereas previously it had always taken place in January.

The Russian political elite was greatly concerned by the wave of so-called colored revolutions that swept through the post-Soviet space during 2003–5, in particular the Orange revolution that took place in neighboring Ukraine.

Some respondents suggested that there is at least a *perception* among officials that overly restrictive antialcohol policies could provoke popular discontent. This thinking is shown in its most basic form in an off-the-cuff comment by the host of the respected Channel 5 discussion show *Otkritaya Studiya*: "Ours is a very specific country. If you made vodka five times more expensive people would riot."[33] Indeed, there is a correlation in Russian history of revolutions following shortly after prohibitions, a fact that has not gone unnoticed by commentators. "First there was the alcohol revolution, then the real revolution," noted a vodka producer with a wry smile, referring to the events of 1914 and 1917. Another respondent, a brewing executive, made a similar observation, but more explicitly: "Many commentators say that expensive vodka reduces the electoral popularity of our president. The more expensive the vodka, the less people will vote for him. The joke has often gone that the last Russian tsar passed a dry law in 1914, and then the communist revolution took place in 1917. Then Gorbachev started fighting with drunkenness in 1985, and in 1991 the Soviet Union ceased to exist. And again, if they start to tackle vodka now, then it'll be death to Putin. Maybe that's what he's afraid of."

In sum, the doublethink in Russian public opinion on alcohol would appear to have a real influence on policy formation. Alcohol is both popular and unpopular at the same time. It is regarded as a threat to society, yet is at the very heart of major celebrations and social rituals. Both pro-alcohol and antialcohol policies are thus regarded as populist, requiring a delicate balancing act by the authorities: being seen to take action on alcohol, while not impacting too severely on drinkers' interests. What this doublethink does not explain is why alcohol consumption has come to be problematized by the Russian authorities at some times more than others in the post-Soviet period. It is to this puzzle that we now turn.

Chapter 10

From Illegality to Demography

Alcohol Policy Paradigms

"A national disaster." President Medvedev's description of Russia's alcohol consumption in 2009 could hardly fail to stick in the mind. Unsurprisingly, the soundbite became a standard reference for journalists around the globe writing on alcohol in Russia—which presumably was the intention. But what was it exactly that made alcohol a national disaster for Russia? And more curiously, why did Russian presidents not make similar warnings in the 1990s and early 2000s, when consumption was even higher than in 2009?

Public and academic discussions of social problems often implicitly assume that the problem is an objective state of affairs independent of the observer. Yet as constructivist scholars have pointed out, there is nothing inherent in a state of affairs that intrinsically makes it a "problem." Rather, problems necessarily involve an element of subjective human judgment: they are *interpretations* of phenomena.[1] Thus with respect to alcohol, the use of alcohol in itself is only a *kind of behavior*: a further normative attitude or judgment is required to designate it as a social problem.[2]

Moreover, the public identification of certain phenomena as social problems at a given place and time does not always have a clear relation to the objective existence of those phenomena. As Joseph Gusfield pointed out, it is doubtful that the emergence of the concern with child abuse from the 1970s onward was due to more abuse actually taking place.[3] And so it was with alcohol in Russia: consumption had already been declining for several years when Medvedev made his famous "national disaster" statement. Thus, part of the task of explaining alcohol policy formation involves analysis of how the problem is defined, and how it came to be so defined. Rather than simply describing the problems themselves, we should seek to understand "how and why conditions become understood as public or social problems and how or why they are defined in particular fashions."[4]

The notion that high per capita alcohol consumption represented a social problem did not become mainstream among Russian political elites until the latter half of the 2000s. And yet, there was a never-ending stream of federal legislation throughout the 1990s aimed at regulating alcohol (see chapter 3). How, then, was alcohol problematized to warrant such constant legislative attention?

In 1997, President Yeltsin delivered a radio address to the nation on the subject of vodka. That the president chose to speak directly to the people on the subject of alcohol indicates the importance of the issue to the political elite at that time. Yeltsin's statements are illustrative of how the alcohol problem was constructed in 1990s policy circles. First, Yeltsin claimed that the very solvency of the federal budget hinged on curbing the illegal alcohol market: "Last December, I led for the first time a session of the Extraordinary Commission on Strengthening Fiscal and Budgetary Discipline. And there I demanded that order be brought to the production and sale of alcoholic drinks. It was clear to me that only then we will be able to rectify the situation with the budget."

Second, Yeltsin's discussion of the public health aspect of the issue made it clear that he viewed consumption of *illegal* alcohol (rather than alcohol consumption per se) as the main risk to people's health: "Illegal production and sale of alcohol is the second most profitable criminal business after financial fraud. And undoubtedly, it is the most dangerous for the health and lives of Russians. Clandestine vodka is made from God knows what. In the last five years alone, mortality from alcohol poisoning has increased almost threefold."

Quality control of alcoholic beverages, he added, "will give a real benefit in terms of strengthening people's health."[5]

Yeltsin's address epitomized the construction of the alcohol problem by the political elite in the 1990s. The policy focus was on *illegal* alcohol production as the problem, rather than the general level of alcohol consumption among the population. This construction of the problem was directly related to the government's urgent need to restore its budgetary revenue streams that had been seriously undermined by the state capture described in chapter 3. Simpura and Moskalewicz found that of the forty-eight legislative acts passed between February 1996 and March 1997 concerning alcohol licensing and control, "only one health-related concern was explicitly stated, that of the health risk caused by poor quality alcoholic beverages."[6] They summarized the prevailing direction of Russian alcohol policy at the turn of the century: "Clearly, the main issue is the need to establish effective control of production and sales. The main motivation for this effort is not public health, but public order and the fiscal interests of the State."[7] Leading Russian epidemiologist Alexandr Nemtsov, who led a failed attempt in the 1990s to push Russian alcohol policy in a more public health direction, reached the same conclusion: "In all this activity of the leadership of the country, one important characteristic of contemporary alcohol policy in Russia was clear: its priorities lay in the economic sphere and principally sought to increase budget receipts. The problem of preserving the health and lives of citizens was taken up only in passing."[8]

It is important to note that the concern with illegal alcohol was publicly expressed in terms of not only fiscal losses to the state but also the rate of alcohol poisoning among the population from poorly distilled, toxic alcohol. There are two aspects to the prevalence of the "poisonings" discourse. First, as a matter of objective fact, there was indeed a large amount of poorly distilled bootleg alcohol on the Russian market at this time, and consequently a large number of poisonings. And second, the "poisonings" aspect offered a more publicly acceptable reason to fight illegal alcohol than losses to the exchequer: concern for the health of its citizens sounds like a more noble cause than filling the state's coffers. Simpura and Moskalewicz observed that "political euphemisms such as consumer protection or the removal of low-quality beverages from the market" were often used to make the government's self-interested aims more publicly acceptable.[9]

In the wake of Russia's financial collapse in 1998, Yeltsin made a statement that bore striking similarities to Stalin's letter to Molotov of over half a century earlier. "As long as the people spend money on vodka, the profits must go to the state," declared Yeltsin. "We will use them to revive our economy."[10]

Alcohol and the Russian Demographic Crisis

While the Russian political elite was focused on how to claw back the state's alcohol revenues, scientific scholars in the 1990s had identified high per capita alcohol consumption as the main contributing factor to what became known as Russia's "demographic crisis."[11] The facts that formed the basis of this demographic crisis[12] were as follows. Following the fall of the Soviet Union in 1991, Russia experienced rapid population decline: the population fell in every year from 1992 to 2008. Male life expectancy also fell dramatically, from 64.2 years in 1989 to 58.3 years in 1995. While there had been a long-term trend decline of male life expectancy since the 1960s (with female life expectancy remaining more or less constant over the same period), the 1990s represented a dramatic acceleration of this trend.[13]

Russia's demographic decline was not confined to the chaotic transition years of the 1990s but continued in the 2000s. At the beginning of 2008 the Russian population stood at 142 million, a fall of 6.6 million from the figure of 148.6 million at the beginning of 1993. But even this large figure does not fully reveal the decline in the native Russian population, which was partly compensated for by immigration. The natural population shrinkage (i.e., not including immigration) between 1993 and 2008 was 12.3 million people, or 8.3 percent of the 1993 population.[14]

The Russia structure of mortality is very different from a Western model of mortality in that causes of death differ substantially. Russia has an exceedingly high proportion of deaths from external causes (accidents, murder, suicide, etc.) contributing to general mortality—three times higher than in the West. External causes account for 18.2 percent of male deaths in Russia. Furthermore, deaths from external causes tend to occur at a very young age—on average 24.3 years for men and 27.9 years for women. This excess middle-age mortality from external causes, especially among men, is the biggest contributing factor to Russia's demographic decline.[15] And a large proportion of these deaths from external causes are due to excessive alcohol consumption—in particular, vodka, which causes rapid intoxication. Studies have found that alcohol is a factor in 72 percent of murders, 42 percent of suicides, and 52 percent of deaths from other external causes.[16] Deaths from cardiovascular diseases associated with high alcohol consumption also make up a large proportion of premature male mortality.[17] Alexandr Nemtsov calculated that, on average, over the period 1980–2001, 23.4 percent of all deaths in Russia were linked to alcohol.[18] Thus, the scholars Andrey Korotayev and Daria Khaltourina concluded, "As far as the demographic crisis is concerned, everything is very simple: we need to drink less."[19]

Failed Attempts to Reframe the Problem

While the scientific evidence for alcohol's central role in Russia's demographic crisis has grown stronger over time, there was already sufficient data by the mid-1990s to raise alarm among Russian public health experts. The Russian Public Health Association (RAOZ, to use its Russian abbreviation—Rossiyskaya Assotsiatsiya Obshchestvennogo Zdorovya) was formed in 1995 as part of a project funded by the United States Agency for International Development (USAID). Professor Andrey Demin, then deputy to the presidential administration's chief adviser on the environment and health, Alexey Yablokov, became RAOZ's long-term president. The first paper published by RAOZ, entitled "Mortality and predicted life expectancy in Russia," concluded that excessive alcohol consumption was one of the main factors in the "crisis in the condition of the nation's health." The association therefore decided that its next paper should focus exclusively on the alcohol factor, and Alexandr Nemtsov's analysis "The alcohol situation in Russia" was duly published later in 1995.[20]

Demin then secured USAID funding to establish a civil society project, the All-Russian Forum "Alcohol and Health," also in 1995. A range of experts, including both state and civil society representatives, participated in the forum. The aim was to shift alcohol policy discourse away from the illegal alcohol narrative and redefine it in terms of the negative consequences of general per capita consumption on the demographic situation. However, once the forum tried to reach out beyond public health experts and engage the wider policy community, the organizers found that such collaboration was possible only by distorting its message into the prevailing "quality not quantity" discourse that problematized only illegal alcohol. The forum ran a series of events titled "Ensuring the quality and safety of alcoholic products" between 30 November and 4 December 1998 in conjunction with the National Alcohol Association, a trade organization representing producers. According to one of the forum's organizers, the National Alcohol Association then used its collaboration with the forum to support its own policy position: "After the conference, they [Pavel Shapkin and his National Alcohol Association] took all the materials from it to substantiate their participation in the Expert Committee on Alcohol in the State Duma. But we were not invited. In fact, they changed the way of thinking, way of developing policy and so on—they emphasized the quality issues."

The forum's work was also used in parliamentary hearings held by the Duma's Health Committee and the Committee for Economic Policy in December 1998, but again, the subject of the hearings was the quality and safety of alcohol rather than per capita consumption. In 1998 the forum published a collected volume of its work, expressing the hope that it be used in the development of a long-term state antialcohol policy.[21] However, this was to be the forum's last act. Soon after, the USAID funding came to an end and was not renewed, and without funding the forum's activities simply fizzled out.

One of the scientists involved in the "Alcohol and Health" forum project, Professor Alexandr Nemtsov, undertook a personal crusade in 1996–97 to persuade the political elite of the threat that excessive alcohol consumption posed to Russian demographics. Waiving his right to anonymity, Nemtsov related how he felt the political elite at the time had no interest in the issue even when it was brought to their attention:

Nemtsov: We gathered data secretly at first [in the USSR], and then in '89 they did away with all this secrecy, and I started to study alcoholic psychoses, deaths and poisonings—at first in Moscow. Then we got the data on the Soviet Union, and then for Russia, and I was horrified to find a huge amount of deaths due to alcohol. And that's when I was trying to tell the government about the alcohol threat to our country.

ALB: And this was when exactly, under Yeltsin?

Nemtsov: Yes, this was under Yeltsin. He was surrounded by this group of advisers. I went to these advisers; no one would let me go any higher, and in general there was such a "couldn't care less" attitude. This was when the price of our oil was falling and the country suffered great losses from it. An adviser to Yeltsin—a total *bolvan* [dimwit]—said to me, "If you can prove to me that the losses from alcohol are greater than the losses from the fall in the price of oil, then I'll take on this subject." In other words he did not know what was happening around him. In the end I tried for a year to get through somewhere and say that we have a tragedy occurring. No one wanted to listen to me—I wrote articles in newspapers, and then eventually published a small book called *Alcohol Mortality*. And no one from the, let's say, "serious people" in the government wanted to read that either. I found one State Duma deputy, who asked me for four hundred copies of the book, to give them out to every Duma deputy. So he stood for a week with my books and only gave out one hundred copies; the rest didn't want to take them. This took place in 1996–7 and for a whole year I didn't do scientific work, I wrote to the president, and all for nothing.

It is clear that, in the latter half of the 1990s, public health activists made repeated attempts to bring alcohol's effect on the demographic situation to the attention of the political elite. They did not lack insider contacts: key personnel were located within the presidential administration, and representatives of government ministries participated in the activities. There was no shortage of information available to political decision makers on the effects of per capita consumption of legal alcohol on the demographic situation. And yet, in spite of all these efforts, there was no real shift in the policy discourse from the issue of "quality" to that of "quantity."

One obscure development that is worth mentioning in this context is the development of a draft policy concept (*kontseptsiya*[22]) of state alcohol policy in the early 2000s by a working group of the State Council headed by Ravil Geniatulin. The policy concept never progressed beyond draft stage and was shelved, leaving hardly any trace of its existence.[23] While we may never know at whose initiative this draft document was developed and why it was abandoned, an anecdote cited by Alexandr Nemtsov suggests that the decision to shelve the project may have been made by Putin himself. According to the anecdote, a draft concept of state alcohol policy was scheduled to be considered at a session of the State Council on the alcohol problem in 2002. Putin reportedly said dismissively, "Do you want me to become a second Ligachev?"

(a reference to the notoriously unpopular initiator of the 1985 antialcohol campaign) and canceled the scheduled session on the alcohol problem.[24]

How can we explain the failure of Russian public health activists in the 1990s to shift the definition of the alcohol problem from that of illegal alcohol to high per capita consumption, in spite of clear scientific evidence that the latter was a major cause of premature mortality? One factor is that Russia in the 1990s suffered from what may be termed "post-Gorbachev alcohol fatigue." The historian Ron Roizen noted that in the United States, alcohol declined as a political issue following the repeal of Prohibition in 1933. He suggested that the divisions and conflicts over Prohibition "exhausted the nation's patience and interest in the subject," and the policy's perceived failure and unpopularity meant that politicians were wary of advocating any kind of alcohol control measures.[25] It seems likely that the divisiveness, unpopularity, and perceived failure of the Soviet antialcohol campaign of 1985–88 cast a shadow over alcohol control policies, as illustrated by Putin's "second Ligachev" comment. "Today it is customary to speak about legislation restricting the consumption of alcohol, or a so-called 'dry law', only with an ironic smile," lamented Vladimir Rebrykov, a consultant to the State Duma's Committee for Economic Policy, in 1998. "Any attempt at a serious conversation, let alone publicly speaking out in favour of legislative restrictions on the trade of alcohol, provokes the most vitriolic attacks."[26] The "1985 factor" arguably still continues to haunt alcohol policy to some extent. Even while praising the beneficial impact of the Gorbachev-era campaign on demographics in 2009, President Medvedev was careful to criticize the "idiotic bans and mistakes" that accompanied it.[27]

Perhaps an even more important factor is that, throughout the 1990s, the Russian authorities had to deal with fundamental crises that threatened the integrity of the state itself. Following the collapse of the USSR in 1991, the political agenda in Russia was taken up with the problems of transition not only to a free market but to a liberal democratic state. This brought with it a succession of financial, fiscal, and constitutional crises. It is easy to forget just how precarious the survival of the fledgling Russian Federation looked at several points in the 1990s. In 1993 the long-running stalemate between President Yeltsin and parliament over a new constitution culminated in an armed attempt by reactionary parliamentarians to seize power. Yeltsin prevailed, but only after the military—which had been avoiding taking either side—eventually decided to back him and shelled the parliament building, the White House. According to the official figures, 187 people were killed in the armed struggle, including many civilians.

Even after Yeltsin's position was secure, the state and economy remained fragile. The government continually struggled to collect enough tax revenues to pay state employees. In August 1998 the situation reached crisis point when the Russian government and the Central Bank were forced to devalue the ruble and default on its debt. Little wonder that the issue of the nation's health—and alcohol's role in it—was placed on the back burner. Indeed, it was difficult to establish a problematization of alcohol in terms of its effect on the demographic situation, when the demographic situation itself was not yet being treated as an urgent social problem by the Russian political elite.

The Politicization of Demography

The demographic crisis needs be treated with the same critical scrutiny as the alcohol problem, for it too is a social construct. It should not be taken for granted that population decline is naturally a social problem. Indeed, the eighteenth-century demographer Malthus famously claimed the opposite— that unchecked population *growth* would result in catastrophe because agricultural production would not be able to keep pace. China introduced a one-child policy in 1979 in a deliberate attempt to suppress population growth, a policy that began to be phased out in 2015. So why is population decline seen as a negative phenomenon, even a crisis in the Russian case?

To answer this question, we need to return to the concept of the political superelite detailed in the previous chapter. The superelite under Putin, it will be recalled, is dependent on public contentment for the regime's stability. Demographic indicators are therefore of great symbolic importance at the domestic level. Life expectancy and the population level are seen as representative of how well the political elite is looking after the Russian people, as the ubiquity of demography as an issue in contemporary Russian political discourse demonstrates.

The Russian political elite also places great value on demographic indicators at the geopolitical level. Political scientist Andrey Yakovlev has described how the superelite differs from the other elites that support it, "in that it has global interests that elevate it above the group from which it arose, which suppress the interests of this group in order to achieve national goals."[28] In other words, the superelite's interests are inextricably intertwined with Russia's success as a state, as it is this that guarantees both their current security in post and their future historical reputation. In terms of Russian national security, the basic thinking is that Russia has a vast territory that requires a large population to maintain and defend it. Related to this, the political elite also has a symbolic interest at the geopolitical level in maintaining a large and stable population, as this has become linked to Russia's symbolic status as a great power.

The sustained fall in Russia's population in the post-Soviet era was widely represented as an undisputed crisis by the mid-2000s, and became a highly politicized topic in Russian domestic politics.[29] "The population issue is a hot potato in the political struggle in the country. The opposition, mostly left, has made the decline of the population a leading item in the list of Putin's sins," observed Russian sociologist Vladimir Shlapentokh.[30] Similarly, Sergey Zakharov, laboratory head at the Centre for Demography and Human Ecology, Institute of Economic Forecasting, commented in 2004: "Domestic demographics have never been so politicized as they are today. Not one party can go without commenting on the current state of affairs in its public pronouncements or policy documents. Demographic difficulties are used by politicians as an argument to criticise the current regime, and as a springboard for their own promises."[31]

Communist Party (KPRF) leader Gennady Zyuganov made the demographic question one of his party's central concerns, declaring in 2004, "Today, each minute, with our silent participation, the great Russian people are disappearing from the Earth." The second point on the KPRF's current "Minimum Programme," second only to "To establish the rule of the working people," is "To stop the extinction of the country."[32] In 2008, two leading oppositionists, Boris Nemtsov (first deputy prime minister of the Russian Federation, 1997–98) and Vladimir Milov (deputy minister of energy, 2002), published their report "Putin: The Results"—a highly critical survey of the Putin regime. One chapter was entitled "Russia is dying out," and criticized Putin for Russia's high mortality rate, alleging that he had "not even tried to do anything about it."[33]

Because of their importance for political elites, it is not uncommon for scientific findings of negative demographic trends to be perceived as propaganda tools, especially among global powers. When scholar Nicholas Eberstadt published the commentary "The Health Crisis in the USSR" in the

New York Review of Books in 1981, he was accused of running a propaganda operation for the newly elected Reagan administration. One of the articles that quickly appeared in a rival American publication to repudiate Eberstadt's conclusions was entitled "Infant Mortality in the Soviet Union: Anti-Sovietism in the United States." A detailed critique of both Eberstadt's commentary and the research by Christopher Davis and Murray Feshbach that he had been reviewing was published a few years later in the USSR. Entitled *The Anti-Sovietism of Bourgeois Demography*, it accused both publications of being "a fundamental part of the anti-Soviet campaign, directed towards the ideological preparation of the population of the USA for the cold war."[34]

The CIA's estimates of Russian population statistics raised some eyebrows when they were published on the agency's website in October 2011. The CIA's figures for Russia's population, life expectancy, birth and death rates were all significantly worse than those given by Rosstat, the Russian state statistical agency. The former suggested that Russia's population was declining at a rate fifteen times faster than the official Russian statistics.[35] How had the two agencies arrived at such different figures, and had one side manipulated them for political reasons? Some of the Russian press hinted at the question, but without making any direct accusation of either side. The liberal Russian newspaper *Nezavisimaya gazeta* suggested that the 140 million mark had become a psychologically important barrier for officials, noting it was significant that any mention of a possible reduction in the population below this threshold was absent from official documents. According to the newspaper, the original draft of Strategy 2020[36] stated that "if current negative tendencies are maintained, by 2020 the population could fall to 138 million people." But a few months later this had been changed to what the paper called "a more politically correct version": "The depopulation that began in the 1990s to early 2000s could lead to the decline of the total population to 140 million people by 2020."[37]

The Fragmented State and Vague Demographic Policy

While population growth is clearly in the interests of the Russian superelite, pursuit of this goal was for many years undermined by the fragmented nature of the state: the fact that individual bureaucratic departments pursue their own interests, which do not necessarily coincide with the national interest or the ruling elite's interests. Put simply, there was no incentive for any individual government department to develop measures aimed at improving the demographic situation in the absence of specific orders or hypothecated funding to make it accountable for doing so.

According to presidential rhetoric, depopulation was at the top of the political agenda from the very start of the 2000s. In his first federal address as president, Putin problematized the demographic situation in the most serious terms:

> Before talking about priorities and setting tasks, I want to point out the most acute problems the country is facing. . . . With each passing year, we citizens of Russia are becoming fewer and fewer in number. For several years now, the country's population has been decreasing by an average of 750,000 annually. If one believes the long-term forecasts . . . fifteen years from now Russia could have 22 million fewer citizens. I ask you to reflect on that figure: one-seventh of the population. If this trend continues, Russia's survival as a nation will be in jeopardy. We are genuinely threatened with the prospect of wasting away as a nation.[38]

But despite the rhetoric of depopulation being one of the most alarming problems that threatened Russia's very survival as a nation, very little policy action was forthcoming. The 2001 *Concept of Demographic Development of the Russian Federation until 2015*, prepared by the Ministry of Labour and Social Development, was the first official document that laid out a demographic policy of the federal government.[39] It claimed to provide "a system of beliefs, principles and priorities in the field of regulation of demographic processes." However, it was a vague document that problematized Russian depopulation—drawing attention to both declining fertility and hypermortality among working-age males—but without proposing any concrete measures to address it. The main stated policy goal was to first stabilize the population level and then achieve population growth. A few other aims such as "increase life expectancy" and "improve reproductive health" were listed as preconditions for this, but without any quantified targets for their achievement. Moreover, no administrative organs or departments were assigned responsibility for developing policies to meet the stated aims. Unsurprisingly, no action was taken in consequence of the 2001 policy concept, and it was left to ossify. It became a sad artifact of attitudes toward demography among the governing elite: a vague wish for depopulation to reverse itself, with no

incentive for any individual ministry to take action in terms of concrete policy measures. Even Putin appeared to have lost interest in the issue in the
years immediately following his 2000 address, with demography noticeably
absent from his public activity.[40]

Signs of more serious interest in demographic problems by the political
elite began to emerge around 2005. In his federal address of that year, Putin
referred to the demographic situation for the first time since 2000, albeit
fleetingly: "I am deeply convinced that successful implementation of our
policies in all areas hinges closely on solving the acute demographic problems that we face. We cannot accept the fact that life expectancy in Russia is
so much shorter than it is in Western Europe—almost 10 years less for
women and 16 years less for men."[41]

Russian sociologist Vladimir Shlapentokh claimed in 2005 that the so-
called catastrophists (those who drew attention to the high mortality rate in
the severity of Russia's demographic situation) occupied the leading role in
the Russian expert community. The State Duma's Committee for Defence
and Security held a seminar in April 2005 at which catastrophist demographers were dominant.[42] The Russian Orthodox Church had also by this time
"incorporated the demographic crisis in its ideological lexicon."[43] In 2004, it
held a church-public forum entitled "The spiritual and moral basis of Russian demographic development." A resolution passed at the forum stated that
"Russia today is experiencing a demographic crisis, manifesting itself in catastrophic population decline. Each year one million less Russians are born
than die." The resolution went on to criticize the government's 2001 policy
concept on demography, complaining that there was "a lack of concrete action to address the crisis."[44]

The real impetus for renewed action on state demographic policy came in
2006, when President Putin identified it as the most important problem facing the nation in his annual federal address, and devoted the majority of
his speech to detailing specific policy proposals. Putin, who by this time had
gained considerable authority in his position as president compared with
when he first won office in 2000, criticized his ministers and officials for their
inactivity in respect of demographic policy—a significant public rebuke:

> What is the most important thing for us? The Defence Ministry knows what
> is most important. . . . Present-day Russia's most pressing problem—
> demography. . . . You know that, on average, the number of people living in

our country is shrinking by almost 700,000 a year. We have raised this subject repeatedly, but we have really done very little about it. . . . The government just recently adopted a traffic safety programme. All that remains now
is one small detail—implementing the intended measures. In connection
with this, I want to direct the government's attention to the sluggishness and
inexcusable bureaucracy with which tasks of this kind are carried out.[45]

Putin's reference to "the Defence Ministry knows what is most important" reflected the growing discourse constructing the demographic crisis as
a threat to Russia's national security. Sergey Mironov, chair of the upper
house of Russia's parliament, warned in 2005 that if Russia's population
trends did not change, "there will no longer be a great Russia. It will be torn
apart piece by piece, and finally cease to exist."[46]

Putin's presidential rebuke served as a kick start for a more proactive demographic policy backed by concrete measures. In 2007 the old 2001 policy concept was superseded by a new policy—*Concept of Demographic Development of
the Russian Federation until 2025.*[47] Unlike the 2001 version, the new concept set
clear targets for population growth and life expectancy, aiming to stabilize the
population level at 142–43 million people by 2015 and "create conditions for its
growth to 145 million people by 2025." Targets for average life expectancy
were set at seventy years by 2015[48] and seventy-five years by 2025. Subsequent
statements by the governing elite consistently reinforced the message that improving the country's demographics was one of its top priorities. In January 2008, prime minister Viktor Zubkov stated that improving the demographic situation was the main task for Russia's federal ministries in the coming
year.[49] Prime Minister Medvedev made a similar statement in November 2012.[50]

Unlike the old 2001 demographic concept, the publication of the 2007
concept was followed by a package of policy measures. However, these were
primarily directed at increasing the birthrate rather than reducing mortality.[51] Where were the policy measures to address the main driver of the
demographic crisis: premature male mortality and, in particular, excessive
alcohol consumption?

In his federal address of 2005, President Putin problematized alcohol as
follows:

I want to dwell at some length on another difficult problem confronting our
society: the consequences of alcoholism and drug addiction. Alcohol poisoning

alone—especially poisoning caused by drinking alcohol surrogates—kills about 40,000 people a year in Russia. These are mainly young men, breadwinners. But this problem cannot be solved by methods based on prohibition. The ultimate goal of our efforts must be to make the younger generation aware of the need to have a healthy lifestyle, to get regular exercise and engage in sports. . . . Yet in looking through the budget programs for next year and the government's investment programs, I didn't see any desire to address this problem at the federal level. . . . I ask the government to please make the necessary changes.[52]

Some commentators have wrongly interpreted Putin's words as marking the beginning of a new concern by the Russian political elite with excessive alcohol consumption. Marya Levintova, for example, regarded it as the "critical point" for alcohol control policy.[53] However, a careful reading of the quote shows that, rather than representing the beginning of a new public health-based problematization of per capita consumption, the ideas Putin expressed were firmly located within the old "quality" discourse. He referred only to alcohol poisoning and the use of surrogates—a small proportion of alcohol-related harms—rather than consumption as a whole; and he explicitly ruled out restrictive measures in favor of the vague idea of promoting "healthy lifestyles." Thus, Putin's characterization of "the problem" in his 2005 address barely differed from that which had been dominant throughout the post-Soviet period—that the problem was illegal alcohol, and it was this rather than excessive consumption of alcohol in general that represented a health threat. It took the efforts of civil society to bring the issue of alcohol consumption to the center of public discourse about tackling the demographic crisis. How this took place is detailed in the next chapter.

Chapter 11

THE NEW ANTIALCOHOL NETWORK

The birth of the baby was preceded by thunder of exceptional strength—
Russia was startled by the piercing heat and unprecedented scope of the campaign against alcoholism. The program was a "common cause" involving
prominent public figures, and videos which told how by magical means a shot
of vodka causes haemorrhages, and a glass of beer turns a man into a woman.
One of the leaders of the campaign was Archimandrite Tikhon. After such
a call, only the enemies of Russia and the Church could question the timeli-
ness of the urgent restoration of order.[1]

So wrote the Russian daily newspaper *Novaya gazeta* in 2011, describing
satirically (but not inaccurately) the critical buildup of civil society pressure
that preceded the launch of a new antialcohol policy by the Russian government in 2009. The net result was that, by the late 2000s, it was politically
impossible to disagree with the urgent need to tackle the alcohol problem,
which had successfully been constructed by a new civil society elite as threatening the very survival of the Russian nation.

From the mid-2000s, a new network of antialcohol activists emerged in Russia. Although this network can be considered part of civil society, it was a professional civil society *elite* rather than a bottom-up, grassroots movement. The network consisted of three main components. The first was the Russian Coalition for Alcohol Control, a loose affiliation made up mainly of public health professionals and academics, with a few core members undertaking lobbying work at the level of the federal government and national media. The second actor was the Russian Orthodox Church, whose activity was mainly channeled through one influential individual: Father Tikhon Shevkunov, who is closely connected with the Russian political elite including Putin himself. The third element of the network was the Russian Public Chamber—a state institution comprising 126 members of Russia's civil society elite, which in 2009 published a widely publicized report entitled *Alcohol Abuse in the Russian Federation: Socio-economic Consequences and Means of Combating It.* This report was to provide a landmark text that set out the main policy proposals of the antialcohol network, winning them significant media coverage.

The Russian Coalition for Alcohol Control

The Russian Coalition for Alcohol Control (Rossiyskaya koalitsiya za kontrol nad alkogolyem) is a loose network of civil society activists, mainly public health specialists. It was formed in 2007 at the initiative of Kirill Danishevsky of the Open Health Institute and Society for Evidence-Based Medicine, and was originally called the Civil Society Initiative Against Alcohol Abuse. The project was modeled on the Anti-Tobacco Coalition that was already active in Russia, and most nongovernmental organizations (NGOs) from the Anti-Tobacco Coalition also joined the Civil Society Initiative Against Alcohol Abuse. A year later the fledgling project received a state grant to cement it as an active alliance, and it was renamed the Russian Coalition for Alcohol Control. Daria Khaltourina and Andrey Korotayev, academic colleagues who had coauthored papers on alcohol's major contribution to the Russian demographic crisis, became codirectors. Khaltourina was an ambitious public health scholar in her twenties, with boundless energy and determination to bring about real changes in Russian public health policy. With her striking long blond hair and reasoned eloquence, she became the recognizable public face of the coalition and a go-to person for journalists and TV producers in need of a charismatic public health representative.

Even at the height of its prominence, the coalition *as a coalition* did not give the impression of being particularly strong or active. One of the senior members of the coalition admitted that "it has not been as effective as with tobacco." Another respondent, whose organization was formally part of the coalition, expressed the opinion that it was little more than a brand rather than a genuinely functioning coalition: "I don't see any sustained function-ing of this coalition. I just see some people going here and there and saying that they are co-chairman of this coalition. . . . My organization is a mem-ber, but I'm thinking about leaving because I do not see any sense in con-tinuing when there's just a brand of an organization and my name is used by some people who do not even communicate with me."

The coalition is best characterized as a civil society elite rather than a grassroots movement. It is composed of a small number of leading public health activists for whom advocacy work is part of their professional activity. It was funded in large part by a grant from the League of National Health, a state body that distributes grants to health-based NGOs. While it would be easy to classify this as an instance of increasing state control over civil society under Putin,[2] it should be noted that the phenomenon of "elite civil society"— funded by the state and with no accompanying grassroots activity—is actually rather typical of public health action groups in the UK too. For example, the antitobacco lobby group Action on Smoking and Health was founded by a small group of medics in 1971 using a £1,500 loan from the Royal College of Physicians, but was unable to attract grassroots donations and quickly became dependent on government funding. Indeed, there is evidence to suggest that its establishment was actively encouraged by the Department of Health to provide a source of external pressure for antitobacco policies that the department itself favored.[3] Similarly, the British antialcohol NGO Alcohol Concern was established with government funding in 1983[4] and continues to receive the bulk of its income in the form of government grants.

The Russian Orthodox Church

The Russian Orthodox Church (ROC) has historically had a rather ambiva-lent relationship with alcohol. Unlike other Christian denominations, the

ROC does not feature sobriety as part of its historical tradition. The church had little involvement in the development of the substantial prohibition movement in late nineteenth- and early twentieth-century tsarist Russia: "Unlike the near universal hostility toward alcohol among Catholic and Protestant denominations, the Orthodox Church at best only reluctantly approved of temperance ideals, given the centrality of alcohol to peasant hospitality and religious celebrations; at worst, the Church was openly antagonistic toward temperance given its close connection to the imperial state and the need to maintain its monopoly on spiritual authority over the peasantry."[5]

In the 1990s the Moscow patriarchate took advantage of the excise privileges detailed in chapter 3 to conduct a lucrative import business through its Department of External Relations, dealing mainly in duty-free cigarettes but also vodka. Allegations about the "business" continue to haunt Patriarch Kirill, who headed the Department of External Relations at the time and went on to become patriarch in 2009.

The development of proactive antialcohol campaigning by the ROC was largely due to the personal efforts of one individual: Father Tikhon Shevkunov. Holding the title of archimandrite (higher abbot), Father Tikhon is officially not particularly high-ranking but wields considerable informal authority due to his close association with Russia's political elite. It is widely rumored that Father Tikhon is confessor to Vladimir Putin, something that Tikhon himself will neither confirm nor deny. The little public knowledge that we have about Putin and Father Tikhon's relationship has been summarized by journalist Charles Clover as follows: "The only details he [Father Tikhon] gives is that Putin, sometime before he became president at the end of 1999 (most likely while he was head of Russia's FSB security service from 1998 to 1999), appeared at the doors of the monastery one day. Since then, the two men have maintained a very public association, with Tikhon accompanying Putin on foreign and domestic trips, dealing with ecclesiastical problems. But according to persistent rumor, Tikhon ushered the former KGB colonel into the Orthodox faith and became his *dukhovnik*, or godfather."[6]

Father Tikhon's appointment as archimandrite of the Sretenskiy monastery in 1995 seems to have played a large role in drawing him into the informal networks of Russia's ruling elite. The Sretenskiy monastery is located on the same street as the Lubyanka, the notorious headquarters of Russia's federal security service the FSB, and its predecessor, the KGB. According to renowned Russian journalist Mikhail Zygar, the Sretenskiy monastery served as an informal meeting place for *siloviki* (Russian security services officials) in the 1990s, and in the 2000s "became the favourite haunt of just about all the country's top officials."[7] Thus it was that Tikhon became "one of the most influential members of the Church hierarchy."[8]

Father Tikhon's personal concern with the alcohol problem in Russia was apparently triggered by his opening a farm in the Ryazan region, where, in the words of one respondent, "he saw that the population of the surrounding villages was completely devastated by alcohol and alcoholism, so he realized that he had to do something." This led to Father Tikhon meeting with the sobriety movement leader Vladimir Zhdanov, and in turn he became well acquainted with leading members of the coalition, notably Daria Khaltourina and Andrey Korotayev. While Father Tikhon is not alone in the ROC in conducting antialcohol activity, it is doubtful that it would have become official ROC policy without his intervention, as the following exchange with a public health respondent illustrates:

ALB: So in terms of the church's activities in the antialcohol campaign, to what extent is it the personal initiative of Father Tikhon?

Respondent: It's his personal initiative. He managed to get Patriarch Kirill on board, so the patriarch is supporting. But generally it's Tikhon's personal project.

ALB: So if there were no Father Tikhon, would anything be happening?

Respondent: No, I don't think so. Maybe small things because there's always been the church brotherhood and they have a lot of members; annual conferences like the Christmas Readings. . . . At the Christmas Readings there were meetings, there were maybe two hundred people coming to Moscow from all regions of Russia and also other countries, but it was not influential at all. Because Father Tikhon was very close—and is still very close—to the decision makers.

ALB: You mean Putin?

Respondent: Putin, Surkov, Zubkov . . . He's perfect in communication—people love him. And he works at quite a high level so he knows all the governors, all the ministers, he socializes with them and so on.

Father Tikhon thus possesses a rare combination of two valuable resources for success in Russian policymaking circles. First, he has the status of an insider in the governing elite and the trust of Vladimir Putin himself. But unlike other members of Putin's circle, he also has the moral authority of a senior churchman, able to appear in the public eye as a guardian of the national interest untainted by private vested interests.

The Legitimizing Institution: The Public Chamber

The Public Chamber of the Russian Federation (Obshchestvennaya Palata Rossiyskoy Federatsii) is an institution created by President Putin in 2004 to enhance dialogue between state and society, and facilitate civil society input into the formation and implementation of public policy. It comprises 166 notable members of Russian civil society (since 2013; previously 126). In 2009, all "socially significant" bills submitted to the State Duma were required to undergo expert examination by the Public Chamber.[9] While the chamber has little formal power to influence the policy process (its unanimous request to the Duma to postpone its deliberations on controversial new NGO legislation in 2005 was simply ignored, for example), it does provide its individual members with an additional platform they can use to push their own policy agendas. Members gain access to such privileged resources as greater access to information, meetings with government officials, and heightened media coverage.[10]

In May 2009 the Public Chamber published a major report entitled *Alcohol Abuse in the Russian Federation: Socio-economic Consequences and Means of Combating It*.[11] Although the Public Chamber was the official author of the report, it was mostly written by public health experts affiliated with the Russian Coalition for Alcohol Control under the patronage of supportive members of the chamber. The major patron was Yevgeniy Yuriev, a member of the chamber's Social and Demographic Development Commission who won the backing of the commission's chair, Alexandra Ochirova, to produce a Public Chamber report addressing the nation's alcohol problem.

Yuriev is perhaps best described as a minor oligarch—in 2010 he ranked 431 in Russian business magazine *Finans*'s ranking of the top five hundred richest people in Russia.[12] Yuriev is reportedly both very religious and very patriotic; he sponsors philanthropic activities including ones associated with the ROC, although he is not connected to Father Tikhon. In 2006 he was elected chair of the Public Council of Central Russia and subsequently became a member of the Public Chamber. He also served as an adviser to President Medvedev between 2010 and 2012. One respondent, a public health activist who has worked with Yuriev, related that like many Russian patriots, Yuriev became concerned by the country's demographic problems. He started developing his own national demographic program, paying experts to assist him. Although he had originally been pushing for pro-natalist and family-oriented measures, the experts who advised Yuriev suggested that he pay more attention to alcohol and tobacco as the major factors behind Russian hypermortality. Yuriev subsequently became acquainted with members of the Russian Coalition for Alcohol Control, which led to collaboration on the Public Chamber's report on alcohol abuse. This report was to play a significant role in helping shift public discourse on alcohol in a more public health direction.

From Illegality to Public Health

Between approximately 2006 and 2009, a major shift in the prevailing conception of the alcohol problem in public discourse took place. This shift was triggered to a large extent by the success of the new civil society elite in gaining major media coverage for their definition of the problem as one of public health rather than illegality.

In 2006, prior to their involvement in establishing the Russian Coalition for Alcohol Control, Korotayev and Khaltourina published an article in the political-economic journal *Ekspert* entitled "The Russian Vodka Cross."[13] The article began by outlining the trend that Russian demographers had labeled the "Russian cross": a dramatic fall in the birthrate in the post-Soviet period coinciding with an equally dramatic rise in the mortality rate, which when plotted on a graph formed an x-shaped cross. The authors observed that while the low birthrate was not exceptional by European standards, the mortality rate was exceptionally high: "In Russia, it is the catastrophic mortality rate of the population which creates a huge gap between births and deaths, resulting in the depopulation of the country." The remainder of the article proceeded to demonstrate that the main factor driving Russia's hypermortality was high per capita alcohol consumption, combined with the dominance of strong alcoholic drinks such as vodka that lead to rapid intoxication. Thus, the authors dubbed the "Russian cross" (a concept that had been in circulation in Russian demographics since the 1990s) the "Russian vodka cross." Korotayev and Khaltourina also explicitly refuted the "quality" discourse that had long dominated discussion on the alcohol problem in Russia: "It is widely believed that the reason for the majority of alcohol poisonings is the increased toxicity of illegal alcohol products. . . . This is not the case. Firstly, any ethanol is a toxic substance and an instantaneous dose of 400 grams of even quality pure alcohol can result in death. Therefore, the very availability of alcohol makes it dangerous. Secondly, toxicological studies have shown that the bulk of *samogon* and counterfeit vodka consumed in Russia is no more—and in some cases less—toxic than quality vodka."[14]

The article caught the attention of some mainstream Russian media outlets—aided by the success of the young, dynamic Khaltourina in actively engaging with journalists. The publicity generated by the "Vodka Cross" piece set in motion a gradual shift in media discourse to high per capita consumption as the problem.

The next major breakthrough for the new antialcohol network in mainstreaming its public health construction of the alcohol problem came through the ROC's Obshcheye Delo (Common Cause) project, an initiative spearheaded by Father Tikhon. The Common Cause project developed a series of hard-hitting documentaries warning of the medical harms caused by alcohol use. Many of the ideas they contained were taken from the lectures of the charismatic sobriety activist Vladimir Zhdanov, who collaborated with Tikhon on the project. In early 2009 Common Cause partnered with Russia's leading national television channel *Perviy Kanal* (First Channel), which broadcast four of the documentary films followed by in-depth discussion shows on the issues they raised. Tikhon himself was a major participant in the discussion shows, which gave him significant airtime to lay out his public health construction of the alcohol problem. Key members of the Coalition for Alcohol Control, government representatives, and celebrities also participated, giving the shows additional authority. The shows were hosted by the well-known television presenters Pyotr Tolstoy and Maria Shukshina, who repeated the antialcohol network's key soundbites about alcohol consumption being a "national disaster" that would condemn Russia to a very bleak future in the twenty-first century unless "urgent measures" were taken.[15] In parallel with this, First Channel also broadcast a series of public service advertisements (*roliki*) developed by Common Cause, which were screened on prime-time advertising slots.[16] Father Tikhon emphasized that these were not aimed at alcoholics, but rather at encouraging "average drinkers" to reduce their consumption.[17]

Two further milestones for the civil society elite in establishing their construction of the alcohol problem were achieved in May 2009. The first milestone was the publication of the Public Chamber's report *Alcohol Abuse in the Russian Federation*. The report took the "threat to national security" discourse that had grown around discussions of the Russian demographic crisis and applied it to alcohol abuse, citing the "harm inflicted on the family, society and the state." "Alcohol abuse" was defined broadly as high per capita consumption. Explicitly arguing against the old "quality" discourse, the report asserted that the biggest problem was everyday people abusing alcohol "in the same way that everyone else does."[18] The report also pushed the policy measures favored by the civil society elite, recommending the urgent introduction of numerous restrictive policies toward alcohol. In order to encourage consumption patterns to shift away from strong alcohol, it was proposed to increase excise duties on strong alcoholic drinks along the models that had already enjoyed success in Poland, Scandinavia, and the Baltic countries. As part of the fight against illegal alcohol, the report recommended introducing a state monopoly on the production of ethanol, with payment of excise duties on vodka *before* the transfer of the raw spirit. The report also recommended a state monopoly on the retail sale of alcohol, plus a range of measures restricting physical access to alcohol, such as reducing the number of outlets selling alcohol, and a ban on selling alcohol at night and on Sundays.[19]

The publication of the Public Chamber report received much positive coverage in the Russian media. It can be considered a significant PR success for the civil society elite in mainstreaming their conception of the alcohol problem and getting their policy recommendations on the political agenda. The Public Chamber "brand" provided not only high-level media coverage but a degree of political legitimacy, and established the document as a key text that could be referred to in support of antialcohol policies, a point made by more than one of the public health activists involved:

Respondent 1: It was distributed—like all Public Chamber reports—to the government agencies, the Duma and so on. For us it was a nice initiative to summarize everything in a short, readable format. . . . When you have a movement, over time you have to create basic texts. We did have basic texts before but they need to be re-created, updated. So it was a nice event for us.

Respondent 2: Yes, it was influential and it is an important reference, and I am very happy that there was no editing or censorship.

The second significant milestone was at the ROC's XIII World Russian People's Congress (Russkiy Narodniy Sobor), held in Moscow on 22–23 May 2009. The congress passed a resolution entitled "On urgent measures for protection against the alcohol threat."[20] Like the Public Chamber report, the resolution explicitly problematized high per capita alcohol consumption and utilized the discourse of national security in establishing the severity of the problem: "One of the main reasons for the deep demographic crisis that threatens the territorial integrity of the Russian Federation, and the very existence of the state, is currently ultra-high alcohol consumption."[21] The resolution went on to claim that alcohol was the cause of around a quarter of total Russian deaths annually, and directly appealed to the president and government of the Russian Federation to adopt a list of specific policies to tackle the "alcohol threat." These included the following:

- A complete ban on the sale of all alcoholic drinks (including beer) at stalls and kiosks
- Recognizing beer over 3.5 percent abv as an alcoholic beverage
- Restricting the sale of alcohol to the hours 11:00 a.m.–7:00 p.m. (with the exception of cafés, restaurants, and bars)
- The tightening of administrative sanctions (including fines and revocation of licenses) for the sale of alcohol to minors
- A ban on drinks that contain both alcohol and caffeine
- Introducing restrictions on the production and sale of perfumes and medical tinctures containing alcohol[22]

Shortly after the adoption of this resolution, the patriarch wrote a letter to President Medvedev asking him to take action accordingly. It is difficult to know to what extent the patriarch's letter was influential in Medvedev's decision to adopt an antialcohol initiative, but it is interesting to note that one

public health respondent who lobbied the federal authorities on alcohol policy believed that the patriarch's intervention was crucial:

> Respondent: I think the campaign—sort of campaign, I don't know if it was
> really a campaign, maybe it was a set of events not particularly connected to
> each other—but if we talk about President Medvedev, he organized the
> meeting in Sochi after a letter from the patriarch, and the patriarch wrote
> this letter on the basis of the resolution of the Russian People's Congress.
>
> ALB: So the church had its congress on alcohol, and that was enough to in-
> fluence the government?
>
> Respondent: No, it was that the patriarch took it seriously. The church has
> many conferences, but the patriarch does not write a letter on every problem
> which has been raised. So the patriarch took it seriously, and the letter from
> the patriarch to the president, yes that was taken seriously by the president. . . .
> *The presidential administration cannot ignore a letter from the patriarch, gener-*
> *ally.* [Emphasis mine]

Following the resolution of May 2009, the ROC established the Church-
Public Council for Protection Against the Alcohol Threat. The Church-
Public Council held a congress in February 2012 at the Church of Christ the
Saviour in Moscow, at which it passed an *obrashcheniye* (appeal) addressed
to the president and government.[23] The measures proposed included gradually reducing the number of points of sale of alcohol to a level that corre-
sponds to the European average, and further reducing the hours for the sale
of alcohol to 11:00 a.m.–7:00 p.m. (i.e., a repetition of the 2009 resolution's
demand; in the meantime, the major alcohol law of 2011 had restricted the
sale of alcohol to 8:00 a.m.–11:00 p.m.). The *obrashcheniye* also called for
eliminating the excise benefits for medicinal and alcohol-containing products such as perfume sold in containers larger than 25 mL. Perhaps the most
intriguing of the new measures proposed was "a ban on the use of plastic
bottles as packaging for the sale of alcoholic beverages, which by virtue of
their volume and affordability stimulate the alcoholisation of the population." A ban on plastic bottles as packaging for alcohol is a proposal that has
for some years been pushed by the vodka lobby to try to impose costs on the
beer industry, which would bear the brunt of such a measure.

Three Public faces, One Powerful Network

At the formal level, the new antialcohol elite that emerged at the end of the 2000s consisted of three separate institutions: the Russian Coalition for Alcohol Control (a public health lobby group), the ROC, and the Public Chamber (a state institution bringing together civil society leaders). But when one examines the actual workings of the antialcohol elite, it is best conceptualized as a single, unified network wearing three public faces. For all three institutions, most of the specialist work of information gathering, drafting policy recommendations, and writing reports was done by a core of public health professionals affiliated with the coalition. These individuals provided the expertise and workload capacity. The ROC provided political clout and moral weight as "protector of the nation" (public opinion surveys have consistently found that the ROC is one of the most highly trusted public institutions in a country where trust in public institutions is woefully low[24]). The ROC and the Public Chamber both acted as useful loudspeakers for the coalition to push its policies into the media and public discourse, because they possess considerable authority and their statements attract major media coverage.

Perhaps one of the key reasons for the shift in the alcohol problem discourse is that the new antialcohol network was successful in engaging the media to relate its narrative. Key members of the coalition already had considerable experience with public health advocacy in other spheres, such as HIV and tobacco. For example, coalition founder Kirill Danishevskiy worked on major HIV prevention projects for the Open Health Institute, and these projects had built up substantial databases of media contacts. This was a new generation of antialcohol activist: young public health professionals, fluent in English and active in the international public health community, who adopted the PR techniques of their Western colleagues. One such activist noted: "You have to build a critical mass of pressure and use the right channels, because if you are not on central TV, if you don't write to the agencies, ministers, and you don't work with journalists and you're not professional enough to be looked upon as credible, you will not have influence."

Another public health respondent made the same point about the importance of successfully engaging the media: "See, before 2007 a lot of scientists were talking about the alcohol issue at scientific conferences. Somewhere around 2006–7 some of the active people, lobbyists like Daria [Khaltourina] etc., started talking about it. That really changes the scene because it's very different when scientists do it and when Daria does it, because she's talking to journalists and the scientists are talking to each other."

The policy measures called for by the ROC in its two resolutions were proposed by key members of the coalition (Danishevskiy, Khaltourina, and Korotayev) together with the sobriety activist Zhdanov. The increasing weight of the ROC as a political actor was illustrated in 2010, when United Russia party officials met with ROC representatives to discuss what they called "questions of cooperation in the sphere of the moral and spiritual development of society." ROC representatives were entitled to view draft bills during the preliminary development phase (before they were submitted to the State Duma) in order to ensure that their views were taken on board. The chair of the State Duma's committee for the affairs of religious associations and organizations, Sergey Popov, related that the Duma had "established a system of cooperation with the ROC when bills undergo second reading."[25] The political weight of the ROC was also suggested by some remarks made by respondents. The idea that the presidential administration "cannot ignore a letter from the Patriarch" has already been related above. Another telling moment was when the head of RAR, Igor Chuyan, appeared as one of the keynote speakers at the Church-Public Council for Protection Against the Alcohol Threat's congress held in February 2012. For a long-standing state vodka industry leader like Chuyan to deliver a keynote speech at a congress full of devout temperance activists could be considered as walking into the lion's den. It is even more remarkable in view of Chuyan's famously secretive nature: he is notorious for almost never speaking in public. I was present at the congress and was struck by how uncomfortable Chuyan looked. Of course, this could be as much due to the rarity with which he speaks in public as the potentially hostile environment, but it was notable that he did not stay to take questions like the other speakers. We cannot be sure, but it seems likely that Chuyan's presence at the congress was due to the informal political authority that the ROC—and in particular Father Tikhon—possesses. One respondent explained simply, "He [Chuyan] wouldn't say no to Father Tikhon."

In fact, Father Tikhon managed to forge a useful working relationship with RAR, something that the public health lobbyists in the Coalition for Alcohol Control had not achieved. When RAR developed the government's alcohol policy concept in 2009 it sent a draft to Father Tikhon for comment but not to the coalition. The case shows how Father Tikhon, possessing the political authority of the ROC and the informal authority of being perceived as close to Putin, acted as a channel for the coalition to exert its influence on policymaking. A senior member of the coalition related the process as follows: "RAR sent it [the draft policy concept] to Father Tikhon; they didn't send it to me. I don't have very good contacts with RAR. Father Tikhon sent it to me, so we all saw the document before. If you influence policy you don't need that many interventions, so I don't think they're in contact on a daily basis, but there is sufficiently good work. . . . So they sent it to Father Tikhon, Tikhon sent it to me, I told him it's ok—because it's not bad, it's not very concrete but it's ok."

The same respondent related how Tikhon built up the relationship with RAR despite the initial doubts of his public health colleagues. The exchange is also interesting because it reveals that the Ministry of Health saw Tikhon's Common Cause project as a rival to its own health promotion activity, rather than an opportunity for cooperation. Inasmuch as RAR and the Ministry of Health were also competing at this time for the turf rights to alcohol control policy, it seems that cooperation with Tikhon may have had strategic benefits for RAR as well as Tikhon:

Respondent: First of all it was Father Tikhon's initial strategy to build friends with RAR and with the Ministry of Health, but he didn't find as much understanding with the Ministry of Health. I think that RAR took this contact with Father Tikhon as a way of legitimizing them, because they were about to be taken very, very negatively in the beginning by the health people. . . . And of course he [Chuyan] is not a health person, although he serves a good function in terms of health. . . . I was also very uncomfortable and I was not very enthusiastic of Father Tikhon working with Chuyan; I thought it would be much smarter to work with and through the Ministry of Health. But he decided to go that way and it proved helpful.

ALB: So the Ministry of Health people aren't interested in links with Father Tikhon?

Respondent: They were interested; the problem was that the Ministry of Health does its own campaign, a public service advertising campaign on alcohol, and they kind of view Father Tikhon a little competitively.

ALB: So he's treading on their turf, from their point of view?

Respondent: Yes, because there is money from the budget for this healthy lifestyles campaign. . . . And they still do have contacts, just Father Tikhon didn't find it too useful, and also there was a general strategy to give more and more authority to RAR on alcohol.

The practice of the coalition's specialists influencing policy by working through an institution possessing greater authority than themselves also occurred with the major alcohol control bill of 2011. This time the Public Chamber provided the front of authority. The Public Chamber submitted an expert commentary on the bill that was published on the bill's official Duma page and circulated to all the relevant agencies. A working group was formed for the preparation of this commentary, in which the public health experts of the coalition played a prominent role. It seems that the Public Chamber's commentary enjoyed success in bringing about some of the changes favored by the public health lobby, such as a ban on the sale of ethyl alcohol in the Far North.[26]

The coalition also successfully worked with the Duma deputy Viktor Zvagelskiy. The public health respondent who had closest dealings with Zvagelskiy noted that they had certain common interests: in particular, reducing the availability of alcohol surrogates and beer. The respondent agreed that they had a strategic alliance, and described their working relationship as a good one: "I come to his [Zvagelskiy's] office, sometimes I write proposals for him. And in general we exchange information. . . . I'm fine with what he's done, he helped with the kiosk thing,[27] and as for taxes—the only area where he could potentially be detrimental—he's not in charge at all. That's not his responsibility. . . . He says some very interesting things to me, he's a very valuable source of information. Until he does something harmful, we'll be cooperating."

The respondent provided some detailed examples of the cooperation in action. On one occasion, the respondent suggested removing a tax break for producers of certain alcohol-containing products. Zvagelskiy enthusiastically agreed and asked the respondent to provide a written proposal. Once the proposal had been amended slightly by Zvagelskiy's lawyers, he duly introduced it.

The assistance the civil society elite provided to Zvagelskiy can be described as an alternative source of expert capacity, a concept the respondent themselves used: "Whenever anybody has a request on alcohol, the request for information now comes to us, because we have alternative expert capacity. Industry has expert capacity, and us, and that's it, nobody else in the country. So basically we write all these requests: to this ministry, to that ministry, to the presidential administration, to that working group, and so on, here and there. To the media, also . . . It's very tiring, it's rapid response and sometimes you have to work on something overnight."

This "expert capacity" was clearly useful to Zvagelskiy as an informal extra source of workload support, but perhaps more importantly, as a scientific knowledge base that he could draw on to provide an objective public health justification for policies advocated by himself and RAR.

By 2009, two major factors had combined to fundamentally shift the prevailing alcohol policy paradigm in Russia. First, the government was taking Russia's demographic situation seriously and beginning to take action accordingly. Second, an influential antialcohol network composed of key members of Russia's civil society elite had succeeded in problematizing high per capita consumption in the media and other channels of public discourse. As a result, the prevailing discourse on the alcohol problem had shifted substantially away from the "quality not quantity" theme that had dominated during the first fifteen years of the post-Soviet era. The stage was set for the launch of a major new government initiative to reduce alcohol consumption in the country.

Chapter 12

Medvedev and the Antialcohol Initiative

"Dmitry Medvedev is starting an anti-alcohol campaign" announced the national daily newspaper *Izvestiya* in the summer of 2009.[1] "Anti-alcohol campaign number two" proclaimed the *Sankt-Peterburgskiye vedomosti*, in a clear reference to the Gorbachev-era campaign of nearly twenty-five years earlier.[2] Western media outlets were quick to pick up on the news of a new antialcohol campaign in Russia. Britain's *Daily Telegraph* reported that Medvedev had "begun the toughest anti-alcohol campaign since the collapse of the Soviet Union,"[3] while *Time* magazine wrote that he had "launched a new war on drinking."[4]

What exactly had triggered these media proclamations of an antialcohol campaign? The occasion was a major executive meeting on developing a national strategy to reduce alcohol consumption, chaired by President Medvedev on 12 August 2009.[5] It was at this meeting, held in the resort city of Sochi, that Medvedev made his now-famous statement that, "frankly speaking, [the alcohol problem] has taken on the proportions of a national disaster."[6] One month after the Sochi meeting, on 11 September 2009, Medvedev issued a list of instructions to the federal government "on measures to reduce alcohol consumption."[7] Prime Minister Putin was listed as responsible for their execution. It was this set of instructions that was to provide the framework for the battles over Russian alcohol policy in subsequent years.

The first step listed in the policy instructions was to develop a national alcohol policy concept "to reduce alcohol abuse" by 15 December 2009. But many specific policies were also included in Medvedev's instructions, including submitting a bill to the State Duma increasing the penalties for selling alcohol to minors; limiting "weak alcoholic beverages" to 330 mL containers; requiring mandatory health warnings on beer and weak alcoholic beverages (to cover not less than 20 percent of the packaging area); and increasing restrictions on the advertising of alcoholic beverages, beer, and similar beverages containing over 5 percent alcohol by volume (abv). The introduction of mandatory minimum retail prices for alcoholic drinks was to be considered, while the government was instructed to "consider the consequences" of introducing a state monopoly on the production and circulation of pure alcohol (ethanol) and alcoholic products. The need to continue the fight against illegal alcohol was once again emphasized, but perhaps unsurprisingly given the apparently intractable nature of the problem, no concrete solutions were proposed, just a vague reference to "developing a set of measures," including "increased control over the production and circulation of alcoholic products."

Medvedev's policy instructions also specified several amendments to be made to Federal Law No. 171, the main law governing the production and sale of alcohol in the country. These included allowing the federal government to restrict the time and place of alcohol sales, granting federal subjects (i.e., regional governments[8]) the right to impose even tighter restrictions on the time and place of sales than the federal requirements, and banning nonstationary points of sale (i.e., kiosks, tents, and stalls) from selling beer stronger than 5 percent abv.

Medvedev himself never described this new policy initiative as an antialcohol campaign, or indeed a campaign of any type. Even if he had privately conceived of it as a campaign, he would have been wary of using the term because of the negative connotations of the antialcohol campaign of the Gorbachev years. It is notable that in his address at the 12 August meeting, Medvedev struck a delicate balance, referring to the "organisational errors" of the Gorbachev campaign while praising its positive effects on male mortality. The official terminology used for the initiative was "measures to reduce alcohol consumption in Russia," thus carefully avoiding the connotation of being opposed to alcohol per se. Of course, the journalists covering the story were not to be so easily deterred: "antialcohol campaign" had a much catchier (and more newsworthy) ring to it.

The alcohol policy concept ordered by Medvedev was published on 30 December 2009, bearing the unwieldy title (typical of Russian government documents) *Concept for the implementation of state policy for decreasing the scale of abuse of alcoholic products and prevention of alcoholism among the population of the Russian Federation, for the period to 2020.*[9] The policy concept fully embraced the antialcohol elite's construction of the alcohol problem. Alcohol was once again cited as a "major threat to national security," and the aim of reducing alcohol consumption was to "improve the demographic situation in the country." The concept explicitly stated three goals for alcohol policy: a significant reduction in alcohol consumption, improving systems for preventing alcohol abuse, and improving management of the alcohol market. While some specific outcome targets were set, other goals were vaguely worded. In the first phase (2010–12) the two main targets were to reduce per capita alcohol consumption by 15 percent and to reduce the share of overall consumption taken by strong alcoholic beverages (although no precise figure was given). The latter was particularly interesting in view of RAR's connections with vodka interests. The target for the second phase (2013–20) was to reduce per capita consumption by 55 percent. It is interesting to note—in view of the difficulties in measuring per capita consumption in Russia described in chapter 9—that the starting figure for per capita consumption was not listed in the concept. Taking the Ministry of Health and Social Development's much-cited 2009 figure of 18 liters as the base figure for per capita alcohol consumption would suggest targets of 15.3 liters by 2012, and 8.1 liters by 2020.[10] The other notable target for the second phase was the "elimination of the illegal alcohol market." This aim could reasonably be regarded as unrealistic given that estimates at the time put the black market at roughly half of the total alcohol market.[11]

One of the most intriguing features of Medvedev's policy instructions was the 5 percent abv threshold for the proposed new restrictions on beer. The president ordered that so-called nonstationary points of sale (i.e., kiosks, tents, and stalls) be banned from selling strong beers, as well as tightening the restrictions on beer advertising. But crucially, these provisions would apply only to beer stronger than 5 percent abv. To put this in context, a standard lager is typically somewhere between 4 and 5 percent abv; Budweiser is exactly 5 percent abv. Given that the majority of beer sold in Russia was less than 5 percent abv, the proposal was not particularly detrimental for either beer manufacturers or kiosk owners. However, ultimately the vodka lobby within the state was able to overturn the 5 percent abv threshold in favor of a total ban, significantly altering the balance of power between beer and vodka producers.

The federal alcohol regulator RAR was made responsible for drafting the alcohol policy concept, but there was clearly competition between RAR and the Ministry of Health and Social Development on this issue. The latter had already drafted its own alcohol policy concept in 2008, which had been circulated among relevant ministries and agencies for comment.[12] So how did it come about that RAR rather than the Ministry of Health became responsible for antialcohol policy development? It is difficult to know the details of what happened inside the "black box" of top-level policy decisions: even the best-informed respondents were unaware of the finer details of the machinations at the ministerial level, but one suggested that "there was a general strategy to give more and more authority to RAR on alcohol," and that there was "a decision from the top to go through RAR." Another respondent, a brewing executive, suggested that making RAR responsible for antialcohol policy was a deliberate strategy by the vodka interests within the state to take alcohol policy out of the hands of public health (e.g., the Ministry of Health or consumer protection agency Rospotrebnadzor), where it would pose a greater threat to their interests.

Explaining the Campaign

There had been several factors pushing for a new, public health–oriented alcohol policy from the mid-2000s onward. The interests of the superelite in the country's demographic situation were channeled into a new antialcohol agenda by the emergence of a small but well-connected civil society elite. However, this apparent new elite consensus on the need to tackle the alcohol threat was ultimately tempered by two major factors. The first was the ambivalent and contradictory attitudes of the general public toward alcohol. When combined with the fear of popular discontent within the Putinite regime, this resulted in a delicate balancing act for the elite: needing to be seen as tackling alcohol-related problems, while keeping alcohol sufficiently affordable for the population. The second factor distorting the development and implementation of antialcohol policies in Russia was an institutional one. It concerned the balance of power among the various bureaucratic departments competing for turf rights over responsibility for alcohol policy. As noted in chapter 6, the emergence of the new alcohol regulator RAR as the dominant bureaucratic actor in the field of alcohol policy represented a power shift in favor of the vodka interests associated with the state. Like the political elite, RAR also had a delicate balancing act to play. As the federal alcohol regulator, it needed to be seen as developing policies to reduce per capita consumption as instructed, while at the same time not alienating the vodka interests with which it had informal ties. In some cases, RAR proved very successful in using the former as moral cover for the latter, such as using the amendment of Law 171 on alcohol control to impose major restrictions on the beer industry (see chapter 13).

One notable feature of the new antialcohol initiative was a disproportionate focus on children and youth drinking as the problem.[13] Given that the main factor in Russian hypermortality is excessive mortality among working-age males, such an emphasis on youth drinking may seem spurious. Nor is Russian youth drinking particularly high in comparative terms. The results of the 2011 survey conducted by ESPAD (the European School Survey Project on Alcohol and Other Drugs) suggested that alcohol use among fifteen- to sixteen-year-old students in Russia was relatively low compared with the European average.[14] It may be argued that reducing underage drinking is a long-term means of reducing the future consumption of those individuals when they become adults. However, this argument was rarely explicitly made, and the focus on underage drinking seemed out of proportion to its potential role in reducing adult consumption.

One influential public health respondent was critical of the focus on youth drinking, which they firmly agreed was much less of a public health problem than consumption by working-age males. Why, then, was there so much focus on the "problem" of underage drinking in Russia?

> Respondent: It's emotional. Like, it's *children*. . . . I think it's an irrational, emotional perception of reality and the real danger is supermortality among young and middle-aged men. We shouldn't get disturbed by our perceptions from the reality.

ALB: Although when you look at things the president [Medvedev] says, he says the priority has to be protecting children from the alcohol threat.

Respondent: Yes, it's a pity that he's disorientated from the real problem.

ALB: So why does he talk about children and adolescents so much? Because he knows it's a popular concern?

Respondent: I think he thinks it's a problem. Also they were very reluctant to do something with alcohol, and "children" seems to be the only argument which works—at least, Father Tikhon does this. So you get other measures for children. But generally I don't like these discussions on children because they distract from more important things.

Measures to tackle youth drinking were an ever-present feature of the legislative activity of the campaign. In December 2010 the State Duma passed a bill giving shop assistants the right to insist on identification if they have doubts about a customer's age.[15] In July 2011 the repeated sale of alcohol to minors by individuals (as distinct from legal entities) was made a criminal offense. A specific offense of selling alcohol to minors was established in the Code of Administrative Offenses, separate from other violations of the law on the retail sale of alcohol and with its own level of fines.[16] The level of fines was increased significantly (as much as tenfold) by a further law of 13 November 2012. The increases are shown in table 12.1.[17]

The ban on selling premixed cocktails in containers larger than 330 mL (which went into effect 1 January 2013) also represented a symbolic attack on the problem of youth drinking, since these drinks are seen as being aimed primarily at teenagers.

Table 12.1 Changes to the level of fines for selling alcohol to minors (November 2012)

Type of seller prosecuted	Old level of fine (RUB)	New level of fine (RUB)
Individuals	3,000–5,000	30,000–50,000
*Officials**	10,000–20,000	100,000–200,000
Legal entities	80,000–100,000	300,000–500,000

*Self-employed businessmen are classified as officials.

Advantage Vodka

The Russian government established a minimum retail price on vodka on 1 January 2010. The price was initially set at 89 rubles per half liter (just under $3 at the exchange rate at the time) but was subject to yearly increases (see table 12.2), more than doubling to 220 rubles by August 2014 (although it decreased slightly in 2015).

When the policy was introduced, it was widely represented by the media as being part of the antialcohol campaign. This seems logical: according to basic economic rules of supply and demand, if the price of vodka is raised, demand for it should fall.

It is surprising to learn that, when one digs a little deeper into the policymaking processes, the impetus to establish a minimum price on vodka actually came from the vodka industry itself, rather than public health interests. The thinking went that when faced with a branded vodka at the minimum price and a counterfeit vodka, the consumer would always choose the branded vodka. Thus, illegal vodka would be rendered unattractive by losing its only competitive advantage: its cheap price.[18] This argument, of course, applies only to the sale of *illegal* alcohol by *legal* retail outlets; there is no reason to think that under-the-counter sales would not continue to be conducted at below the minimum price. Nevertheless, the policy appears to have been strongly lobbied by vodka industry organizations. In the summer of 2007 the Union of

Table 12.2 Minimum retail price of vodka, 2010–16

Effective date	Price (RUB)/0.5L
1 January 2010	89
1 January 2011	98
1 July 2012	125
1 January 2013	170
10 March 2014	199
1 August 2014	220
1 February 2015	185
13 June 2016	190

Alcohol Producers publicly called for the introduction of a minimum vodka price on the grounds that it would help combat illegal production. A bill was duly introduced to the Duma by United Russia deputy Vladimir Pekarev in October 2007, which proposed establishing a minimum vodka price of 78 rubles per half liter. Pekarev, who first entered the Duma in 1999, was a "vodka king": he founded the major vodka distiller OST-Alko.[19] While Pekarev's bill did not pass, the idea of a minimum price on vodka became well established in industry discourse. Notably, Rosspirtprom's PR director Dmitry Dobrov spoke out in favor of the policy at the time of Pekarev's initiative.[20] Once the new alcohol regulator RAR was established in 2009, it seemed inevitable that it would introduce a minimum price for vodka: the government decree of 24 February 2009 that officially created RAR explicitly listed among the new agency's powers the right to set minimum prices for strong alcohol (over 28 percent abv). Thus, the introduction of the minimum retail price for vodka on 1 January 2010 was coincidental with, rather than part of, the new antialcohol initiative, though framing the policy as part of an antialcohol campaign was convenient for all concerned.

The minimum retail price for vodka is far from the only policy that has been represented as part of the antialcohol campaign while in fact benefiting the vodka industry. Vodka gained a relative competitive advantage over beer in 2010 due to dramatic changes in the rate of excise duty. In 2010, excise duty was increased *threefold* (i.e., 200 percent) on beer, while the corresponding increase on strong alcohol was just 9.9 percent (which in real terms represented a freeze given that inflation was running at 10 percent that year). As table 12.3 shows, even though vodka was subject to slight above-inflationary excise increases in subsequent years, nothing before or since has even come close to the 200 percent increase imposed on beer.

How can we explain this targeting of beer but not vodka in the midst of the antialcohol campaign? It will be recalled that one of the official goals of state policy as set out in the alcohol policy concept was reducing the share of overall consumption taken by strong alcoholic beverages, and yet this excise policy seemed to encourage the exact opposite.

The answer lay in the tasks facing the Ministry of Finance (Minfin) at this time, combined with the apparent effect of insider vodka lobbying. In 2009, when the budget plans for 2010 were being prepared, Russia was experiencing the consequences of the global financial crisis. Minfin was facing a huge fall in budgetary incomes, and finance minister Alexey Kudrin was

Table 12.3 Rate of increase in excise duty and inflation in the Russian Federation (as percentage of previous year)

	2006	2007	2008	2009	2010	2011	2012
Inflation (indeks potrebitel'skikh tsen (IPTs)—consumer price index)	9	11.9	13.3	8.8	10	6.5–7*	5–6*
Indexation of duty rate on strong alcohol	8.9	1.9	7.1	10.1	9.9	10	19.9
Indexation of duty rate on wine	0	0	6.8	10.6	34.6	42.9	20
Indexation of duty rate on beer	9.1	8.4	32.4	9.5	200	11.1	20

*Predicted inflation.
Source: Table reproduced from the Russian language original with kind permission of the Gaidar Institute. Gaidar Institute for Economic Policy, "Analiz tekushchego sostoyaniya nalogooblozheniya alkogol'noy otrasli v Rossii i otsenka posledstviy povysheniya stavok aktsiza na alkogol'nuyu produktsiyu" [Analysis of the current taxation structure of the alcohol industry in Russia and assessment of the consequences of the increase in excise rates on alcoholic products], PowerPoint presentation, October 2011.

desperately searching for ways to generate extra income to reduce the large budget deficit. Minfin proposed trebling excise duty on beer, with a much smaller (though still considerably more substantial than in previous years) increase of 30 percent on excise duty on strong alcohol. However, while the government approved the increase for beer, it vetoed Minfin's proposed increase for spirits. One respondent, a specialist in excise duties, hinted that Putin may have played a role in scrapping the proposed increase in the rate on strong alcohol, and that insider vodka lobbying was a factor:

> ALB: So why in 2010 did the government put up excise duty so steeply on beer and not on vodka?
>
> Respondent: There was the effect of lobbying; and note that it was decided at the very highest echelon, almost at Putin's level.
>
> ALB: And who exactly lobbied?
>
> Respondent: I don't want to name any names, it's sufficient to look at the structure of the market; you'll see that a lot of them (as I understand it) belong to the Rotenberg family. That's more than 10 percent of the market, they're very strongly affiliated to and acquainted with Mr Putin. At the level of the prime minister [i.e., Putin at this time], there was, let's say, a nod given to go more easy on the indexation of strong alcohol. Whereas beer on the whole, if you look at our beer market they're all foreigners.

In fact, it appears that there was an attempt within the presidential administration to scale back the enormous increase in beer excise. Presidential aide (and subsequent deputy prime minister) Arkady Dvorkovich issued a written observation (*zamechaniye*) forcefully criticizing the increase, stating, "This could substantially complicate the realisation of state policy on the reduction of consumption of strong alcohol among the population." It is not known to whom Dvorkovich sent his *zamechaniye*, but we do know that President Medvedev subsequently issued an order to Prime Minister Putin, instructing the government to monitor the structure of consumption with respect to strong alcohol and beer, and to "consider the possibility of introducing changes to the Tax Code . . . increasing excise rates in accordance with the strength of the beverage."[21] Yet as we have seen, no such modifications took place.

The apparent effects of insider lobbying aside, there is another reason why increasing excise duty on beer was more attractive from a revenue-raising perspective than an increase on vodka. The efficiency of excise tax collection on beer in Russia was close to 100 percent; that is, avoidance of

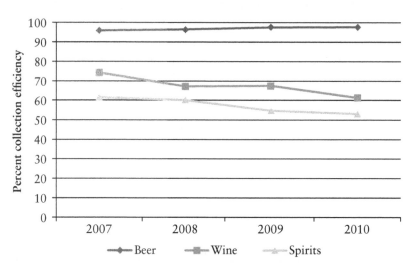

Figure 12.1 Efficiency of excise duty collection in the Russian Federation. Figures calculated by the Gaidar Institute, Moscow, using Euromonitor data. Gaidar Institute for Economic Policy, "Analiz tekushchego sostoyaniya nalogooblozheniya alkogol'noy otrasli v Rossii i otsenka posledstviy povysheniya stavok aktsiza na alkogol'nuyu produktsiyu" [Analysis of the current taxation structure of the alcohol industry in Russia and assessment of the consequences of the increase in excise rates on alcoholic products], PowerPoint presentation, October 2011.

excise duty was almost nonexistent. For spirits, by contrast, the efficiency rate was only 50–60 percent, and excise avoidance tends to rise with increases in the rate (see figure 12.1). Thus, an excise increase on beer would guarantee the additional expected revenues, while an excise increase on vodka would not necessarily generate significant (or indeed, any) extra income to the budget.

The following year, 2010, Minfin again proposed increasing excise rates on strong alcohol, but was again rebuffed by the government. The proposal was for an increase of 30 percent every year. This would have involved the minimum price for a half liter of vodka rising to 120 rubles in 2011, 160 rubles in 2012, and 200 rubles by 2013—more than doubling in three years.[22] However, following a meeting of the government chaired by Prime Minister Putin on 30 June 2010, Minfin's proposed increases were again rejected,[23] and once again spirits escaped with a rise of 10 percent.

Thus, in the year following President Medvedev's instructions on measures to reduce alcohol consumption, there had been the *impression* of significant action: measures to tackle youth drinking, a minimum price for vodka, and a trebling of excise duty on beer. Yet only the first of these measures actually resulted from the antialcohol agenda. What of the other measures that had been instructed by Medvedev in September 2009? These were the subject of a major government bill that was at the center of a fierce lobbying battle. The next chapter shows how certain provisions in the bill were hijacked by the vodka lobby to target its major competitor—the multinational beer industry.

Chapter 13

Alcohol Policy as Battleground

The 2011 Alcohol Law

In July 2011, Western media outlets reported—with scarcely contained bemusement—on changes to Russian alcohol law. What could prompt international media interest in such a niche area of regulation, typically of interest only to policy wonks and industry specialists? The answer was that, apparently, Russian law did not regard beer as an alcoholic drink but merely a foodstuff—on a par with fruit juice or soda. The unspoken implication was clear. Those crazy Russians! So consumed by their vodka-soaked drinking culture that they do not even regard beer as alcohol! Until now, of course. The Russian authorities were at last facing up to the country's disastrous alcohol problem and turning "an apparently self-evident truth into law—that beer is an alcoholic drink."[1]

As so often in the sphere of Russian alcohol policymaking, this simplistic narrative was extremely misleading. First, take the notion that beer was not classified as alcohol. In technical legal terms this was true: beer's production and sale were governed by a set of laws different from those of other alcoholic drinks. But if this conjured up visions of Russian children buying a beer as casually as their Western counterparts might buy a cola, they would be wide of the mark. Beer not being legally classified as alcohol did not mean that its sale was unrestricted. It could not be sold to minors. It was subject to excise tax. Its advertising was constrained by numerous restrictions. In short, in Russia beer was already being regulated in much the same way as in Western countries.

Second, the idea that the reclassification of beer as alcohol was a straightforward result of Medvedev's antialcohol initiative, passed with the aim of reducing consumption among the population, is an extreme simplification. This chapter examines in detail the development and eventual passage in July 2011 of the government bill amending Law 171, the main law that regulates the production and sale of alcohol.[2] While the impetus to amend Law 171 was indeed provided by President Medvedev's orders to the federal government on measures to reduce alcohol consumption, the final content of the new law was far from predetermined by his instructions. This provides a revealing case study of what is known in policy studies as the advocacy coalition framework (ACF): that policy formation is a constant battleground between stakeholders, and policy outcomes are the ad hoc results of those battles. The final version of the bill amending Law 171 represented just such an ad hoc outcome of clashes between diverse political forces and vested interests. No single actor was in overall control, but RAR and the vodka interests close to it proved to be the most powerful.

The Battle Begins

In his policy instructions to the government of September 2009, Medvedev had listed quite specific details of amendments to be made to Law 171. A federal norm restricting the time and place of alcohol sales was to be introduced. Regional governments would be granted the right to impose even tighter restrictions on the time and place of sales than the federal requirements, to accommodate the fact that some already had such restrictions in place. Another set of measures would promote the idea of discouraging consumption of stronger alcohol (including strong beers) by differentiating between beer under and over 5 percent abv. For example, various restrictions on advertising alcohol would be extended to all except weak beers, and non-stationary points of sale (i.e., kiosks, tents, and stalls) would also be prohibited from selling beer stronger than 5 percent abv.

What was most striking about the process of amending Law 171 from a political scientist's perspective was the inordinate amount of time each stage took. Every step in the process seemed to be subject to mysterious delays, unexplained postponements, and long periods of silence. This is an indication of just how fierce the struggle was over the law's precise content. Anyone who expected the amending bill to simply implement the president's instructions as gospel, with no alterations and no additions, was in for a very rude awakening. The wide range of actors involved in this struggle included not only industry lobbyists but a whole range of state actors, including government departments and the presidential administration, who had conflicting opinions on what measures should be included and were involved in fierce battles behind the scenes. This was reflected in the large number of very different draft versions of the bill that were in circulation: two respondents independently stated there were at least ten.

RAR was appointed the profile agency for the bill amending Law 171, that is, the agency responsible for drafting the bill, mediating the feedback from other ministries, and submitting an agreed version to the government. As described in chapter 6, RAR has close ties to the state- and *sistema*-sponsored vodka industry. It is thus no surprise that RAR was pushing for some of the more radical anti-beer measures contained in the numerous versions of the draft bill in circulation, such as introducing licensing for beer production and extending EGAIS to beer.[3] The view in the brewing industry was that, rather than having a public health rationale, RAR's main motivation for reclassifying beer as an alcoholic product was that it was a precondition for the agency to be able to extend its policy reach to the brewing industry. As one brewing executive expressed this belief: "We understood that RAR, having been established, would try to grab the beer industry under its control. Formally they couldn't do it as long as beer was not an alcoholic product: according to Russian legislation and RAR's statute, it could only concern itself with alcoholic products. It was quite obvious, it was only a matter of time."

This respondent was a GR specialist for a major brewer at the time of the bill's development. Their account of the process of preparing a government bill is revealing for understanding how Russian government departments other than the profile agency are able to block or force modification of individual provisions in a bill. First, the profile agency (in this case RAR) prepares the first draft of the bill. Responsibility for the bill then passes to a deputy prime minister (Viktor Zubkov in this instance), who has to include in the dialogue other ministries that have a policy interest in the subject of the bill. In our case, those ministries included the Ministry of Health, Ministry of Internal Affairs, Ministry of Trade, Ministry for Economic Development, and of course RAR itself. The ministries provide their positions and comments on the bill's provisions, which together form a process of discussion in the government. Once the bill is broadly agreed upon by all ministries, the final version moves to the Government Commission on Legislative Work, which determines whether to support the bill at the government level or reject it for further review. If the bill is supported by the commission, it proceeds to the State Duma as a government bill.

The GR executive described how they and their fellow brewing industry lobbyists managed to gain the support of other ministries to oppose RAR behind the scenes, forcing RAR to make some concessions to the brewers in the version of the bill that went to first reading:

> We started actively trying to interfere with the contents of this bill, because over time it changed from very extreme proposals like installing the EGAIS system and excise stamps on beer bottles, up to very mild and moderate versions where beer was legally treated as alcohol, but de facto regulation was almost the same as brewers had before 2011. . . . We managed to get the support of other ministries in the government—the Ministry for the Economy, Ministry of Trade, Ministry of Agriculture and so on—who created quite a strong opposition to the extreme proposals. They agreed generally with the idea that beer can be regulated by the same law, but of course they were strictly against kiosk bans, EGAIS, licensing and so on. So we managed to create a big opposition to the draft law in the government, and RAR had to make some concessions, remove some extreme proposals.

The ultimate arbiter between all these competing factions within the government was the Government Commission for Regulating the Alcohol Market, which convened to consider the draft bill on 11 June 2010. The business broadsheet *Kommersant* obtained a copy of the commission's minutes and reported the amendments it had made to the draft bill, summarized in table 13.1.

Table 13.1 Government Commission for Regulating the Alcohol Market's amendments to RAR's draft bill

Proposed by RAR	Government Commission's decision
Reclassify beer as alcohol	Approved
Introduce compulsory accounting and declaration of beer production	Excluded
Introduce licensing of beer production and sale	Excluded
Restrict alcoholic beverages under 7 percent abv to containers of 330 mL*	Withdrawn by RAR
Introduce a ban on the sale of beer over 5 percent abv at nonstationary retail outlets (e.g., kiosks, tents)	Approved
Prohibit the retail sale of alcohol 9 p.m.–11 a.m.	Approved Minpromtorg's alternative proposal—11 p.m.–8 a.m.

* This proposal was a source of much confusion, even for insiders. It had been listed in President Medvedev's policy instructions of 11 September 2009, but it is not clear whether it was intended to apply to beer or only to premixed cocktails (the instructions stated simply "weak alcoholic beverages"). In the explanatory notes to the bill drafted by RAR, the measure was specifically described as applying to "weak alcoholic products, beer and beer-based beverages" (see original documents leaked in Elizaveta Nikitina, "Zakon o trezvom budushem" [Law for a sober future], Slon.ru, 2 December 2009, accessed 11 December 2009, http://slon.ru/articles/201384/?sphrase_id =154857). However, when the 330 mL provision reappeared in the bill presented at first reading, and indeed was retained in the version eventually passed by the Duma, it applied only to cocktails, not beer. Had the provision applied to beer it would certainly have caused considerable inconvenience and cost to brewers, as most Russian beer is sold in containers of at least 500 mL. What is interesting is that two brewing executives, working for different companies, independently assured me that the 330 mL measure had *never* been intended to apply to beer; one suggested that it had simply been "a misunderstanding, because the media could not distinguish between beer and low-alcohol drinks with added ethanol." But this is contradicted by RAR's draft, which as noted specifically stated that the measure applied to beer. It is hard to explain this contradictory information.
Source: Oleg Trutnev, "Pivo eshchyo ne okreplo" [Beer isn't yet strong enough], *Kommersant*, No. 113, 28 June 2010.

Perhaps surprisingly given its vodka industry links, RAR's original proposal for time restrictions on the retail sale of alcohol had been relatively strict: the agency proposed banning all alcohol sales between the hours 9 p.m. and 11 a.m. This proposal had faced opposition from other government departments, namely, Minpromtorg (the Ministry of Trade) and the MVD (Ministry of Internal Affairs). Both ministries argued that such a restriction would too drastically restrict citizens' right to buy legal alcohol in shops, and would cause the illegal alcohol trade to rise.[4] In the end, Minpromtorg's compromise proposal of 11 p.m.–8 a.m. was accepted by the Government Commission for Regulating the Alcohol Market.

The beer industry particularly feared RAR's proposal to extend the licensing and declaration systems to beer production, claiming that it would inflict "immeasurable" losses on the industry. The brewers had observed the way in which RAR appeared to be using its licensing powers to control and consolidate the vodka industry, and naturally feared that a similar fate awaited the beer industry should it be subject to licensing.[5] They expressed concerns that what they perceived as the corrupt nature of the alcohol licensing system would impose additional financial and administrative burdens on the industry that could not be avoided simply by complying with the law. "The licenses themselves aren't particularly expensive," observed Heinekin Russia's corporate affairs director Kirill Bolmatov. "But we know from the experience of the vodka sector that the licensing requirements are very blurred, which creates a fertile ground for corruption. RAR can refuse licenses on the most contrived pretexts, which has already led to the halting of major producers."[6]

When asked on a live radio program why the bill was taking so long to be submitted to first reading, United Russia's alcohol policy representative, Viktor Zvagelskiy, was evasive. The exchange is worth relating in full, since it gives a good overview of the difficulties in understanding the factors behind the bill's progress—the opaqueness of the process, the behind-the-scenes fights between different ministries, and the convenience (and insufficiency) of using "lobbying" as an explanation of slow legislative progress:

Host: But there's been no decision as yet . . .

Zvagelskiy: The government says "yes," the administration says "yes," but there's no movement.

Host: Why not?

Zvagelskiy: Probably because of very strong lobbying tendencies.

Host: What, "lobbying tendencies" come up to your colleagues carrying suitcases, or what? What does "strong lobbying" mean? I want to understand how it actually happens.

Zvagelskiy: You know what it is? You shouldn't over-estimate the power of deputies and the Duma in this regard, unfortunately.

Host: But you pass laws.

Zvagelskiy: Unfortunately, any bills which we try to get passed must receive approval in the government of any relevant department, and in the present case there can be a great deal of them. For example, in order to get a positive outcome for your bill, it's necessary to pass eight relevant authorities, eight ministries which, if you look them in the eye will say yes, but in fact there are a whole host of pretexts on which they say no.

Host: And can you name those ministries and agencies which are holding up the passing of this law?

Zvagelskiy: Practically all ministries and government bodies that we went to—the Department of Justice, the Ministry of Health. Apart from the specialist agency Rosalkogolregulirovaniye, which now, thank God, has been created, and it seems to agree with this; but almost all agencies for one reason or another, perhaps from their point of view thinking that it's correct, but they say "not yet." We pass through all this with great difficulty. As soon as . . .

Host: Viktor, again speculation. But anyway tell me, is it corruption? Why don't these ministries give a positive outcome?

Zvagelskiy: You know, not exactly corruption. Maybe to constantly label everything "corruption" isn't always correct. It's officials' fear for their places. Until the "first person" says something, until the president says something, the head of the government—after he said that beer is alcohol, they supported it—some veiled, and some openly. After that, the fear disappeared instantly, and now we are getting positive feedback. And before that we were fighting . . .

. . .

Host: Viktor, anyway let's clarify this principal moment. You're saying that officials are scared for their chairs, places and so on, until the "first person" or "second person" says to the team "attack!"

Zvagelskiy: Well, it's not always like that, but I'm narrowing the question down to just my tiny problem. That's what I come up against, it's how it is in this case.

Host: But it's not a tiny problem. You can't get a bill agreed with these government bodies—it's a very serious problem.[7]

In fact, it seems that Zvagelskiy may have had a trick up his sleeve to speed the bill's progress along. The case suggests that he collaborated with RAR to help the agency secure its policy goals. Zvagelskiy allegedly took the text of RAR's draft bill, and in late 2010 introduced it to the State Duma as his own legislative initiative. According to one respondent's testimony, the text was directly copied and pasted from RAR: the author and file properties of Zvagelskiy's draft bill published on the Duma website were exactly the same as the RAR draft bill that had been circulating. Zvagelskiy's bill was adopted at first reading, probably in no small part due to his position as a United Russia deputy and major contributor to the party's regional election fund in Moscow. As the respondent observed, the intended effect of Zvagelskiy's move was to put pressure on the government and its ministries to finalize the official bill, or risk Zvagelskiy's bill being passed in any case. And it appears that it did the trick. The official bill was submitted to the State Duma by the government on 11 January 2011, and on 22 February comfortably passed first reading.

And so, by February 2011, after a seemingly never-ending struggle, the first stage in the battle was over. RAR's bill had suffered some modifications during the long struggle of intergovernment negotiations but had made it to the Duma and was safely past first reading. Now a second battleground lay ahead: detailed consideration of the bill at committee stage, to be overseen by none other than Viktor Zvagelskiy himself.

Outwitting the Brewers

Although RAR had benefited from its friendly ruling party deputy, Viktor Zvagelskiy, putting pressure on the government to submit its bill to the State Duma, the alcohol regulator by no means had the upper hand at this point. It had been forced to compromise on several measures, and overall the package was not particularly detrimental to the beer industry; as one brewing executive put it, it was "not 100 percent ok, but let's say 70 percent ok." It was between the first reading on 22 February 2011 and the second reading on 6 July 2011 that the vodka lobby within the state was able to operate strategically to push through important changes that significantly heightened the bill's impact on the brewing industry.

As noted at the beginning of this chapter, the provision of the bill that was most commented on in the media was the official recategorization of beer as an alcoholic product—a reversal of the law of December 1996 that had declassified beer as alcohol. This bill, if passed, would change that situation: beer would be governed by Law 171 just like wine and spirits. But even then, this did not necessarily mean that beer would be subject to the *same* restrictions as those stronger drinks. To understand how beer would continue to be more loosely regulated than vodka under the version of the bill passed at first reading, it is worth looking at the provisions of the bill as a whole and the numerous exemptions made for beer.

RAR had already been forced by opposition from other government departments to drop several of its proposals from the version of the bill submitted to the Duma, including the licensing and declaration of beer production. Furthermore, the bill made several exemptions for weaker beers (defined as 5 percent abv or under, which in fact accounted for the majority of sales in the Russian market). Thus, the version of the bill passed at first reading would prohibit the sale of alcohol at places of "mass gathering" and "potential heightened risk"—such as railway stations, airports, metro stations, wholesale grocery markets, military facilities—but beer under 5 percent abv could continue to be sold. Similarly, kiosks and other nonstationary places of retail sale would no longer be able to sell beer over 5 percent abv, but could continue to sell weaker beer as before. The bill also stipulated a ban on the retail sale of alcohol between 11 p.m. and 8 a.m. local time, with regional governments given the right to introduce tighter restrictions up to a full ban[8]; but again, beer under 5 percent abv was excluded from the ban. As discussed in the previous chapter, the 5 percent abv threshold was contained in Medvedev's policy instructions to the federal government of September 2009. The inclusion of this threshold in the government bill was therefore simply a fulfillment of the president's instructions. Finally, beer was exempt from the provision that weak alcoholic beverages (defined as those under 7 percent abv) could be sold only in containers of 330 mL or less.

Following the passage of the bill at first reading on 22 February 2011, the second reading was scheduled to take place soon after, in March 2011.[9] However, the bill was again delayed, with behind-the-scenes struggles over proposed amendments to it seemingly the cause. Once again the bill was the battleground for competing policy interests, but this time the site of the battle was the legislature rather than the executive. In accordance with Duma legislative procedure, after first reading bills go to committee stage, where the provisions are debated and deputies can propose amendments. In the case of the bill amending Law 171, it was the Duma's Committee for Economic Policy that administered the committee stage. Viktor Zvagelskiy was deputy chair of the committee, and chair of its subcommittee on the state regulation of excisable goods. At first glance, Zvagelskiy's influence over the bill at committee stage may not seem that different from RAR's influence as "profile agency" when the bill was being drafted for the government. But there was a subtle difference: since any amendments made at this stage were formally those of the legislature rather than the executive, they did not need to go through the arduous process of interdepartmental discussion that had thwarted several of RAR's original measures aimed at beer. And sure enough, soon after first reading the committee indicated that it was looking to strip weaker beers of the "unreasonable preference" that the current version of the bill granted them.[10]

Unsurprisingly, Zvagelskiy was responsible for drafting the Duma's official package of amendments to the bill. The amendments not only proposed reinstating most of the clauses relating to the brewing industry that RAR had been forced to remove before first reading (e.g., licensing and declaration of beer production), but also included a new measure that threatened the brewers' interests: banning the sale of beer in plastic bottles, known as PET.[11] The pretext for this amendment was the harmonization of regulations within the customs union of Russia, Belarus, and Kazakhstan; Kazakhstan had long had a ban on the sale of beer in plastic bottles.[12] But the measure would also have acted as a de facto way to increase the unit cost of beer, since PET is a cheaper form of container than glass.

However, Zvagelskiy and the Committee for Economic Policy did not have carte blanche to push through any amendments they wished. They were required to submit their package of proposed amendments to the Government Commission for Regulating the Alcohol Market, which considered them at a session held on 27 April 2011. While this was not a formal requirement of Duma legislative procedure, as an instruction from the government it could hardly be ignored. Zvagelskiy was present at the session, as were representatives of the main ministries that had opposed RAR's anti-beer measures prior to first reading: the Ministry for Economic Development and the Ministry of Trade. The dynamics of this committee were very much a mystery of the policymaking "black box." Even respondents who were very close to the policy process were divided as to whether it actually made decisions or simply rubber-stamped decisions already made elsewhere. The chair of the committee, it will be recalled, was deputy prime minister Viktor Zubkov, who has strong formal and informal ties to state-sponsored vodka interests: board member of Rosspirtprom, founder of RAR, and trustee of Arkady Rotenberg's Yawara-Neva Judo Club. The deputy chair of the committee was RAR head Igor Chuyan. This would appear to give the committee's leadership a significant vodka bias. However, the committee rejected three of Zvagelskiy's most radical anti-beer amendments: beer licensing, extending EGAIS to brewers, and a ban on beer in PET containers. It did, however, agree that beer under 5 percent abv should *not* be exempt from three bans: sale in kiosks, nighttime sales, and advertising. Thus, the brewers lost the magical "5 percent abv threshold" that would have prevented the bill having a major impact on their business. This is an intriguing outcome that cannot be fully explained until we have a better insider knowledge of how the Government Commission for Regulating the Alcohol Market operated. Even one key public health respondent, despite their close involvement in the policy process, confessed they still did not know how exactly the vodka lobby was able to overcome the presidential administration's opposition to a total ban on beer sales in kiosks: "There was pressure from the Expert Department of the presidential administration on kiosks, to lighten things on beer such that kiosks should be able to continue selling it, but still they managed to push through the kiosk ban. The presidential administration was not the only force there, there was RAR, Zvagelskiy, and a lot of vodka industry allies, so they managed to push it through, although I don't know how they did it. I was actually positively surprised myself that they managed to get beer out of kiosks. It was such a gift, so nice!"

But if the vodka lobby's victory on kiosks was impressive, how do we account for the failure of its amendments on beer licensing, declaration, and PET containers? Were the other ministerial representatives on the commission so opposed to these measures that it was politically impossible for the commission to approve them, regardless of Zubkov's and Chuyan's personal preferences? Did Zvagelskiy never seriously expect his more radical amendments to be passed, but simply included them to be bargained away in return for securing the kiosk and advertising bans—as one brewer respondent suggested? It is also possible that one of the characteristics that made the brewing industry fair game for punitive measures under Putin's regime— its multinational character—may have served to protect it from some of the vodka lobby's more radical proposals. One respondent suggested that the decision to drop the proposal for licensing of beer production was taken on high in the Russian government because of concerns that the large multinational brewing companies could be frightened off from continued inward investment in Russia. It is difficult to verify such claims, but the idea that the brewers' status as "foreigners" could work both for and against them is certainly a plausible one.

Since the consideration of the Duma's package of amendments by the Government Commission for Regulating the Alcohol Market was, procedurally speaking, an informal arrangement, in theory Zvagelskiy could have ignored their changes and retained all of his own amendments in the version of the bill put to second reading. However, it would have been politically impossible for him to go against Zubkov, the deputy prime minister and trusted colleague of Putin, in this way. Both the government and the president have representatives in the Duma who can suspend a bill indefinitely should they choose to do so. Moreover, as one brewing executive suggested, Zvagelskiy's alleged concealed interests in the alcohol industry mean that his own position could easily have been compromised if he had become more troublesome than useful. This represents the flip side of *sistema* membership: one is as much trapped as empowered by its collective ties and systems of informal control.[13] Thus, in reality Zvagelskiy alone did not possess the power to go against the Government Commission for Regulating the Alcohol Market.

Nevertheless, it seems that even after the Government Commission for Regulating the Alcohol Market had given its verdict on the package of amendments, further machinations continued behind the scenes. The commission had met on 27 April, and the second reading had been planned for May.[14] But when May came, the much-anticipated second reading did not materialize. In mid-May, the brewers held a round table to discuss the proposed amendments that would impact most heavily on them. Zvagelskiy was present, and reportedly stated that while he was prepared to reconsider his position on PET containers, he would continue to press his other amendments to second reading.[15] Whether this was simply a bluff on Zvagelskiy's part or whether he had the support of someone senior within the government to go against the commission's decision we do not know.

The weeks came and went with no sign of the bill's second reading. But just as it seemed that the bill would not be passed before summer recess, it dramatically reappeared on the Duma's schedule, passing second reading on 6 July and third reading on 7 July—the penultimate day of the Duma's spring session. The bill was passed almost unanimously: 441 deputies voting in favor, none against, and just one abstention, demonstrating both the compliant nature of the Russian parliament and the political undesirability of being seen to oppose (moderate) alcohol control measures. In the final reck-

Table 13.2 Changes in provisions affecting beer in successive incarnations of the government bill amending Law 171, 2010–11

	Leaked RAR draft (December 2010)	First reading version (February 2011)	Duma's proposed amendments (April 2011)	Final version passed into law (July 2011)
Licensing of beer production	Yes	No	Yes	No
Beer production declaration (extending EGAIS to beer)	Yes	No	Yes	No
All beer banned from sale in nonstationary outlets	Yes	No—only beer over 5 percent abv	Yes	Yes
Beer included in nighttime retail sale ban	Yes (9 p.m.–11 a.m. for strong alcohol, 11 p.m.–10 a.m. for beer)	No—11 p.m.–8 a.m. ban for all alcohol *except* beer under 5 percent abv	Yes	Yes—11 p.m.–8 a.m. ban for all alcohol
Ban on beer advertising on TV and billboards	No	No	Yes	Yes
Ban on selling beer in plastic containers (PET)	No	No	Yes	No

Table 13.3 Effective dates of measures contained in the 2011 law amending Law 171

Effective date	Provision
Immediate effect (22 July 2011)	Ban on the sale of alcohol stronger than 1.5 percent abv (with the exception of beer) 11 p.m.–8 a.m. local time
	Ban on the sale of beer stronger than 5 percent abv at kiosks
22 July 2012	Beer can no longer be advertised on TV, on the radio, or on billboards/outdoors
1 January 2013	Complete ban on the sale of alcoholic beverages (>0.5 percent abv), including beer, at street stalls and kiosks
	Complete ban on the sale of any alcoholic beverages (>0.5 percent abv), including beer, from 11 p.m. to 8 a.m. local time
	Alcoholic beverages with ethyl alcohol content added during the manufacturing process (i.e., cocktails, not beer) up to 7 percent abv cannot be sold in containers larger than 330 mL.

oning, the bill that was eventually passed in July 2011 impacted beer more harshly than the version that passed first reading in February of that year, but the control measures that the brewers feared most—licensing and EGAIS—were not included (see table 13.2).

The bill was signed into law by President Medvedev on 20 July 2011.[16] The measures it contained went into effect in several stages (see table 13.3). In particular, additional time was granted to allow the brewers and businesses dependent on their products (notably advertisers and owners of non-stationary retail outlets) to prepare for the impact of the new legislation. By 1 January 2013 the full range of restrictions had gone into effect, including a complete ban on the sale of beer at kiosks and other forms of nonstationary retail outlets, and a ban on the retail sale of all alcohol (including beer) between the hours of 11 p.m. and 8 a.m. local time.

In sum, the final version of the law passed in July 2011 was significantly different from that originally envisaged by Medvedev's policy instructions of September 2009. This shows that, even in a highly presidential system like the Russian Federation, policy cannot be straightforwardly dictated from on high. Indeed, when a commodity such as alcohol is involved, with so many interested parties both within and outside the state, policy will continually be tugged this way and that, as advocacy coalitions fight for their own preferred measures. Although the passage of a new law could be seen as representing the end of a policy battle, in reality such endings are illusory. As the next chapter will show, the eventual passage of the 2011 alcohol law did not make permanent the settlement that it represented between the various advocacy coalitions. On the contrary, many of the same policy battles continued to be fought as before.

Chapter 14

The Campaign Is Over, but the Battle Continues

Following the passage of the 2011 law, what had become known in Russia as the antialcohol campaign gradually fizzled out. Official state discourse on the alcohol problem faded away, and by 2013 media references to a campaign had all but vanished. There was a sense with the passage of the 2011 law that all of the obvious policies to try to reduce consumption had already been passed. As with any policy initiative, the topic became tired and public and media interest waned.

Yet alcohol regulation naturally continued, and the powerful interests that in practice determined the finer details of alcohol policy remained very much active. The policy activity of the campaign period of 2009–12 should be seen as just one phase in a broader trend of alcohol policy development: the ongoing struggle between the domestic vodka industry and the multinational beer industry for regulatory advantage. Contemporary Russian alcohol policy continues to take the form of a battle between these two opposing sides, as both the vodka and beer industries try to secure regulations that give them a competitive advantage and impose costs on their rivals.

Although the beer industry lost ground to the vodka industry in the 2011 law, it had successfully resisted three important policies: expansion of EGAIS to brewing, the introduction of licensing of beer production, and a proposed ban on selling alcohol in plastic bottles (PET). Yet, needless to say, the advocates of these policies did not give up. The beer industry may have won the battle with regard to keeping these provisions out of the 2011 law, but the war very much continued. These three policies illustrate the unrelenting role of lobbying and anti-lobbying by the vodka and beer industries in shaping federal alcohol policy in Russia, and demonstrate that the beer lobby continued to lose ground to the vodka lobby in the years after the 2011 law.

The first attempt by RAR to expand EGAIS to the brewing industry following its rejection from the 2011 law took place as early as February 2012. It appears that, rather than relying on primary legislation, RAR decided to act unilaterally and put the requirement in an executive order of its own. According to RAR order No. 31 of 20 February 2012, beer producers would have to be switched to EGAIS by 1 January 2015. What happened next is not clear, but it is possible that the government determined that such a requirement could not be made by executive order, only by primary legislation, for RAR subsequently drafted a bill (No. 686588-6) containing the same requirement, to take effect 1 July 2015. The bill spent many months stuck in the process of interdepartmental negotiation, but eventually received approval from the Government Commission for Legislative Activity on 15 December 2014. After RAR agreed to postpone the date by which brewers were required to go live on EGAIS by a year (to 1 July 2016), the bill was passed by the Duma and signed into law in June 2015.

Why was the EGAIS issue so important for the brewing industry? First, it entailed substantial implementation costs. Anadolu Efes, for example, estimated that it would need to spend over $1 million to connect to EGAIS.[1] It is also important to note that once connected to EGAIS, brewers cannot use the same equipment to produce nonalcoholic beverages. According to the Union of Russian Brewers, this would affect 80 percent of brewers, who produced around 50 percent of kvass (the popular Russian soft drink made from black bread) and 40 percent of all nonalcoholic beverages on the Russian market.[2] These companies would be forced to either invest in new production lines or cease production of nonalcoholic beverages, which could have a dramatic effect on the structure of the soft drink market. Second, there was the very real risk of EGAIS not functioning properly and paralyzing the entire brewing industry, just as it did when it was introduced for strong alcohol in 2006. Brewers expressed concerns about how accurately the system could measure the volume of the liquid given that beer froths.

RAR has been proposing licensing of beer production more or less since its own establishment in 2009. For the agency, this would represent a significant expansion of its powers and authority. Despite its failed attempt to have beer licensing included in the 2011 alcohol bill, RAR continued to push for the policy. In September 2014, the agency tried a more nuanced approach by submitting proposals to deputy prime minister Alexandr Khloponin for licensing the production of so-called beer-based beverages (*pivnyye napitki*),[3] arguing that it was necessary to combat illegal trade (RAR statistics suggested that 49 percent of the market for these drinks was illegal, although Rosstat statistics gave a much lower figure of 6 percent).[4] However, nothing more was heard of these proposals, indicating that the government rejected them.

A bill (No. 463846-6) proposing the licensing of the production and sale of both beer and beer-based beverages had been submitted to the State Duma some months before the RAR proposals detailed above, on 3 March 2014. Unlike the bill extending EGAIS to beer, this was a bill authored by individual Duma deputies rather than RAR or another government department. Deputy Zvagelskiy was one of the initial signatories of the bill, but he withdrew his name from it the following year, on 31 March 2015. First reading of the bill was repeatedly postponed, and it remained in limbo. Eventually, on 25 September 2015, the bill was considered at a plenary session of the State Duma. The government in its official review of the bill did not support it, and the Duma's Legal Department pointed to errors in its text. When it came to voting on the bill, a quorum was not reached, and consequently the bill was rejected.[5] Thus, it appears that the threat to the brewers of beer licensing was quelled—at least for the foreseeable future.

For the brewers and their supporters, fighting proposed bans on selling beer in plastic bottles (PET) remained a constant defensive battle even after the measure was rejected from the 2011 law. A bill that proposed banning alcohol from sale in PET containers was registered in the State Duma in May 2013—initiated not by the government or RAR but rather by a group of deputies from the governing party United Russia. Viktor Zvagelskiy was not listed among the authors, despite the fact that he was the initiator of the rejected amendment to include a ban on PET in the 2011 alcohol bill. Much to-ing and fro-ing ensued, with the government proposing a softened version in response, and the authors revising the bill as a "counteroffer" that was a slight step down from a full ban, but nevertheless much stricter than the government proposal.[6] Meanwhile, the brewers were sufficiently panicked to adopt preemptive defensive measures. On 3 October 2013 those brewers affiliated with the Union of Russian Brewers announced their own voluntary code, according to which they would prohibit themselves from selling beer in plastic bottles larger than 2.5 liters beginning 1 January 2014.

An intriguing instance of "black PR" inflamed the passions of the ongoing lobbying battle over beer sold in PET containers. On 1 June 2015 a mysterious advertising campaign was launched with the melodramatic slogan, "We'll ban plastic bottles—and save Russia!" Advertising banners with the name of the National Union for the Protection of Consumer Rights—an authoritative-sounding but in fact unknown organization registered to former vodka industry representative Pavel Shapkin—appeared on the websites of the leading newspapers *Vedomosti* and *Kommersant*, as well as on billboards on the Rublevskoe Shosse, a major Moscow highway.[7] The Federal Antimonopoly Service (FAS) began investigating the legality of what it called the *antireklama* (literally "anti-advertisement") on the basis that it could constitute unfair competition.

To bring an end to the legislative ping-pong, Prime Minister Medvedev instructed four government departments to jointly assess the proposed restrictions and provide recommendations. The Ministry for Economic Development reported on the results on 25 August 2015. Only RAR was in favor of a ban; the other three departments (the Ministry of Energy, FAS, and the Ministry for Economic Development itself) were against.[8] Yet, this still did not put the issue to bed. In the same month, the Union of Russian Brewers was sufficiently worried to announce that it would be tightening its voluntary code, with the maximum plastic bottle size to be reduced from 2.5 liters to 1.5 liters beginning 1 July 2016. Unlike the 2.5-liter restriction, 1.5 liters was a radical restriction for a voluntary industry measure—the union estimated that 15 percent of all beer produced in the country was sold in plastic bottles larger than 1.5 liters.[9] That the union's member companies were prepared to submit themselves to such a restriction indicates just how concerned they were that a full ban was still in the cards. In the end the government settled on the 1.5-liter compromise, with the amended bill being passed and signed into law in June 2016.[10]

The development of the Eurasian Economic Union (EAEU) between certain countries of the former Soviet Union looks set to provide a new arena for battles for regulatory advantage. Established in 2010 as the Eurasian Customs Union between Russia, Belarus, and Kazakhstan, it became the EAEU on 1 January 2015, with Armenia and Kyrgyzstan becoming the fourth and fifth member states later that year. In institutional terms, the EAEU is in its infancy, and it is not yet clear if and how it will work in practice. In principle, however, much like the European Union (EU) it provides an additional, supranational layer of legally binding regulation—and thus an additional site for lobbyists and policymakers to do battle. Unlike the EU, the fact that there are currently only five member states means that representatives from individual countries will be able to exert greater influence over union regulations—and Russia as the largest and most powerful member is likely to wield disproportionate influence.

RAR was quick to use what was then the Customs Union to try to introduce a ban on selling alcohol in plastic bottles (PET) by the back door. While the Russian government rejected the proposed amendment to include a ban on PET in the 2011 law, RAR at this time produced a draft *tekhreglament* (technical regulation) for the Customs Union, entitled "On the safety of alcoholic products."[11] Kazakhstan was in favor of a union-wide PET ban, as it has had such a ban in place at the national level since 1998. Belarus, however, lies at the other end of the spectrum: PET accounts for a much larger share of the beer market than in Russia. The proposed *tekhreglament* was not passed, apparently bogged down in unresolvable disagreements between the member states. Whether the EAEU can become a genuine supranational source of alcohol regulation in the future remains to be seen.

While the multinational ownership of the main brewing companies has made it an easy target for hostile populist rhetoric from politicians, it is also possible for the brewers' status as "foreigners" to work in their favor. The most striking example of this is the effect that Russia's hosting of the 2018 FIFA World Cup had on its domestic alcohol policy. One of the World Cup's official sponsors is Budweiser, the iconic American beer produced by Anheuser-Busch InBev. The identity of this high-profile sponsor sat rather uncomfortably with Russia's bans on beer advertising in sports stadiums, on television, and in print media. It is not clear at what level pressure was applied—from FIFA, from the brewing industry, from the managing boards of stadiums desperate not to lose out on advertising revenue, or possibly from a combination of actors—but in July 2014 the State Duma obligingly passed a law suspending the advertising bans for beer until the end of 2018 (i.e., after the World Cup). This shows that even Russia is far from immune from the forces of globalization in its domestic policymaking.

The pro-beer lobby not only has been fighting defensive battles against further regulation, but has also made attempts to reverse some elements of the new status quo laid out in the 2011 law. For example, in 2014–16, FAS and Minpromtorg were actively pushing proposals to overturn the ban on selling beer in kiosks and sports stadiums. The latter produced a report entitled "Proposals on the restrictions on the retail sale of alcohol," which claimed the return of beer to kiosks was needed to stem the sharp decline in the number of small retail outlets as well as tackle illegal alcohol sales.[12] In late 2016, the Ministry for Economic Development backed a policy concept developed by Moscow's Higher School of Economics in conjunction with the brewing industry to return to a separate regulatory system for beer, which would liberate the brewers from control by RAR.[13] However, nothing came of any of these efforts.

Indeed, it is hard to see how any initiative to improve the brewers' regulatory lot could succeed given the present balance of power between the state actors involved. It will be recalled from the beginning of chapter 6 how, at a parliamentary hearing in November 2015, Federation Council chair Valentina Matviyenko savaged both RAR and its enigmatic head, Igor Chuyan, citing allegations of corruption and referring the matter to the Anticorruption Committee. Given the severity of the accusations, Chuyan's position seemed untenable, and even the future of RAR itself looked in doubt. And yet, incredibly, both Chuyan and RAR survived. RAR suffered the indignity of being brought under the control of the Ministry of Finance, but to date this appears to have had little impact in policymaking terms. Nothing more was heard of the corruption investigation formally requested by the Federation Council—it literally vanished without a trace. If even Matviyenko—commonly regarded as a close Putin ally—could not take on Chuyan's RAR and win, who could? Until there is a dramatic shift in the balance of power among Russia's governing elite, the beer industry's constant defensive battle against an increasing regulatory burden will continue.

Conclusion

What Alcohol Tells Us about Russian Politics

When I conducted fieldwork interviews in Moscow in early 2012, it was fascinating to note how divided respondents' opinions were on the nature of the government's antialcohol initiative—the defining paradigm of alcohol policy at the time. Moreover, this division was not a reflection of those actors' roles in the policy process. Both public health and industry respondents were strikingly divided between those who believed that a genuine campaign was taking place and those who thought that "antialcohol campaign" was a deeply misleading label—resulting from either lazy journalism or a deliberate attempt by the government to give the impression it was taking action while not really doing so. For example, at least two public health respondents, while cautious about applying the label "antialcohol campaign" unquestioningly, agreed that the general policy direction of the government was antialcohol, a sincere attempt by the government to reduce consumption. In contrast, another public health respondent was scathing of the description "antialcohol campaign," calling it "simulation" and "falsification of antialcohol activity."

Such diverse perceptions of the same policy initiative reveal much about the complexity of alcohol policy in Russia. They bring to mind the famous Indian proverb about a group of blind men who feel an elephant's body to discover what the creature is like; each man touches a different part of the elephant—leg, trunk, tusk, and so on—and so they all come to very different conclusions. Yet there are elements of truth in all of them.

Of course, the Russian government's antialcohol initiative of 2009–12 was in no way comparable to the Gorbachev-era antialcohol campaign of 1985–88, as some of the media implied at the time. But nor could we expect it to be, given that the political and economic environments were totally different. Many of the features of the Gorbachev campaign were particular to the Soviet system and could not be replicated outside it, such as the dramatic curtailment of the supply of alcohol, the destruction of vineyards, and the atmosphere of a witch hunt and search for the "enemies within."

Yet there was undoubtedly some substance to the new policy initiative, in the sense of real policy changes intended (by some of the initiators at least) to reduce consumption. To dismiss the activity of 2009–12 as pure simulation is simply inaccurate. The elite civil society movement that developed in the second half of the 2000s was active and influential in redefining the alcohol problem in terms of public health, with leading actors who possessed genuine ideological interests in reducing consumption. The interests of the political superelite in addressing the demographic crisis were no less real, despite the fact that many of the gains would be symbolic: the prestige of a powerful nation abroad, and a reputation for taking care of the population at home. The interests of the political and civil society elites converged, and the result was the formation of a new form of antialcohol political correctness in Russia: to publicly deny the need to reduce population-level alcohol consumption became unthinkable. There is little doubt that there was a genuine desire among the Russian political elite to reduce alcohol consumption—to the extent that this would secure a significant improvement in mortality and life expectancy. But as one respondent—an industry expert—wisely pointed out, at the level of high politics what matters is not so much desires but priorities. Desires, after all, are infinite; only priorities determine action, especially where desires conflict with each other. Inasmuch as maintaining his popular approval rating was necessarily a high priority for Putin and his circle, antialcohol policy could be pursued only to the extent that it did not provoke popular discontent. The point at which approval would turn into discontent was unclear due to the alcohol doublethink in Russian public opinion, but both poll data and received political wisdom suggested that major price increases on vodka were out of the question.

Although it would be inaccurate to dismiss the policy activity of 2009–12 as mere simulation, it is also true that it was given a false sense of cohesiveness and intentionality by media discourse of an antialcohol campaign. There was a significant gap between superficial appearance and reality: policies that were widely represented as part of the perceived campaign had quite different origins. Thus, minimum vodka pricing was actually a policy that was pushed by the vodka lobby and had nothing to do with reducing consumption, and the dramatic 200 percent increase in beer excise duty was a budget-filling initiative by the Ministry of Finance. Increased restrictions on the sale and advertising of weaker beers were pushed by the vodka lobby informally integrated within the state, although they were also backed by civil society antialcohol lobbyists. It would be misleading to describe any of these measures as part of an antialcohol campaign, but the discourse of a campaign provided a convenient, politically correct justification for all of them. As we have seen, they became integrated into the public and media consciousness as elements of the antialcohol campaign.

Implications for Public Policy Research

Alcohol policy is a fascinating area of study due to its complexity. That complexity results from the ambivalences of alcohol, and manifests itself in both the diversity of policy actors with a stake in the outcome, and the range of ideological views that inform their stances. Accordingly, it is doubtful that a single theory of public policy could satisfactorily account for all aspects of alcohol policy formation. Rather, the insights of several theories can be combined to illustrate different aspects of the process.[1]

The shift in the prevailing understanding of the alcohol problem detailed in chapters 10 and 11 illustrates the important role that agenda setting can play in public policy. Agenda setting can be defined as "an ongoing competition among issue proponents to gain the attention of media professionals, the public, and policy elites."[2] The successful agenda setting by the new civil society elite in the latter half of the 2000s saw their definition of the alcohol problem in terms of demographics become mainstreamed both in public discourse and among the political elite. This set a new framework for the development of alcohol policy—both figuratively in terms of what policy discourse was politically acceptable, and literally in the form of President Medvedev's policy instructions of September 2009. Yet it is important to note that this was just a framework—the *setting* for the negotiation of policy measures between advocacy coalitions, not the determinant of policy details.

Policy actors are in competition to ensure that their preferred policy is the one adopted, and they are motivated by a combination of ideology and material interests. Central to the latter is the role of rent seeking, which public choice theory sees as a key driver of state regulation. Rent seeking—typically pursued through lobbying in modern economies—is a logical and natural consequence of free market competition, as firms (and often whole economic sectors) seek to exploit state institutions to gain a competitive advantage over their rivals.[3] Chapters 7, 8, 13, and 14 all illustrated how two sectors of the alcohol market that are in direct competition with each other—vodka and beer—use lobbying to try to gain regulatory advantage and impose costs on the other side. This underlines the importance of not assuming that the alcohol industry is a unified actor when it comes to alcohol policy advocacy, as some public health accounts have tended to do. Producers of different types of alcoholic beverages are in competition with each other for a share of the total beverage market. While it may sometimes be in their interests to cooperate with each other in promoting or opposing certain policies, it may also be in their interests to seek to gain a competitive advantage over a rival sector of the industry. The Russian case demonstrates how the latter form of competition to capture rents can actually be a driving force behind policy outcomes, even if the policy agenda is not expressed in those terms.

Yet if the battles between the vodka and beer industries are a key driver of policy formation, what role is left for bureaucratic actors? The answer is that their role is probably the most crucial of all. The advocacy coalition framework (ACF) helps us make sense of this apparent paradox. The ACF emphasizes that government departments are not neutral arbiters of policy, but may also form part of "advocacy coalitions" lobbying for or against a given policy.[4] Policy stances of bureaucratic departments may be motivated not only by self-interest (such as expanded powers or increased budget) but also by shared beliefs, such as an ideological commitment to free-market principles (the most plausible explanation for the Federal Antimonopoly Service's repeated opposition to the regulatory tendencies of RAR, for example). Soviet alcohol policy is a particularly revealing illustration of just how divided the state can be on alcohol issues, simply because neither private commercial interests nor civil society activism existed at this time. As shown in chapter 2, changes in alcohol policy tended to be caused by a shift in the relative power of different branches of the state, combined with shifting ideological perceptions of how alcohol either helped or harmed the state's interests. With regard to post-Soviet alcohol policy, it is notable that the increase in policy activity aimed at tightening beer regulation coincided with the growth of vodka interests integrated—both formally and informally—within the state. Furthermore, the brewing lobby could not have been successful in combating some of the policies that were pushed by RAR and Zvagelskiy without certain government departments backing its cause, notably the Federal Antimonopoly Service, Ministry of Trade, and Ministry for Economic Development. In principle, the institutional resources possessed by bureaucratic departments mean that they should have more influence over policy than their nongovernmental advocacy coalition allies.[5] But there is an important caveat. The large number of government departments with interests in alcohol policy means that the process of settling on an agreed policy *within* government is not easy. As chapter 13 illustrated, alcohol policy generates such substantial disagreements between different government departments in Russia that it typically results in considerable delays to the policy process, and sometimes even deadlock.

The ACF is a more representative model of Russian alcohol policymaking than traditional concepts of "policy communities" or "iron triangles." Policy communities are conceived as insular and harmonious groups of policy actors, mainly located within the state, with a shared understanding of the issue and how to address it. They seek policy stability by defining issues so as to exclude others with dissenting views. The ACF, on the other hand, sees its "policy sub-systems" as containing a wide variety of policy actors, with their interaction characterized by conflict and even the demonization of opponents.[6] As we have seen, conflict, intrigue, and vilification have become the essence of contemporary Russian alcohol policymaking.

The Realities of Russian Governance and Policymaking

"Calculations show that if Russians began to drink the same amount of pure alcohol as they do now, but in the form of weaker beverages, namely beer and wine, the death rate in Russia would be significantly lower."[7] So wrote Khaltourina and Korotayev in their influential "Vodka Cross" article of 2006. This point was not lost on the Russian government: its 2009 alcohol policy concept set a goal of not only reducing general per capita consumption but also reducing the share of that consumption taken by strong alcohol. If a single, unified alcohol policy could be dictated from on high by a single government actor, implemented obligingly by officials, it would indeed aim to encourage consumers to replace vodka with beer or wine.

Yet as we have seen, the range of state actors and economic interests connected to alcohol makes such a rational policy approach impossible. Actors pushing public health agendas certainly exist in Russia, within both the state and civil society. But at every stage of policy formation they are in competition with rival advocacy coalitions pursuing very different interests. Minfin naturally prioritizes maximizing incomes to the state budget, while RAR has emerged as a powerful force for control over the vodka market. As chapters 13 and 14 in particular demonstrated, each policy decision is a fresh battleground where these actors compete with each other anew. In this sense, there is no unified federal alcohol policy, but only a series of ad hoc policy outcomes. Official state policy, such as that laid out in the 2009 alcohol policy concept, provides the framework for these policy struggles but does not determine the final outcome.

The case of Russian alcohol policy also reveals much about Russian policymaking and governance more generally. While alcohol's many ambivalences mean that a consistent policy toward it is always difficult to achieve, such inconsistencies are multiplied by the kleptocracy inherent in Russia's political economy. There will always be conflicts between the state's various interests in alcohol, for example, reducing alcohol-related harms versus maintaining the treasury's alcohol revenues. But Russia's crony capitalist regime adds an extra dimension of conflict, between formal and informal state priorities. Ledeneva has observed that informal *sistema* networks can have a distorting effect on state policymaking: formal state priorities may be undermined by the priorities of various power networks. Policies that the government claims have one aim may in fact have a different aim entirely ("doubledeed"), and official state policy discourse can become far removed from how things are discussed behind the scenes.[8] Such a contradictory dual function can be seen in the state-owned alcohol company Rosspirtprom, ostensibly formed to provide the state with lucrative alcohol revenues, but in practice appearing to serve more as a source of enrichment for private individuals close to Putin.

The distorting effects of informal power networks can also be observed in the way that an official strategy of reducing the share of spirits consumption was transformed into policy measures that effectively did the opposite: eliminate the comparative regulatory advantage beer previously enjoyed over vodka in the name of treating all alcoholic beverages equally. When Medvedev's presidential instructions passed through the policy process, they were distorted into policy outcomes that, by eliminating the intended regulatory advantage for weaker beers, effectively improved the competitiveness of vodka relative to beer. In particular, banning the advertising of even weak beers on television and completely eliminating beer sales in kiosks—both measures that were primarily driven by the pro-vodka tandem of RAR and Deputy Zvagelskiy—were able to be presented as antialcohol policies due to the existence of the government's antialcohol initiative and support for the measures from public health activists. Thus, to some extent, the public health actors were complicit in this game, cooperating with the vodka interests to tighten regulation of beer and secure partial victories for the antialcohol movement, presumably hoping to win even stricter regulations on vodka further down the line.

Perhaps the most important lesson of this book is that, in order to fully understand issues of policymaking and governance in Russia, it is insufficient to rely solely on study of formal policymaking institutions and official policy discourse. The distorting effects of informal networks mean that there may well be much more to a policy decision than first meets the eye. The nontransparency of this system can make it hard to penetrate what is really going on, even for those involved in the policy process. And yet, such insiders, despite often feeling more like outsiders, share surprisingly similar interpretations of what is happening and why. This underlines the importance of uncovering who owns what, where vested interests lie, and how those vested interests are connected (whether formally or informally) to the state and the governing elite.

Appendix 1

Methodology and Research Methods

The analysis contained in this book is based on qualitative data gathered from a range of sources: semistructured interviews conducted during fieldwork in Russia, interviews and extended discussions of alcohol policy already in the public domain, government documents and other official publications, and contemporary media articles and opinion polls.

I conducted semistructured interviews with a total of eighteen respondents. The first fifteen interviews were conducted during a fieldwork trip to Moscow from February to April 2012. Three additional respondents were interviewed during a brief trip to Russia in November 2012. Follow-up interviews were conducted with three respondents during another short stay in Moscow in November 2013. All interviews were recorded with the exception of one respondent, who requested not to be recorded. During this interview I made extensive notes and asked the respondent to repeat important points to ensure accuracy; I also added to these notes from memory immediately after the interview. Interviews ranged in length from seven minutes (snatched briefly before the start of an official event) to nearly three hours. The vast majority of interviews were thirty to sixty minutes.

A list of respondents (anonymized using generic categorizations) is given in appendix 2. To my knowledge, all respondents were Russian nationals residing permanently in Russia. One respondent requested that no information whatsoever about their identity be revealed; this respondent is listed simply as "anonymous respondent." After careful thought I decided against giving more specific information about my respondents (such as age, gender, and length of experience). This is to protect respondents' anonymity. The sphere of Russian alcohol policymaking contains relatively few actors, and even such basic information could be sufficient to reveal a respondent's identity. For the same reason I have not attributed quotes to specific respondents in the text, but simply described the type of respondent who is speaking. If quotes had been attributed, it may have been possible by reading all the quotes made by one respondent to ascertain their identity. A full list of interview questions is contained in appendix 3.

The respondent interviews were supplemented by twenty-nine live interviews, presentations, and extended discussions with eighteen prominent policy actors/experts already in the public domain. These were drawn from television debate shows, a special daylong press conference dedicated to alcohol policy held by RIA Novosti, and the Congress of the Church-Public Council for Protection Against the Alcohol Threat, which I attended at the Church of Christ the Saviour in Moscow on 16–17 February 2012. To this were added thirteen in-depth print interviews with nine individuals, all in the public domain. A full list of all these sources is given in appendix 2.

The book draws on nearly two hundred articles and fifteen television and radio broadcasts. Many of the articles were sourced via the Eastview database, which contains Russian national and regional newspapers and journals from the entire post-Soviet period. I also consulted fourteen opinion polls conducted between 2004 and 2012 by the two major Russian polling agencies VTsIOM (The All-Russian Centre for the Study of Public Opinion) and FOM (Public Opinion Fund), which I utilized for the analysis of public opinion on alcohol in Russia. Finally, I made use of a wide range of official documents as primary sources. These included official government publications such as plans, strategies, and policy concepts (*kontseptsii*); transcripts of government meetings; internal government documents (some leaked by the media and some leaked to me by respondents); reports of the State Accounting Chamber; and reports and resolutions produced by institutions that fall into the gray area between state and civil society, notably the Public Chamber and the Russian Orthodox Church.

Appendix 2

LIST OF RESPONDENTS AND STATEMENTS IN THE PUBLIC DOMAIN

i) List of Respondents

1. Sobriety activist
2. Public health activist
3. Professor of medical science, specialist on alcohol and demography
4. Public health activist
5. Former beer industry executive (government relations)
6. Alcohol industry journalist for major national newspaper
7. Russian alcohol industry expert
8. Expert on lobbying in Russia
9. Anonymous respondent
10. Former vodka industry employee
11. Beer industry public relations director
12. Russian alcohol industry expert
13. Sobriety activist

14. Economist, excise duty specialist
15. Beer industry public relations director
16. Vodka producer (owner)
17. Public health expert
18. Member of the Public Chamber of the Russian Federation

ii) Public Discussions and Debates

Maxim Chernigovskiy, general director of the Club of Alcohol Industry Professionals, Saint Petersburg:
  (a) "Tema discussiya: Polusukhoy zakon" [Theme of discussion: Semi-dry law], *Otkritaya Studiya* [Open Studio], Kanal 5 [Channel 5], 12 March 2012. Accessed 12 November 2014, https://www.youtube.com/watch?v=O6TYjgj5iEY.
Nikolay Burlyaev, actor and temperance advocate:
  (a) "Tema: Sukhoy Zakon" [Theme: Dry law], *Poyedinok* [Duel], Rossiya 1 [channel Russia 1], 9 December 2010. Accessed 12 November 2014, https://www.youtube.com/watch?v=BCPNwkmO3Gk.
Kirill Danishevskiy, cochair, Russian Coalition for the Control of Alcohol:
  (a) "Tema discussiya: Surrogati vmesto pivo?" [Theme of discussion: Surrogates instead of beer?], *Otkritaya Studiya* [Open Studio], Kanal 5 [Channel 5], 2 August 2011. Accessed 12 November 2014, https://www.youtube.com/watch?v=8f1akOpWEbU.
Dmitry Dobrov, chair, Union of Alcohol Producers:
  (a) "Situatsiya na alkogol'nom rinke: perviye itogi zakonodatel'nykh izmeneniy" [The situation on the alcohol market: Initial results of the legislative changes], press conference, RIA Novosti Press Centre, Moscow, 19 October 2012. Accessed 11 November 2014, http://pressria.ru/media/20121019/600926565.html.
Vadim Drobiz, director, Centre for the Study of Federal and Regional Alcohol Markets (TsIFRRA):
  (a) "Tema discussiya: Polusukhoy zakon" [Theme of discussion: Semi-dry law], *Otkritaya Studiya* [Open Studio], Kanal 5 [Channel 5], 12 March 2012. Accessed 12 November 2014, https://www.youtube.com/watch?v=O6TYjgj5iEY on 12 November 2014.

(b) "Tema discussiya: Vodku zapretyat?" [Theme of discussion: Will vodka be banned?], *Otkritaya Studiya* [Open Studio], Kanal 5 [Channel 5], 14 January 2011. Accessed 12 November 2014, http://www.5-tv.ru/programs/broadcast/506106/?page =1#c174196.

(c) "Tema discussiya: Zapret na vodku" [Theme of discussion: A ban on vodka], *Otkritaya Studiya* [Open Studio], Kanal 5 [Channel 5], 13 December 2010. Accessed 12 November 2014, http://www.5-tv .ru/programs/broadcast/505984/.

Daria Khaltourina, cochair, Russian Coalition for Alcohol Control:

(a) Congress of the Church-Public Council for Protection Against the Alcohol Threat, Church of Christ the Saviour, Moscow, 16– 17 February 2012 (attended by author)

(b) "Tema discussiya: Vodku zapretyat?" [Theme of discussion: Will vodka be banned?], *Otkritaya Studiya* [Open Studio], Kanal 5 [Channel 5], 14 January 2011. Accessed 12 November 2014, http:// www.5-tv.ru/programs/broadcast/506106/?page=1#c174196.

Diakon Ioann Klimenko, executive secretary of the St. John the Baptist brotherhood "Sobriety":

(a) Congress of the Church-Public Council for Protection Against the Alcohol Threat, Church of Christ the Saviour, Moscow, 16– 17 February 2012 (attended by author)

Dmitry Konstantinov, chief doctor, Saint Petersburg City Narcological Hospital:

(a) "Tema discussiya: Surrogati vmesto pivo?" [Theme of discussion: Surrogates instead of beer?], *Otkritaya Studiya* [Open Studio], Kanal 5 [Channel 5], 2 August 2011. Accessed 12 November 2014, https://www.youtube.com/watch?v=8f1akOpWEbU.

(b) "Tema discussiya: Skazhem pivu "net"?" [Theme of discussion: Should we say "no" to beer?], *Otkritaya Studiya* [Open Studio], Kanal 5 [Channel 5], 4 August 2010. Accessed 12 November 2014, https://www.youtube.com/watch?v=YqtB3Z3EKZU.

Elena Ovcharova, head of the Administrative Rights Defence of Business Group, Pepeliaev Group:

(a) "Situatsiya na alkogol'nom rinke: perviye itogi zakonodatel'nykh izmeneniy" [The situation on the alcohol market: Initial results of the legislative changes], press conference, RIA Novosti Press Centre, Moscow, 19 October 2012. Accessed 11 November 2014, http://pressria.ru/media/20121019/600926565.html.

Aleksandr Petrochenkov, journalist, historian of beer:

(a) "Tema discussiya: Surrogati vmesto pivo?" [Theme of discussion: Surrogates instead of beer?], *Otkritaya Studiya* [Open Studio], Kanal 5 [Channel 5], 2 August 2011. Accessed 12 November 2014, https://www.youtube.com/watch?v=8f1akOpWEbU.

Viktor Pyatko, vice president, Heineken Russia:

(a) "Tema discussiya: Surrogati vmesto pivo?" [Theme of discussion: Surrogates instead of beer?], *Otkritaya Studiya* [Open Studio], Kanal 5 [Channel 5], 2 August 2011. Accessed 12 November 2014, https://www.youtube.com/watch?v=8f1akOpWEbU.

(b) "Tema discussiya: Zapret na vodku" [Theme of discussion: A ban on vodka], *Otkritaya Studiya* [Open Studio], Kanal 5 [Channel 5], 13 December 2010. Accessed 12 November 2014, http://www.5-tv.ru/programs/broadcast/505984/.

(c) "Tema discussiya: Skazhem pivu "net"?" [Theme of discussion: Should we say "no" to beer?], *Otkritaya Studiya* [Open Studio], Kanal 5 [Channel 5], 4 August 2010. Accessed 12 November 2014, https://www.youtube.com/watch?v=YqtB3Z3EKZU.

Alexandr Romanov, general director, Committee of Alcohol Producers:

(a) "Situatsiya na alkogol'nom rinke: perviye itogi zakonodatel'nykh izmeneniy" [The situation on the alcohol market: Initial results of the legislative changes], press conference, RIA Novosti Press Centre, Moscow, 19 October 2012. Accessed 11 November 2014, http://pressria.ru/media/20121019/600926565.html.

Pavel Shapkin, head of the Centre for the Development of National Alcohol Policy:

(a) "Situatsiya na alkogol'nom rinke: perviye itogi zakonodatel'nykh izmeneniy" [The situation on the alcohol market: initial results of the legislative changes], press conference, RIA Novosti Press Centre, Moscow, 19 October 2012. Accessed 11 November 2014, http://pressria.ru/media/20121019/600926565.html.

Archimandrite Tikhon (Shevkunov), cochair of the Church-Public Council for Protection Against the Alcohol Threat:

(a) Congress of the Church-Public Council for Protection Against the Alcohol Threat, Church of Christ the Saviour, Moscow, 16– 17 February 2012 (attended by author).

Aleksey Timofeyev, deputy of the Legislative Assembly of Saint Petersburg:

(a) "Tema discussiya: Zapret na vodku" [Theme of discussion: A ban on vodka], *Otkritaya Studiya* [Open Studio], Kanal 5 [Channel 5], 13 December 2010. Accessed 12 November 2014, http:// www.5-tv.ru/programs/broadcast/505984/.

Nataliya Travkina, head lawyer, Pepeliaev Group:

(a) "Situatsiya na alkogol'nom rinke: perviye itogi zakonodatel'nykh izmeneniy" [The situation on the alcohol market: Initial results of the legislative changes], press conference, RIA Novosti Press Centre, Moscow, 19 October 2012. Accessed 11 November 2014, http://pressria.ru/media/20121019/600926565.html.

Yury Yakhin, senior lawyer, Pepeliayev Group:

(a) "Situatsiya na alkogol'nom rinke: perviye itogi zakonodatel'nykh izmeneniy" [The situation on the alcohol market: Initial results of the legislative changes], press conference, RIA Novosti Press Centre, Moscow, 19 October 2012. Accessed 11 November 2014, http://pressria.ru/media/20121019/600926565.html.

Viktor Zvagelskiy, Duma deputy, United Russia Party:

(a) "Situatsiya na alkogol'nom rinke: perviye itogi zakonodatel'nykh izmeneniy" [The situation on the alcohol market: Initial results of the legislative changes], press conference, RIA Novosti Press Centre, Moscow, 19 October 2012. Accessed 11 November 2014, http://pressria.ru/media/20121019/600926565.html.

(b) "Tema discussiya: Polusukhoy zakon" [Theme of discussion: Semi-dry law], *Otkritaya Studiya* [Open Studio], Kanal 5 [Channel 5], 12 March 2012. Accessed 12 November 2014, https://www .youtube.com/watch?v=O6TYjgj5iEY.

(c) "Tema discussiya: Surrogati vmesto pivo?" [Theme of discussion: Surrogates instead of beer?], *Otkritaya Studiya* [Open Studio], Kanal 5 [Channel 5], 2 August 2011. Accessed 12 November 2014, https://www.youtube.com/watch?v=8f1akOpWEbU.

(f) "Tema discussiya: Vodku zapretyat?" [Theme of discussion: Will vodka be banned?], *Otkritaya Studiya* [Open Studio], Kanal 5

[Channel 5], 14 January 2011. Accessed 12 November 2014, http://www.5-tv.ru/programs/broadcast/506106/?page=1#c174196.

(g) "Tema: Sukhoy Zakon" [Theme: Dry law], *Poyedinok* [Duel], Rossiya 1 [channel Russia 1], 9 December 2010. Accessed 12 November 2014, https://www.youtube.com/watch?v=BCPNwkmO3Gk.

(h) "Populizm ili real'naya bor'ba za zdorov'e natsii? Pivo predlagayut priravnyat' k alkogolyu" [Populism, or a real struggle for the health of the nation? It is proposed to equate beer to alcohol], 99.6 Finam FM, 11 May 2010. Accessed 11 November 2014, http://finam.fm/archive-view/2495/.

iii) Published Interviews

Dmitry Dobrov, chair, Union of Alcohol Producers:
(a) Petrova, Arina, "Alkogol'naya sostavlyayushchaya reforma" [Alcohol-containing reform], "Tax in Practice" supplement, *Kommersant*, 29 June 2011.

Vadim Drobiz, director, Centre for the Study of Federal and Regional Alcohol Markets (TsIFRRA):
(a) Shabaeva, Valeria, "Ekspert Vadim Drobiz—o zakone, priravnivayushchem pivo k alkogolyu" [Expert Vadim Drobiz—on the law equating beer to alcohol], Svobodanews.ru, 6 July 2011. Accessed 11 November 2014, http://www.svobodanews.ru/content/article/24257169.html.

(b) Transcript of radio interview on program "Ot pervogo litsa" [First person], Radio Rossii, 29 December 2011. Accessed 11 November 2014, http://www.radiorus.ru/issue.html?iid=353292&rid.

Vladimir Ivanov, director general, Rosspirtprom:
(a) Trutnev, Oleg, "Administrativnoye davleniye vsegda budet vizivat" obratnuyu otrizhku" [Administrative pressure will always give rise to a backward reaction], *Kommersant*, No. 103 (4403), 10 June 2010.

Daria Khaltourina, cochair, Russian Coalition for Alcohol Control:
(a) "Polusukhoy zakon" [Semi-dry law], Pravoslavie.ru, 9 August 2011. Accessed 2 December 2014, http://www.pravoslavie.ru/guest/48003.htm.

(b) "Aktsizniye voyni" [Excise wars], *Tribune*, 10 September 2009. Accessed 2 December 2014, http://www.tribuna.ru/articles/2009/09/10/article5444/.

Vladimir Mishelovin, head of the Federal Anti-Monopoly Service of the Russian Federation (FAS):

(a) "V. Mishelovin: Mi nablyudaem revolutsionnuyu situatsiyu na alkogol'nom rinkye" [V Mishelovin: We are witnessing a revolutionary situation on the alcohol market], Alcoexpert.ru, 30 January 2012. Accessed http://www.alcoexpert.ru/analitika/7757-v-mishelovin-my-nablyudaem-revolyucionnuyu-situaciyu-na-alkogolnom.html.

Yury Shefler, founder, Soyuzplodimport vodka company:

(a) Prokhorov, Victor, "The Object of the Campaign against Soyuzplodimport Is to Take Our Business from Us . . . ," *Kompaniya*, 11 March 2002.

Pavel Tolstykh, general editor, web-portal Lobbying.ru:

(a) "Rynok vodki—eto ogromniy rynok tenovogo kesha dlya regionalnykh elit" [The vodka market is an enormous market of black cash for regional elites], *RBK Daily*, 26 March 2012. Accessed 27 March 2012, http://www.rbcdaily.ru/2012/03/26/market/562949983360637.

Leonid Vigdorovich, director of Strategic Development, Kazyonka; chair of the Presidium of the Expert Council on Alcohol of the State Duma:

(a) "Leonid Vigdorovich—Igri zakonchilis" [Leonid Vigdorovich—the games are over], Alcohole.ru (*sic*), 26 November 2010. Accessed 2 December 2014, http://www.alcohole.ru/news/plans/9299/.

Viktor Zvagelskiy, State Duma deputy, United Russia Party:

(a) Yevplanov, Andrei, "Deputati popravyat zdorov'e. Gosduma vzyalas' za alkogol' vser'ez" [The deputies improve health. The State Duma has gotten serious with alcohol], *Rossiyskaya Biznes-gazeta*, No. 841 (12), 27 March 2012.

(b) Nikitina, Elizaveta, "'V ideale mi dolzhni priyti k kontrafaktomu rinku alkogolya okolo 10 percent'—Deputat Gosdumi Viktor Zvagelskiy" ["Ideally we need to reduce the market for counterfeit alcohol to around 10 percent"—State Duma Deputy Viktor Zvagelskiy], Slon.ru, 7 April 2011. Accessed 30 November 2014,

http://slon.ru/economics/v_ideale_my_dolzhny_priyti_k
_kontrafaktnomu_rynku-577891.xhtml.

(c) "Gosudarstvennoye regulirovaniye rinka alkogol'noy produktsii"
[Government regulation of the market for alcoholic products],
Consultant.ru, 10 February 2011. Accessed 23 February 2011,
http://www.consultant.ru/law/interview/zvagelski.html.

Appendix 3

List of Interview Questions

1. Introductory

Firstly, could you please tell me a little about you and your organization's involvement in alcohol policy. What do you do exactly?

I would like to start by asking you a very open-ended question. Who do you think has most influence and control over state alcohol policy in Russia?

2. Antialcohol Campaign (general)

I would like to ask you some questions about the initiative to lower alcohol consumption which began under President Medvedev in 2009. The Russian media often refer to President Medvedev's antialcohol campaign. Do you think the term "antialcohol campaign" is an accurate description of current government policies?

Why has the antialcohol campaign happened when it has? (for example, why did it only begin in 2009, when Putin raised the issue in his 2005 address to the Federal Assembly?)

We now know that it is likely that Putin will once again become president of Russia. How is this likely to affect the antialcohol campaign? How is it likely to affect alcohol policy more generally?

3. Antialcohol Policy Concept and Presidential Orders

I would now like to ask you some questions on the presidential orders to the government of September 2009 on alcohol policy, and the government's Anti-Alcohol Plan of 30 December 2009. Who/what institutional apparatus worked out the content of the list of presidential orders of September 2009 on alcohol policy? On whose initiative were these orders drafted?

Who advised the measures in the antialcohol plan, including that beer cannot be sold in containers larger than 330 mL?

In the original proposals agreed upon by the government (the *Kompleks Mer* of 14 December 2009), why was 5 percent decided on as the cutoff point for beer legislation (kiosks, advertising, etc.)?

4. Alcohol Control Bill 2011

I would like to ask you some questions about the bill on alcohol regulation passed by the State Duma in July 2011, which amongst other things reclassified beer as an alcoholic product. What happened between the first and second readings to bring about such dramatic changes to the bill's provisions, in particular the change from 5 percent to 0.5 percent for drinks that can't be sold in kiosks and are encompassed by the after 11 p.m. sales ban?

How was the recategorization of beer as alcohol able to pass the Duma and Federation Council in 2011, when such a law has already been rejected by parliament numerous times in recent years? What has changed?

Why were the provisions for beer production to be licensed and subject to the same regulation as stronger alcohol dropped from the final bill?

In the president's comments on the bill dated 29 March 2011 he complained that the ability of the regions to take the retail sales restrictions further, up to and including a full ban, hadn't been included as specified in his orders of 10 September 2009. Why would he want to have the possibility of a full ban after the deep unpopularity of the Gorbachev campaign? Doesn't this go against the "power vertical" principle?

5. Excise Duty and Minimum Vodka Price

Why in 2010 did the government steeply increase excise duty on beer but not vodka? Why did it only increase excise on vodka from 2011? Why not back in 2010 when it increased it on beer?

Who was for and who was against the large increase in excise duty to take place 2012–14? How was it eventually pushed through when it seemed it had been defeated? Should it be seen as an initiative as part of the antialcohol campaign, or was it a separate budgetary consideration?

6. Rosalkogolregulirovaniye (RAR)

On whose authority was RAR formed? Who lobbied for its formation?

It seems that alcohol producers lobbied for the formation of RAR, and yet now producers are complaining about "heavy handed" and unfair regulation by RAR. How do we explain this apparent paradox? Is the market divided into companies which RAR protects and those it targets, or did producers unwittingly create "Frankenstein's monster" when they lobbied for the creation of RAR?

We often hear that there is a strong alcohol lobby. If RAR is threatening their interests, why have they not lobbied more strongly against RAR?

7. Rosspirtprom

How strong are the links between Rosspirtprom and RAR? Does Rosspirtprom have any influence over alcohol policy?

In 2007 Rospirtprom announced that it would produce a new, super-cheap "people's vodka" so that poor people would not resort to illegal vodka.

But it seems the idea did not materialize. What happened to the "people's vodka" idea?

8. Alcohol Lobby Groups

What lobby groups try to influence government alcohol policy? What is the role of trade organizations, such as the Union of Russian Brewers and the Union of Alcohol Producers?

How does a given lobby group attempt to influence federal alcohol policy? Through what mechanisms?

How does your organization try to influence state alcohol policy? By what means?

How has alcohol and beer lobbying changed over the years? Are there any differences between now and ten years ago, for example?

9. State Duma

What role does the State Duma Committee for Economic Policy under Viktor Zvagelskiy play in alcohol policy formation?

10. State Monopoly on Alcohol

How likely is it that the government will bring in a state monopoly on alcohol? Why was Putin originally proposing the idea then turned against it?

11. Demographic Situation

When did the demographic situation in Russia first become a serious concern for the Russian government?

Why did the demographic situation begin to concern the government only then, why not sooner?

When did the Russian government first begin to recognize that excessive alcohol consumption is a major contributing factor to the demographic crisis in Russia?

12. Contacts

Could you recommend other individuals who it may be useful for me to interview while I'm in Moscow? Would it be possible for you to give me their contact details?

Notes

Introduction

1. "Excerpts from Transcript of Meeting on Measures to Reduce Alcohol Consumption in Russia," Kremlin.ru, 12 August 2009. Accessed http://www.kremlin.ru/eng/text/speeches/2009/08/12/1845_type82912type82913_220798.shtml on 13 August 2009.

2. Nemtsov, *Alkogol'naya Istoriya Rossii*, 264.

3. "Hazardous drinking" was defined as nonbeverage alcohol consumption (such as medical tinctures, chemicals, or eau de cologne) or excessive consumption of alcoholic beverages or both. Leon et al., "Hazardous Alcohol Drinking and Premature Mortality in Russia."

4. Zaridze et al., "Alcohol and Cause-Specific Mortality in Russia."

5. Sabatier, "An Advocacy Coalition Framework of Policy Change and the Role of Policy-Oriented Learning Therein," 131.

6. Ibid., 133.

7. Like many types of institutions, bureaucracies tend to acquire departmental ideologies that reflect the perceived importance and desirability of their own work. Thus, the leaders of a department with responsibility for alcohol licensing, for example, may genuinely believe that stricter licensing would be in the public interest, aside from the

budgetary and power benefits it would bring to the organization. See Downs, *Inside Bureaucracy*, 237–46.

8. Ibid., 213–15.

9. Simmons et al., "Bootleggers, Baptists, and Political Entrepreneurs," 367–81.

10. Gusfield, *Contested Meanings*, 17–30.

11. Thom, "A Social and Political History of Alcohol," 22–25; Bunton, "Regulating our Favourite Drug," 104–17.

12. Tkatchenko et al., "Public Health in Russia," 164–69; Vishnevsky and Bobylev, *National Human Development Report Russian Federation 2008*, 66–67.

13. Cairney, *Understanding Public Policy*, 13.

14. Babor et al., *Alcohol*, 48–49.

15. Cook and Moore, "The Economics of Alcohol Abuse and Alcohol-Control Policies," 128.

16. Babor et al., *Alcohol*, 53, 55.

17. Heath, "Why We Don't Know More about the Social Benefits of Moderate Drinking," S72.

18. Babor et al., *Alcohol*, 60–62.

19. Room, "The Idea of Alcohol Policy," 7.

20. Mäkelä and Viikari, "Notes on Alcohol and the State," 151–79.

21. Public Chamber of the Russian Federation, *Zloupotreblenie Alkogolem v Rossiyskoy Federatsii*, 45.

22. Room, "The Idea of Alcohol Policy," 7.

23. Ibid., 8.

24. Christian, *Living Water*, 38.

25. "Rent" in this sense is an economic concept, which in simple terms means "something for nothing." Rents are the product of rent seeking: "spending time and money not on the production of real goods and services, but rather on trying to get the government to change the rules so as to make one's business more profitable." Black et al., *A Dictionary of Economics*. It represents a transfer of wealth rather than the generation of new wealth. See also Simmons, *Beyond Politics*, 62.

26. For an in-depth study of *sistema* see Ledeneva, *Can Russia Modernise?*

1. Feeding the State: Vodka from Tsarism to Communism

1. Christian, *Living Water*, 27.

2. Ibid., 3.

3. Ibid., 5, 43. It is worth noting that alcohol revenues provided a comparable proportion of government revenues in England in the nineteenth century. Ibid., 11.

4. Pokhlebkin, *A History of Vodka*, 46.

5. Christian, *Living Water*, 8.

6. Ibid., 372.

7. Quoted in Takala, *Veseliye Rusi*, 102.

8. Ibid., 107, 115.

9. For an in-depth account, see Herlihy, *The Alcoholic Empire*, 129–45.

10. Ibid., 130–32.

11. Levine, *The 1985 Alcohol Reform in the USSR*, 130.

12. Quoted in Herlihy, *The Alcoholic Empire*, 137.

13. Schrad, *The Political Power of Bad Ideas*, 119.

14. Ibid., 129.

15. Herlihy, *The Alcoholic Empire*, 138–39.

16. Schrad, *The Political Power of Bad Ideas*, 129–30; Herlihy, *The Alcoholic Empire*, 139.

17. Schrad, *The Political Power of Bad Ideas*, 131, 138.

18. Ibid., 132; Herlihy, *The Alcoholic Empire*, 142–45.

19. Pravda, "Ideology and the Soviet Policy Process," 237.

20. V. I. Lenin, "Zaklyuchitel'noye slovo po dokladu o prodovol'stvennom naloge" (Concluding remarks on the report on the food tax), Tenth Party Conference, 27 May 1921. In V. I. Lenin, *Polnoye sobraniye sochinenii,* Izd. 5 (Moscow): 326.

21. *Pravda*, 12 July 1923. Quoted in Transchel, *Under the Influence*, 68.

22. Stone, "The Soviet Government and Moonshine," 359.

23. White, *Russia Goes Dry*, 17.

24. Stone, "The Soviet Government and Moonshine," 360.

25. Ibid., 361.

26. Ibid., 363.

27. Weissman, "Prohibition and Alcohol Control in the USSR," 362.

28. Ibid., 353.

29. Stone, "The Soviet Government and Moonshine," 374.

30. Phillips, *Bolsheviks and the Bottle*, 22.

31. *Pravda*, 2 November 1922, quoted in Stone, "The Soviet Government and Moonshine," 365.

32. Quoted in Levine, *The 1985 Alcohol Reform in the USSR*, 140.

33. Phillips, *Bolsheviks and the Bottle*, 21.

34. Weissman, "Prohibition and Alcohol Control in the USSR," 358.

35. Phillips, *Bolsheviks and the Bottle*, 23.

36. *Za noviy byt*, no. 7–8 (1928): 22, quoted in White, *Russia Goes Dry*, 23.

37. Phillips, *Bolsheviks and the Bottle*, 23–25.

38. White, *Russia Goes Dry*, 23–24.

39. For a detailed account of the fall of Bukharin and Stalin's elimination of the Right Opposition, see Cohen, *Bukharin and the Bolshevik Revolution*, 270–336.

40. Phillips, *Bolsheviks and the Bottle*, 24–25; White, *Russia Goes Dry*, 25.

41. Stalin to Molotov, 1 September 1930. Reproduced in *Pis'ma I. V. Stalina V. M. Molotovu 1925–39*, letter no. 62: 209–10.

42. White, *Russia Goes Dry*, 25.

43. Levine, *The 1985 Alcohol Reform in the USSR*, 142.

2. Soviet Policy Doublethink

1. Orwell, *Nineteen Eighty-Four*, 223.

2. Shlapentokh, *Public and Private Life of the Soviet People*, 18–21.

3. Shabalin, "P'yanka, vypivka, popoyka," 21.

4. Levine, *The 1985 Alcohol Reform in the USSR*, 142–44. Gorbachev himself cited the "propaganda" that there were no objective reasons for alcoholism to exist in socialist society as a reason for government inaction in the decades prior to his leadership. Gorbachev, *Zhizn' i reformy*, 339.

5. Connor, "Alcohol and Soviet Society," 575.

6. Levine, *The 1985 Alcohol Reform in the USSR*, 142.

7. *Bol'shaya Sovetskaya Entsiklopediya* [*Big Soviet Encyclopaedia*], 2nd izd., tom 2 (Moscow: Bol'shaya sovetskaya entsiklopediya, 1950), 117.

8. Korolenko, Minevich, and Segal, "The Politicization of Alcohol in the USSR," 1270.

9. White, *Russia Goes Dry*, 32.

10. Literally meaning "self-publication," *samizdat* referred to the unofficial, typically clandestine production and circulation of texts in the USSR as a means of avoiding state censorship. See Forsyth, "Samizdat".

11. Krasikov, "Commodity Number One (part 1)." Krasikov was actually a pseudonym of former *Izvestiya* journalist and Trotsky follower Mikhail D. Baitalskiy, a fact that was revealed only after his death. See Schrad, *Vodka Politics*, 244–45.

12. Krasikov, "Commodity Number One," 96–101.

13. Ibid., 111.

14. Segal, *The Drunken Society*, 178.

15. Levine, *The 1985 Alcohol Reform in the USSR*, 142.

16. *Spravochnik partiinogo rabotnika*, vyp. 2 (1959), 404–8.

17. Takala, *Veseliye Rusi*, 252–53.

18. *Spravochnik partiinogo rabotnika*, vyp. 13 (1973), 182–86.

19. White, *Russia Goes Dry*, 59–60.

20. Zaigraev, "Gosudarstvennaya politika kak factor alkogolizatsii naseleniya," 109–10.

21. Tarschys, "The Success of a Failure," 12.

22. Reitan, "The Operation Failed, but the Patient Survived," 248.

23. Tarschys, "The Success of a Failure," 14.

24. Connor, "Alcohol and Soviet Society," 581.

25. Christian, *Living Water*, 7.

26. Levine, *The 1985 Alcohol Reform in the USSR*, 144.

27. *Bol'shaya Sovetskaya Entsiklopediya*, 2nd izd., 116–120; *Bol'shaya Sovetskaya Entsiklopediya*, 3rd izd., tom 1 (1970) (Moscow: Sovetskaya entsiklopediya), 442–43.

28. *Bol'shaya Sovetskaya Entsiklopediya*, 2nd izd., 117.

29. Ibid., 118.

30. *Bol'shaya Sovetskaya Entsiklopediya*, 3rd izd., 218.

31. Tarschys, "The Success of a Failure," 13.

32. Levine, *The 1985 Alcohol Reform in the USSR*, 60–75.

33. Reitan, "The Operation Failed," 246.

34. Ryzhkov, *Desyat let velikikh potraseniy*, 95.

35. Gorbachev, *Zhizn' i reformy*, 340.

36. Treml, "Soviet and Russian Statistics on Alcohol Consumption and Abuse," 224.

37. White, *Russia Goes Dry*, 38.

38. Treml, "Soviet and Russian Statistics," 224.

39. Tarschys, "The Success of a Failure," 14–16.

40. Levine, *The 1985 Alcohol Reform in the USSR*, 243.

41. Ibid., 243–44.

42. Central Committee of the CPSU, "O merakh po preodoleniyu p'yanstva i alko-golizma" [On measures to overcome drunkenness and alcoholism] (resolution), 7 May 1985. Published in *Pravda*, 17 May 1985, 1. English translation available in *Current Digest of the Soviet Press* 37, no. 20 (12 June 1985): 1–4.

43. Ibid.

44. White, *Russia Goes Dry*, 74–75.

45. Ibid., 61; Tarschys, "The Success of a Failure," 17.

46. White, *After Gorbachev*, 10–11.

47. Schrad, *Vodka Politics*, 257–58.

48. Ryzhkov, *Desyat let velikikh potraseniy*, 94.

49. Tarschys, "The Success of a Failure," 9.

50. Ligachev, *Inside Gorbachev's Kremlin*, 337.

51. White, *Russia Goes Dry*, 66–68; Levine, *The 1985 Alcohol Reform in the USSR*, 84–87; Schrad, *Vodka Politics*, 268–71.

52. Schrad, *Vodka Politics*, 268; Levine, *The 1985 Alcohol Reform in the USSR*, 84.

53. Levine, *The 1985 Alcohol Reform in the USSR*, 85.

54. Gorbachev, *Zhizn' i reformy*, 338–42.

55. Levine, *The 1985 Alcohol Reform in the USSR*, 248–54.

56. Schrad, *Vodka Politics*, 271–72; White, *Russia Goes Dry*, 68.

57. Hough and Fainsod, *How the Soviet Union Is Governed*, 477.

58. Levine, *The 1985 Alcohol Reform in the USSR*, 257.

59. Tarschys, "The Success of a Failure," 9.

60. Quoted in Tarschys, "The Success of a Failure," 21.

61. Korolenko, Minevich, Segal, "The Politicization of Alcohol in the USSR," 1271.

62. Tarschys, "The Success of a Failure," 10.

63. Ibid., 11–12; Levine, *The 1985 Alcohol Reform in the USSR*, 78.

64. Tarschys, "The Success of a Failure," 11, 22.

65. Levine, *The 1985 Alcohol Reform in the USSR*, 59–61.

66. Nemtsov, *Alkogol'naya Istoriya Rossii*, 20.

3. The Parasites Feed: State Capture under Yeltsin

1. Nemtsov, *Alkogol'naya Istoriya Rossii*, 102.

2. Ibid.

3. Harper, *Moscow Madness*, 232.

4. Although several scholarly socioeconomic accounts of 1990s Russia refer to a phenomenon of state capture, there is no single, agreed-upon definition of the term. Joel Hellman and colleagues define state capture as the ability of private enterprises to influence government legislation and bureaucratic policy through private payments to public officials. Yet this is quite a narrow definition, involving only one method of extracting rents from the state (influencing policy) through only one means (paying bribes). More

comprehensive is Timothy Frye's definition of state capture as state agents giving preferential treatment to private individuals/firms for relatively little in return. Frye distinguishes state capture from elite exchange, where state agents gain substantial benefits in return for their preferential treatment to firms. An example of the latter was factory management receiving favored treatment during privatization in return for supporting Yeltsin in his political struggles. See Hellman, Jones, and Kaufmann, "Seize the State, Seize the Day"; Frye, "Capture or Exchange?"; Ledeneva, "Introduction: Economic Crime in the New Russian Economy"; Yakovlev, "The Evolution of Business."

5. Treisman, "Death and Prices," 310, 312.

6. Ibid.

7. Takala, *Veseliye Rusi*, 273.

8. Treisman, "Death and Prices," 313; Nemtsov, *Alkogol'naya Istoriya Rossii*, 97.

9. Hoffman, *The Oligarchs*, 192–93.

10. Fituni, "Economic Crime in the Context of Transition to a Market Economy," 17.

11. Zaigraev, "P'yanstvo v Rossii kak real'naya ugroza natsional'noy bezopasnosti," 71.

12. Ibid., 75. A "dal" is equivalent to a deciliter (one-tenth of a liter) and is a standard measurement of beverage production in Russia.

13. On Soviet organized crime, how it evolved into the *mafiya* of the 1990s, and how the term *mafiya* came to be used to describe organized crime, see Handelman, *Comrade Criminal*.

14. Ledeneva, "Introduction: Economic Crime in the New Russian Economy," 5; Galeotti, "The Mafiya and the New Russia," 418.

15. Fituni, "Economic Crime in the Context of Transition to a Market Economy," 17; Handelman, *Comrade Criminal*, 110–14, 335–42.

16. For a comprehensive account of what he calls "the privatization of the power ministries," see Volkov, *Violent Entrepreneurs*, 126–54. On the ability of former employees to still enjoy use of state resources, see Volkov, "Organised Violence, Market Building, and State Formation in Post-Communist Russia," 57.

17. Shleifer and Treisman, *Without a Map*, 2.

18. Nemtsov, *Alkogol'naya Istoriya Rossii*, 100.

19. Ibid.

20. Fituni, "Economic Crime in the Context of Transition to a Market Economy," 18.

21. Harper, *Moscow Madness*, 162.

22. Nemtsov, *Alkogol'naya Istoriya Rossii*, 101.

23. Ledeneva, "Introduction: Economic Crime in the New Russian Economy," 4.

24. Galeotti, "The Mafiya and the New Russia," 424.

25. Ledeneva, "Introduction: Economic Crime in the New Russian Economy," 4.

26. Harper, *Moscow Madness*, 162–63.

27. Nemtsov, *Alkogol'naya Istoriya Rossii*, 102.

28. Ibid., 105.

29. Ibid.

30. Ibid.

31. Nemtsov, *Alkogol'naya Istoriya Rossii*, 105–6, 116–17; Schrad, *Vodka Politics*, 314.

32. Ukaz Prezidenta Rossiyskoy Federatsii No. 918 "O vosstanovlenii gosudarstvennoy monopolii na proizvodstvo, khraneniye, optovuyu i roznichnuyu prodazhu alkogol'noy produktsii" [Decree of the President of the Russian Federation No. 918 On measures to reestablish the government monopoly on the production, storage, and wholesale and retail sale of alcohol products], *Sobraniye aktov Prezidenta i Pravitel'stva Rossiyskoy Federatsii*, No. 24, 14 June 1993, article 2235.

33. Postanovleniye Pravitel'stva Rossiyskoy Federatsii No. 358 "O merakh po vosstanovleniyu gosudarstvennoy monopolii na proizvodstvo, khraneniye, optovuyu i roznichnuyu prodazhu alkogol'noy produktsii" [Resolution of the Government of the Russian Federation No. 358 On measures to reestablish the state monopoly on the production, storage, and wholesale and retail sale of alcoholic products], 22 April 1994, *Sobraniye zakonodatel'stva Rossiyskoy Federatsii*, No. 1, 2 May 1994, article 21, 19–22.

34. Postanovleniye Pravitel'stva Rossiyskoy Federatsii No. 1088 "Ob utverzhdenii Poryadka roznichnoy torgovli alkogol'nymi napitkami i pivom na territorii Rossiyskoy Federatsii" [Resolution of the Government of the Russian Federation No. 1088 On the establishment of the Order of retail sale of alcoholic beverages and beer on the territory of the Russian Federation], 26 September 1994, *Sobraniye zakonodatel'stva Rossiyskoy Federatsii*, No. 23, 3 October 1994, article 2567, 3480–83.

35. Takala, *Veseliye Rusi*, 274; Nemtsov, *Alkogol'naya Istoriya Rossii*, 103.

36. A. Aboronov, "Vodka i monopoliya. Aktual'noye interv'yu" [Vodka and monopoly. A topical interview], *Ekonomika i Zhizn'*, 23 November 1996.

37. FZ No. 171-F3 "O gosudarstvennom regulirovanii proizvodstva i oborota etilovogo spirta i alkogol'noy produktsii," 22 November 1995, *Sobraniye zakonodatel'stva Rossiyskoy Federatsii*, No. 48, 27 November 1995, article 4553, 8491–99.

38. Nemtsov, *Alkogol'naya Istoriya Rossii*, 118.

39. Ibid., 119.

40. FZ No. 15 F-3 "O vnesenii izmeneniy i dopolneniy v Federal'nyy zakon 'O gosudarstvennom regulirovanii proizvodstva i oborota etilovogo spirta i alkogol'noy produktsii'" [On the amendment of federal law "On State Regulation of the Production and Sale of Ethyl Alcohol and Alcoholic Products"], 10 January 1997, *Sobraniye zakonodatel'stva Rossiyskoy Federatsii*, No. 3, 20 January 1997, article 359, 606–7.

41. Takala, *Veseliye Rusi*, 281.

4. Regaining State Control under Putin

1. The term "corporate raiding," or *reiderstvo*, has a very different meaning in the Russian context than in Anglo-Saxon economies. In the latter it refers to the aggressive but legal activity of buying up shares in a target company to acquire control of its management. In Russia, by contrast, corporate raiding involves acquiring the company by semilegal, illegal, or possibly corrupt transfer of property rights. See Ledeneva, *Can Russia Modernise?*, 188; Mesquita, "Reiderstvo."

2. Alex Nicholson, "Warrant Issued for Vodka Magnate," *Moscow Times*, 31 July 2002.

3. Yury Zarakhovich, "Fighting Spirits," *Time*, 23 June 2002, accessed 27 November 2014, http://www.time.com/time/magazine/article/0,9171,265361,00.html.

4. Quoted in Zarakhovich, "Fighting Spirits."

5. Svetlana Mentyukova, Dmitry Butrin, and Elena Kiseleva, "Soyuzplodimport Is Getting Out of Bottle," *Business and Economic Reports*, 13 August 2008.

6. Zarakhovich, "Fighting Spirits."

7. Zarakhovich, "Fighting Spirits."

8. A more precise dating of the transition from state capture to business capture is provided by Andrei Yakovlev, on the basis of industrial and business surveys. Yakovlev found that business dominance over the state peaked in the summer of 1996. The early 2000s were a period of "balance of power" between business and the state, while the full dominance of state over business occurred in the summer of 2004 onward. Yakovlev, "The Evolution of Business—State Interaction in Russia," 1033–56.

9. Ibid.; Ledeneva, *Can Russia Modernise?*, 69.

10. It is not always clear who exactly benefits from business capture: the state in its own right or private individuals who work within the state. The answer would appear to be both, depending on the instance of business capture that is being described. Conceptually, it could be argued that where people benefit *as private individuals*, this is simply a new form of state capture. There cannot be a simple dichotomy between state capture and business capture, precisely because the dividing line between business and state is itself blurred in Russia. In part, this reflects the legacy of porous boundaries between public and private domains in communist societies, and the insecure property rights of the postcommunist elites. See Ledeneva, *Can Russia Modernise?*, 54–55.

11. Gulnaz Sharafutdinova sees both state capture and business capture as variants of crony capitalism, with the difference being which category of actor is more powerful. State capture is a case of venal corruption where business interests corrupt politics, whereas business capture is a type of systematic corruption where the state controls access to valuable economic activity, thus making economic success and property rights conditional upon continued support for the regime. Sharafutdinova, *Political Consequences of Crony Capitalism inside Russia*, 138–42.

12. White, *Understanding Russian Politics*, 172.

13. Barnes, *Owning Russia*, 172–73.

14. Ibid., 173–74.

15. There was contradictory evidence as to whether Berezovsky committed suicide by hanging himself or was strangled (i.e., unlawful killing). The coroner recorded an open verdict.

16. "Ob uchrezhdenii federal'nogo gosudarstvennogo unitarnogo predpriyatiya 'Rosspirtprom'" [On the establishment of the federal state unitary enterprise "Rosspirtprom"], 6 May 2000, *Sobraniye zakonodatel'stva Rossiyskoy Federatsii*, No. 21, 22 May 2000, article 2240, 4500–4508.

17. Galina Lyapunova and Dmitry Dobrov, "Russia Loses Alcohol Independence," *Current Digest of the Post-Soviet Press* 52, no. 21 (21 June 2000): 16; Igor Semenenko, "State Sets Up Holding Unifying Alcohol Assets," *Moscow Times*, 31 May 2000.

18. Ibid.

19. Nemtsov and Milov, *Putin i Gazprom*, 4.

20. Ibid.; see also Treisman, *The Return*, 115.

21. Dawisha, *Putin's Kleptocracy*, 280–81.

22. Ibid., 281–82.

23. "Natsional'niy proyekt 'Dostupniy alkogol'" [The "Affordable Alcohol" national project], *Ekspert*, 19 February 2007, accessed 27 November 2014, http://expert.ru/siberia /2007/07/rynok_alkogolya_editorial/.

24. For a comprehensive account of Putin's establishment of centralized control ("new federalism") during his first two presidencies, see Sakwa, *Putin: Russia's Choice*, 186–213.

25. Yulia Latynina, "Inside Russia: Heavyweights Still Waging Centralization," *Moscow Times*, 20 September 2000.

26. Petrov, "Kak v kaple vodki," 140–41.

27. Nina Petlyanova, "Soobrazili na svoikh" [Divided up between themselves], *Novaya gazeta*, No. 23, 4 March 2011.

28. Latynina, "Inside Russia."

29. Schrad, *Vodka Politics*, 701–4.

30. Dmitry Dobrov, "Who Owns Russia? Trends in the Sector," *Russia Journal*, 2 November 2001.

31. Latynina, "Inside Russia."

32. "Vodka Monopoly's Manager Found Stabbed in Apartment," *Moscow Times*, 3 June 2002.

33. Alex Nicholson, "Kasyanov Sacks Chief of State Vodka Holding," *Moscow Times*, 30 July 2002.

34. At the very least an ethyl alcohol monopolist, if not a vodka monopolist—a distinction that is often fudged even in official discourse. Ethyl alcohol is pure alcohol (*spirt* in Russian) and is the raw ingredient from which vodka is made. Thus, it would be possible to have a state monopoly on ethyl alcohol responsible for selling this ingredient to private vodka producers.

35. ALB=Anna L. Bailey, the author.

36. Natalya Alyakrinskaya, "Russia. Will the State Take Over the Alcohol Market?" *Moscow News*, 19 October 2005.

37. Ibid.

38. To my knowledge, this letter is not in the public domain. A copy of it was passed to me by one of my respondents. I have no reason to doubt that the letter is genuine, but at the same time it has not been possible to independently verify its authenticity.

39. Ben Cooper, "Putin Puts Monopoly Plans Firmly in Play," Just-drinks, 19 July 2005, accessed 1 March 2010, http://www.just-drinks.com/analysis/putin-puts -monopoly-plans-firmly-in-play_id85132.aspx?d=1.

40. Alyakrinskaya, "Russia: Will the State Take Over the Alcohol Market?"

41. Transcript of press conference with the Russian and foreign media, Round Hall, the Kremlin, Moscow, 1 February 2007, accessed 1 November 2014, http://eng.pda .kremlin.ru/transcripts/8490.

42. Quoted in Julian Evans, "Moscow Rediscovers Its Taste for State Alcohol," *The Times*, 13 November 2006.

43. Ibid.

44. Accounting Chamber of the Russian Federation, 2008, 98.

45. "Sberbank Invited to Become Shareholder of Largest Alcohol Producer," *FK-Novosti* (English version), 3 June 2010.

46. "Russia Needs to Be Strong and Competitive. Russian President V.V. Putin's Message to the Russian Federation Federal Assembly," *Current Digest of the Post-Soviet Press* 54, no. 16 (15 May 2002): 4.

47. Accounting Chamber of the Russian Federation, 2008, 109.

48. This remark was prompted by one account that stated that when set up, Rosspirtprom "employed a group of security types from St Petersburg." See Latynina, "Inside Russia." For a scholarly account of the role of the *siloviki* in business under Putin, see Treisman, "Putin's Silovarchs."

5. The Judo Gang: Informal Networks and Perceptions of Power

1. Putin, *First Person*, 19.

2. For an in-depth academic analysis of *sistema* and how it operates under Putin, see Ledeneva, *Can Russia Modernise?*

3. Dawisha, *Putin's Kleptocracy*, 36–37, 317–18; Sharafutdinova, *Political Consequences of Crony Capitalism inside Russia*, 72.

4. Nina Petlyanova, "Soobrazili na svoikh" [Divided up between themselves], *Novaya gazeta*, No. 23, 4 March 2011.

5. For more details on the Rotenbergs' business interests and how the brothers have benefited from contracts awarded by the state, see Dawisha, *Putin's Kleptocracy*, 92–94.

6. Catherine Belton and Charles Clover, "Putin's People," *Financial Times*, 30 May 2012.

7. Simon Shuster, "Vladimir Putin's Billionaire Boys Judo Club," *Time*, 1 March 2011, accessed 8 June 2013, http://www.time.com/time/world/article/0,8599,2055962,00.html.

8. US Department of the Treasury, "Treasury Sanctions Russian Officials, Members of the Russian Leadership's Inner Circle, and an Entity for Involvement in the Situation in Ukraine" (press release), 20 March 2014.

9. Petlyanova, "Soobrazili na svoikh"; Rinat Sagdiyev, "Kremlyovskiy spirtoupolnomochenniy," *Vedomosti*, No. 2340, 20 April 2009.

10. Ibid.

11. Ibid.

12. Market analyst Vadim Drobiz uses this term to refer to the collaboration of RAR, Rosspirtprom, and Putin's friends to clear the market of unwanted producers and dominate it themselves. Quoted in Petlyanova, "Soobrazili na svoikh."

13. Petlyanova, "Soobrazili na svoikh."

14. "Korporatsiya 'Rossiya'" [Russia Inc.], *New Times*, No. 36 (221), 31 October 2011, cited in Schrad, *Vodka Politics*, 355.

15. Schrad, *Vodka Politics*, 358.

16. Denis Puzyrev, "Rassledovaniye RBK: kto zarabatyvayet na deshevoy vodkye" [An RBK investigation: Who's making money from cheap vodka], *RBK Daily*, 25 October 2015, http://www.rbc.ru/business/12/10/2015/561a74a69a79474b921fc62d.

17. Oleg Trutnev, "'Putinka' teryayet protsenti" [Putinka is losing percentage], *Kommersant*, 29 July 2016, http://kommersant.ru/doc/3049657.

18. Denis Puzyrev and Igor Terentyev, "Druzya 'Putinki': kto zarabotal na glavnykh vodochnykh brendakh Rossii" [Friends of Putinka: Who made money from Russia's main vodka brands], *RBK Daily*, 9 November 2014, http://www.rbc.ru/business/09/11 /2014/545fc573cbb20f85e14cfbad.

19. Oleg Trutnev, "'Rosspirtprom' i polyaki mutyat vodku" [Rosspirtprom and the Poles stir up vodka], *Kommersant*, No. 172 (4713), 15 September 2011, http://www .kommersant.ru/doc/1773740; Denis Puzyrev, "Vodka dlya milliardera" [Vodka for a billionaire], *RBK Daily*, No. 45, 16 March 2016, 16; "Rosspirtprom i VEDK razdelyayut distributsiyu svoikh brendov" [Rosspirtprom and VEDK share distribution of their brands], Spirt-Express.ru, 15 October 2013, http://spirt-express.ru/novosti/novosti -kompaniy/1662/.

20. "Rosspirtprom i VEDK razdelyayut distributsiyu svoikh brendov."

21. Denis Puzyrev and Irina Malkova, "Milliarder Anisimov vstupil v tyazhbu za aktsii byvshego vodochnogo lidera" [Billionaire Anisimov in lawsuit for shares of former leading vodka], *RBK Daily*, 14 April 2016, http://www.rbc.ru/business/14/04/2016 /570fb3b39a79479e65ea192b.

22. "Samiye prodavayemiye vodochniye brendy v Rossii" [The bestselling vodka brands in Russia], *Kommersant*, 29 July 2016, http://kommersant.ru/doc/3049716.

23. Puzyrev, "Vodka dlya milliardera."

24. Rinat Sagdiyev, "Vodka so svyazyami" [Vodka with connections], *Vedomosti*, No. 4042, 28 March 2016.

25. Denis Puzirev, "Status-grupp podveli zavody" [Status Group loses factories], *RBK Daily*, No. 52, 25 March 2016, 16.

26. Sagdiyev, "Vodka so svyazyami."

27. Puzyrev, "Rassledovaniye RBK: kto zarabatyvayet na deshevoy vodkye."

28. Ibid.; Sagdiyev, "Vodka so svyazyami."

29. Ledeneva, *Can Russia Modernise?*, 53, 214–24.

30. Both of these models are cited in Ledeneva, *Can Russia Modernise?*, 53, 59–60.

31. Ibid., 53.

32. Alex Nicholson, "Kasyanov Sacks Chief of State Vodka Holding," *Moscow Times*, 30 July 2002.

33. Accounting Chamber of the Russian Federation, 2003.

34. "Business in Brief: Vodka Case Opened," *Moscow Times*, 26 March 2003.

35. Elizaveta Nikitina, "Zivenko obvinyayut v bankrotstvye" [Zivenko accused of bankruptcy], *Vedomosti*, No. 102, 5 June 2012.

36. Rinat Sagdiev, "Krupnym planom: Razlili ne po-bratski" [Close-up: Poured not in a brotherly way], *Vedomosti*, No. 29, 18 February 2010. Scholar Andrew Barnes has described the Russian phenomenon of using bankruptcy proceedings to seize control over a rival's asset as "political bankruptcy." It is also known in Russia as *zakaznoye bankrotstvo*, or "bankruptcy to order." See, respectively, Barnes, *Owning Russia*, 170; Mesquita, "Reiderstvo."

37. Sagdiev, "Krupnym planom: Razlili ne po-bratski."

38. Ibid.
39. Nemtsov and Milov, *Putin i Gazprom*, 11.
40. Ibid., 13–14.
41. U.S. Department of the Treasury, "Treasury Sanctions Russian Officials."
42. Nemtsov and Milov, *Putin i Gazprom*, 18.
43. Shuster, "Vladimir Putin's Billionaire Boys Judo Club."
44. Ledeneva, *Can Russia Modernise?*, 149.
45. Kryshtanovskaya and White, "Inside the Putin Court," 1065.
46. Pavlovsky, "Russian Politics under Putin."
47. Ledeneva, *Can Russia Modernise?*, 80.

6. An All-Powerful Regulator

1. Quoted in Evgeniy Kalyukov and Ksenia Shamakina, "Matviyenko prigrozila glavye Rosalkogol'regulirovaniya proverkoy" [Matviyenko threatens the head of Rosalkogolregulirovaniye with investigation], *RBK Daily*, 25 November 2015. A video transcript of the full hearing can be viewed at https://www.youtube.com/watch?v=-c1_2YJaaL0.

2. Ukaz Prezidenta Rossiyskoy Federatsii [Decree of the president of the Russian Federation] No. 1883 "Ob obrazovanii Federal'noy sluzhby po regulirovaniyu alkogol'nogo rynka" [On the formation of the Federal Agency for Regulating the Alcohol Market], 31 December 2008, *Sobraniye zakonodatel'stva Rossiyskoy Federatsii*, No. 1, 5 January 2009, 350–51.

3. "Alcohol industry" in this context means mainly the vodka industry. Beer was not classified as alcohol until 2011, while the wine and non-vodka spirits industries represented tiny proportions of the domestic market.

4. Downs, *Inside Bureaucracy*, 264.

5. Ibid., 213–15.

6. Svetlana Mentyukova, "Otvetstvennogo za alkogol'niy krizis sozdadut s nulya" [Body answerable for the alcohol crisis to be set up from scratch], *Kommersant*, No. 158, 28 August 2006, 7.

7. Ekaterina Ignatova, "Uprava na vodku" [Vodka management], *Kommersant Business Guide*, in *Kommersant*, No. 46 (4101), 17 March 2009, accessed 26 July 2010, http://www.kommersant.ru/doc.aspx?DocsID=1128454.

8. Mentyukova, "Otvetstvennogo za alkogol'niy krizis sozdadut s nulya."

9. Elena Denisenko, "Mnogoznachitel'noye molchaniye" [Significant silence], *Ekspert*, 4 December 2006, accessed 27 November 2014, http://expert.ru/northwest/2006/45/mnogoznachitelnoe_molchanie/.

10. "Russia to Create Federal Alcohol Control Service in One Month," Interfax, 13 November 2008.

11. Alena Chechel', Sof'ia Korepanova, and Filipp Sterkin, "Alkogol'niy organ" [Alcohol body], *Vedomosti*, No. 215, 13 November 2008.

12. Wilson, *Bureaucracy*, 179–95.

13. Mentyukova, "Otvetstvennogo za alkogol'niy krizis sozdadut s nulya."

14. Ignatova, "Uprava na vodku."

15. Sofia Zyryanova, "Aleksey Gordeyev ukhodit s polya" [Aleksey Gordeyev leaves the stage], *Trud*, No. 28, 17 February 2009, 3.

16. Ignatova, "Uprava na vodku."

17. Ukaz Prezidenta Rossiyskoy Federatsii [Decree of the president of the Russian Federation] No. 1883 "Ob obrazovanii Federal'noy sluzhby po regulirovaniyu alkogol'nogo rynka" [On the formation of the Federal Agency for Regulating the Alcohol Market], 31 December 2008, *Sobraniye zakonodatel'stva Rossiyskoy Federatsii*, No. 1, 5 January 2009, article 95, 350–51.

18. Postanovleniye Pravitel'stva Rossiyskoy Federatsii No. 154 "O Federal'noy sluzhbe po regulirovaniyu alkogol'nogo rynka" [On the Federal Service for Regulating the Alcohol Market], *Sobraniye zakonodatel'stva Rossiyskoy Federatsii*, No. 9, 2 March 2009, article 1119, 2692–93.

19. Nina Petlyanova, "Soobrazili na svoikh" [Divided up between themselves], *Novaya gazeta*, No. 23, 4 March 2011.

20. Natalia Travkina, presentation at "Situatsiya na alkogol'nom rinke: perviye itogi zakonodatel'nykh izmeneniy" [The situation on the alcohol market: Initial results of the legislative changes] (press conference, RIA Novosti Press Centre, Moscow, 19 October 2012), accessed 11 November 2014, http://pressria.ru/media/20121019/600926565.html.

21. "Tema discussiya: Vodku zapretyat?" [Theme of discussion: Will vodka be banned?], *Otkritaya Studiya* [Open Studio], Kanal 5 [Channel 5], 14 January 2011, accessed 12 November 2014, http://www.5-tv.ru/programs/broadcast/506106/?page=1#c174196.

22. Pyotr Mordasov, "Lobbizm krepkiy, vyderzhanniy" [Robust, vintage lobbying], *Nezavisimaya gazeta*, 15 April 2011.

23. Quoted in Petlyanova, "Soobrazili na svoikh."

24. Petlyanova, "Soobrazili na svoikh."

25. Ovcharova and Travkina, "Problemy litsenzirovaniya na alkogol'nom rynkye," 143. This in itself is an interesting finding, given that the independence of the Russian judiciary from the state is often called into question. These cases would appear to support Kathryn Hendley's finding that the arbitration courts are generally prepared to defend private enterprises against the state: interference from political authorities in the judicial process is the exception rather than the rule. Hendley, "The Role of Law," 95, 98.

26. Petlyanova, "Soobrazili na svoikh."

27. Elena Ovcharova, presentation at "Situatsiya na alkogol'nom rinke: perviye itogi zakonodatel'nykh izmeneniy" [The situation on the alcohol market: Initial results of the legislative changes] (press conference, RIA Novosti Press Centre, Moscow, 19 October 2012), accessed 11 November 2014, http://pressria.ru/media/20121019/600926565 .html.

28. In the cases described by Ovcharova and Travkina, RAR takes over a month at best, and several months at worst, to act on the court judgment and eventually issue the license.

29. Ovcharova and Travkina, "Problemy litsenzirovaniya na alkogol'nom rynkye," 138.

30. On *reiderstvo*, see Ledeneva, *Can Russia Modernise?*, 188–94; Mesquita, "Reiderstvo."

31. Ledeneva, *Can Russia Modernise?*, 189.

32. Ibid., 190–91; Michael Rochlitz, "The Raider and the Modernizer."

33. Quoted in Nina Petlyanova, "Soobrazili na svoikh."

34. Ibid.

35. "Alcohol Market Regulator Charged with Abuse of Competition," *FK-Novosti* (English version), 14 December 2010.

36. Oleg Trutnev, "'OST-Alko' nakapalo Viktoru Zubkovu na Rosalkogolregulirovaniye" [OST-Alko complained to Viktor Zubkov about Rosalkogolregulirovaniye], *Kommersant*, No. 226, 7 December 2010, 12.

37. Ibid.

38. Rafail Bikmukhametov, "FAS zashchishchaet alkogol" [FAS protects alcohol], *Ekonomika i zhizn'*, No. 23, 17 June 2011, 20.

39. Rosstat, *Tsentral'naya Baza Statisticheskikh Dannykh* [Central Statistical Database], accessed 14 March 2016, http://www.gks.ru.

7. Beer: The New Pretender on the Russian Alcohol Market

1. Other countries traditionally exhibiting the North European pattern include Russia's northeast European neighbors Poland, Ukraine, and the Baltic states, as well as the Nordic countries. Popova et al., "Comparing Alcohol Consumption in Central and Eastern Europe to Other European Countries," 465.

2. Deconinck and Swinnen, "From Vodka to Baltika," 289.

3. Colen and Swinnen, "Beer-Drinking Nations," 130.

4. Deconinck and Swinnen, "From Vodka to Baltika," 289. It is interesting to note that having a large population can make a country a major beer market even if its per capita consumption is relatively low. For example, in 2005 China was the world's largest beer market, accounting for one-fifth of the entire global market, although its per capita consumption was just 24 liters. Colen and Swinnen, "Beer-Drinking Nations," 129.

5. Nemtsov, *Alkogol'naya Istoriya Rossii*, 126.

6. Deconinck and Swinnen, "From Vodka to Baltika," 307, n. 1.

7. Nemtsov, *Alkogol'naya Istoriya Rossii*, 125.

8. Nevertheless, small Russian-owned brewers, which are represented by the "others" category in industry data, have been steadily increasing their market share. Thus, the market share taken by "others" doubled from 13 percent in 2009 to 26 percent in 2015. See Baltika Breweries LLC, *2015 Sustainability Report*, 13.

9. Harper, *Moscow Madness*.

10. Morris, "Drinking to the Nation."

11. Deconinck and Swinnen, "From Vodka to Baltika," 301. For more on the ambiguous evidence with respect to partial advertising bans, see Babor et al., *Alcohol: No Ordinary Commodity*, 194–96.

12. Morris, "Drinking to the Nation," 1387.

13. Deconinck and Swinnen, "From Vodka to Baltika," 302.

14. Ukaz Prezidenta Rossiyskoy Federatsii No. 427 (28 April 1997) "O dopolnitel'nykh merakh po predotvrashcheniyu nezakonnogo proizvodstva i oborota spirta etilovogo i

alkogol'noy produktsii" [Decree of the President of the Russian Federation "On additional measures to prevent illicit production and trafficking ethyl alcohol and alcoholic beverages"], *Sobraniye zakonodatel'stva Rossiyskoy Federatsii*, No. 18, 5 May 1997, article 2134, 3465–66.

15. Deconinck and Swinnen, "From Vodka to Baltika," 305.

16. Tullock, "Rent Seeking."

17. Quoted in "Rynok vodki—eto ogromniy rynok tenevogo kesha dlya regional'nykh elit" [The vodka market is a large market of shady cash for the regional elite], RBC Daily, 26 March 2012, accessed 27 March 2012, http://www.rbcdaily.ru/2012/03/26/market/562949983360637.

18. Multinational spirits producers operating in Russia are represented by the Alcoholic Beverages Committee, which includes such international giants as Bacardi, Diagio, and William Grant & Sons.

19. Orttung, "Business and Politics in the Russian Regions," 49.

20. Quoted in "Rynok vodki."

21. Daucé, "Dzhinsa."

22. FZ No. 15 F-3 "O vnesenii izmeneniy i dopolneniy v Federal'nyy zakon 'O gosudarstvennom regulirovanii proizvodstva i oborota etilovogo spirta i alkogol'noy produktsii'" [On the amendment of federal law "On State Regulation of the Production and Sale of Ethyl Spirit and Alcohol Products"], 10 January 1997, *Sobraniye zakonodatel'stva Rossiyskoy Federatsii*, No. 3, 20 January 1997, article 359, 606–7.

23. Public Chamber of the Russian Federation, *Zloupotreblenie Alkogolem v Rossiyskoy Federatsii*, 66–69.

24. WHO, Country Alcohol Profile: Russian Federation, 2014. Available at http://www.who.int/substance_abuse/publications/global_alcohol_report/profiles/en/ .

25. Mikhail Vorobyov, "Beer Ads Are Going Into the Night—and Also to the Inside Pages of Newspapers and Magazines," *Current Digest of the Russian Press* 56, no. 31 (1 September 2004): 16.

26. Morris, "Drinking to the Nation," 1387, n. 1.

27. *Sobraniye zakonodatel'stva Rossiyskoy Federatsii*, No. 34, article 3530. See also "Russia: Federation Council Votes to Restrict Advertising in Broadcast, Print Media," Interfax, 8 August 2004.

28. "Tema discussiya: Skazhem pivu 'net'?" [Theme of discussion: Should we say "no" to beer?], *Otkritaya Studiya* [Open Studio], Kanal 5 [Channel 5], 4 August 2010, accessed 12 November 2014, https://www.youtube.com/watch?v=YqtB3Z3EKZU.

29. Pipiya Besik, "Vladimir Putin—kryostniy otets 'Baltiki'" [Vladimir Putin is Baltika's godfather], *Nezavisimaya gazeta*, 19 July 2000, http://www.ng.ru/regions/2000-07-19/4_baltika.html.

30. "OAO 'Pivovarennaya kompaniya 'Baltika'—soorganizator 'Kubka Prezidenta Rossii' po dzyudo 2003 goda" [The Baltika brewing company is a co-organizer of the 2003 Russian President's Cup in judo], Baltika (press release), 20 November 2003, http://corporate.baltika.ru/m/3049/oao_piwowarennaya_kompaniya_baltika_-_soorgani.html.

31. Ibid.

32. Besik, "Vladimir Putin—kryostniy otets 'Baltiki.'"

8. The Brewers' Nemesis in the Duma

1. Tatyana Kosobokova, "Kto finansiruyet predvybornuyu kampaniyu 'Yedinoy Rossii'" [Who is financing United Russia's election campaign], RBC Daily, 3 October 2011, reproduced at http://lobbying.ru/content/sections/articleid_7734_linkid_63.html, accessed 27 March 2012; "Rynok vodki—eto ogromniy rynok tenevogo kesha dlya regional'nykh elit" [The vodka market is a large market of shady cash for the regional elite], RBC Daily, 26 March 2012, accessed 27 March 2012, http://www.rbcdaily.ru/2012/03/26/market /562949983360637.

2. "Rynok vodki—eto ogromniy rynok tenevogo kesha dlya regional'nykh elit."

3. Aleksei Polukhin and Olga Osipova, "Vodka so vkusom lobbi" [Vodka with a taste of lobbying], *Novaya gazeta*, No. 33, 30 March 2011, 11.

4. Elizaveta Nikitina, "'V ideale mi dolzhni priyti k kontrafaktomu rinku alkogolya okolo 10 percent'—Deputat Gosdumi Viktor Zvagelskiy" ["Ideally we need to reduce the market for counterfeit alcohol to around 10 percent"—State Duma deputy Viktor Zvagelskiy], Slon.ru, 7 April 2011, accessed 30 November 2014, http://slon.ru/economics /v_ideale_my_dolzhny_priyti_k_kontrafaktnomu_rynku-577891.xhtml.

5. Ilya Zinenko, "FAS khochet oshtrafovat' sozdateley vodka 'Kazyonka'" [FAS wants to fine the founders of the vodka Kazyonka], RB.ru, 5 May 2009, accessed 30 November 2014, http://www.rb.ru/article/fas-hochet-oshtrafovat-sozdateley-vodki-kazyonka /5818737.html.

6. "FAS Rossii oshtrafovala rasprostraniteley reklami vodki 'Kazyonka' pod vidom reklami odnoimennogo fil'ma" [FAS Russia has fined the distributors of an advert for Kazyonka vodka under the guise of an advert for a film of the same name], Fas.gov.ru, 30 March 2010, accessed 8 July 2013, http://www.fas.gov.ru/fas-news/fas-news_29687.html.

7. "A bil li uchreditel'?" [But was he the founder?], *Novaya gazeta*, No. 74, 12 July 2010.

8. Pyotr Lavrov, "Blog Maxima Isayeva: Tsenzura v SMI propakhla vodkoy" [The Maxim Isayev Blog: Press censorship cultivated by vodka], *Moscow Post*, 1 March 2013, accessed 2 June 2013, http://www.moscow-post.ru/redactor/tsenzura_v_smi_propaxla _vodkoj8575/.

9. Polukhin and Osipova, "Vodka so vkusom lobbi."

10. "Rynok vodki—eto ogromniy rynok tenevogo kesha dlya regional'nykh elit."

11. "Tema discussiya: Surrogati vmesto pivo?" [Theme of discussion: Surrogates instead of beer?], *Otkritaya Studiya* [Open Studio], Kanal 5 [Channel 5], 2 August 2011, accessed 12 November 2014, https://www.youtube.com/watch?v=8f1akOpWEbU.

12. "Vodka, chast' 1: Istoriya vserossiyskogo zastol'ya" [Vodka, part 1: The history of the Russian feast], NTV, 8 October 2010, accessed 12 November 2014, https://www .youtube.com/watch?v=lc_N6MxKL7s&spfreload=10.

13. Boris Gryzlov, chairman of the State Duma 29 December 2003–14 December 2011 and parliamentary leader of United Russia for most of this period.

14. "Tema: Sukhoy Zakon" [Theme: Dry law], *Poyedinok* [Duel], *Rossiya-1* [channel Russia-1], 9 December 2010, accessed 12 November 2014, https://www.youtube.com /watch?v=BCPNwkmO3Gk.

15. For an analysis of *cherniy piar* in post-Soviet Russia, see Ledeneva, *How Russia Really Works*, 28–57.

16. Nikitina, "'V ideale mi dolzhni.'"

17. "Tema discussiya: Surrogati vmesto pivo?" [Theme of discussion: Surrogates instead of beer?], *Otkritaya Studiya* [Open Studio], Kanal 5 [Channel 5], 2 August 2011, accessed 12 November 2014, https://www.youtube.com/watch?v=8f1akOpWEbU.

18. Irina Novoselova, "Deputatskaya artel" [A deputy's artel], Vek.ru, 29 April 2010, accessed 11 November 2013, http://wek.ru/deputatskaya-artel.

19. "Tema discussiya: Surrogati vmesto pivo?"

20. "Sud otkazal v udovletvorenii iska SRP k Zvagel'skomu" [Court has dismissed SRP's lawsuit against Zvagelskiy], Foodmarkets.ru, 31 March 2011, accessed 8 June 2013, http://foodmarkets.ru/news/topic/4026.

21. Rafail Bikmukhametov, "Rossii'skoe pivo ob'iavili surrogatom" [Russian beer declared as surrogate], *Ekonomika i zhizn'*, No. 6, 18 February 2011.

9. "Vodka Is Our Enemy, but Who Said We're Afraid of Enemies?"

1. Schrad, *Vodka Politics*, 77–78.

2. Public Chamber of the Russian Federation, *Zloupotreblenie Alkogolem v Rossiyskoy Federatsii*, 40.

3. Dafflon, *Youth in Russia—The Portrait of a Generation in Transition*. It should be noted that the term "alcoholism" is used in common Russian parlance to refer not to a medical condition as in the West but high alcohol consumption in general.

4. As one would expect, estimating the size of the illegal alcohol market is a difficult task. There are no official state statistics on this. The Accounting Chamber of the Russia Federation estimated in 2007 that illegal spirits accounted for up to 50 percent of the Russian market. The chamber's estimate for 2012 was "just" 30 percent, but this rose to over 50 percent for 2013 following a rise in excise duty that year. Some wildly varying estimates were reported in 2015: RAR put the share of the illegal spirits market at just 22.5 percent, while the chair of Russia's upper house of parliament cited expert estimates that put illegal production at 65 percent (although the sources were not given). See respectively: "SP: Situatsiya s neligal'nym alkogolem v RF ne uluchshayetsya" [Accounting Chamber: The situation with illegal alcohol in the RF is not improving], *RBK Daily*, 22 June 2007, accessed on 1 December 2014, http://top.rbc.ru/society/22/06/2007/107231 .shtml; "Nam i dvesti po plechu" [We can shoulder two hundred], *Rossiyskaya gazeta*, 28 February 2014, accessed 19 September 2015, https://rg.ru/2014/02/28/spirtnoe.html; "Dolya nelegal'nogo krepkogo alkogolya v RF sostavlyaet 22,5%" [The share of illegal strong alcohol in the RF is 22.5%], TASS, 25 November 2015, accessed 19 June 2016, http://tass.ru/ekonomika/2471766; "Matviyenko: dolya legal'no proizvedennogo v 2015 g. alkogolya snizilas' do 35%" [Matviyenko: The share of legally manufactured alcohol fell to 35% in 2015], TASS, 25 November 2016, accessed on 19 June 2016, http://tass.ru /politika/2470191.

5. See, for example, statement by the Ministry of Health and Social Development, reported in "Over 3 Million Russians Abuse Drugs and Alcohol—Ministry," Itar-Tass, 12 November 2008; and Medvedev's speech at the Sochi meeting, "Nachalo soveshchaniya o merakh po snizheniyu potrebleniya alkogolya v Rossii" [The start of

discussions on measures to reduce alcohol consumption in Russia], Kremlin.ru, 12 August 2009, accessed 13 August 2009, http://news.kremlin.ru/transcripts/5171.

6. Nemtsov, *Alkogol'naya Istoriya Rossii*, 235–59.

7. Bobrova, "Gender Differences in Drinking Practices in Middle Aged and Older Russians," 573.

8. World Health Organization, 2014 Country Alcohol Profiles. Available at http://www.who.int/substance_abuse/publications/global_alcohol_report/profiles/en/

9. FOM (Public Opinion Fund), "Otnosheniye k povysheniyu tsen na vodku" [Attitudes to the increase in vodka prices], 9–10 June 2012, accessed 12 September 2012, http://fom.ru/obshchestvo/10569.

10. McKee and Rose, *Smoking and Drinking in Russia, Ukraine and Belarus*, 9.

11. The WHO data on abstention rates in 2000 are given in the 2010 edition of the Country Alcohol Profiles.

12. Public Chamber of the Russian Federation, *Zloupotreblenie Alkogolem v Rossiyskoy Federatsii*, 44.

13. Nikolayeva, "Opyt sotsiologicheskogo izucheniya sotsial'no-priemlemykh praktik alkogol'nogo potrebleniya v Pskovskoy oblasti," 175.

14. Gusfield, *Symbolic Crusade*.

15. Levada, "Homo Praevaricatus: Russian Doublethink."

16. Ledeneva defines blat as "the use of personal networks and informal contacts to obtain goods and services in short supply and to find a way around formal procedures." The concept is very much particular to the Soviet economy, which was highly bureaucratized and suffered from shortages of many consumer goods. Ledeneva, *Russia's Economy of Favours*, 1–4.

17. Ibid., 60.

18. VTsIOM (The All-Russian Centre for the Study of Public Opinion), "Popravki v zakon ob oborote alkogolya: Obshchestvennaya otsenka" [Changes to the law on circulation of alcohol: Public appraisal], press release No. 1849, 26 September 2011, accessed 12 September 2012, http://wciom.ru/index.php?id=459&uid=112019.

19. Yury Levada, "Homo Praevaricatus," 314.

20. Ibid., 320.

21. Segal, *The Drunken Society*, 100–102.

22. McKee and Rose, *Smoking and Drinking in Russia, Ukraine and Belarus*, 12–13.

23. VTsIOM, "Popravki v zakon ob oborote alkogolya."

24. The pollster's question incorrectly stated that the provision applied to both beer and premixed cocktails, whereas in fact it applies only to the latter. This misconception was also widely reproduced in the national press.

25. Gusfield, *Contested Meanings*, 4.

26. The term "managed democracy" was used by Kremlin spin doctors early on in Putin's first presidential term, and has since become a common scholarly characterization of the political system that has emerged under Putin. See Lipman and McFaul, "'Managed democracy' in Russia: Putin and the Press"; Sakwa, *Putin: Russia's Choice*, 116. On the creation of "virtual" opposition, see Wilson, *Virtual Politics*, 33–48, 260–65.

27. Treisman, *The Return*, 240–61.

28. Zudin, "Rezhim V. Putina: konturi novoy politicheskoy sistemi," 69.

29. Ibid., 75.

30. Diana Khachatryan, "Sukhoy larok" [Dry stall], *Novaya gazeta*, No. 73, 8 July 2011.

31. "Populizm ili real'naya bor'ba za zdorov'ye natsii? Pivo predlagayut priravnyat' k alkogolyu" [Populism, or a genuine fight for the health of the nation? It is proposed to reclassify beer as alcohol], 99.6 Finam FM, 11 May 2010, accessed 12 November 2014, https://www.youtube.com/watch?v=Y_Z_HynDn0w&spfreload=10.

32. Andrew Roth, "Desperate Measures: History Shows That Heightened Excise Taxes on Alcohol Can Have Severe Political Repercussions," *Russia Profile*, 8 April 2011.

33. "Tema discussiya: Surrogati vmesto pivo?" [Theme of discussion: Surrogates instead of beer?], *Otkritaya Studiya* [Open Studio], Kanal 5 [Channel 5], 2 August 2011, accessed on 12 November 2014, https://www.youtube.com/watch?v=8f1akOpWEbU.

10. From Illegality to Demography: Alcohol Policy Paradigms

1. Gusfield, *Contested Meanings*, 4.

2. Mauss, "Science, Social Movements, and Cynicism," 188.

3. Gusfield, *Contested Meanings*, 12.

4. Ibid., 5–12.

5. Boris Yeltsin, "Perekryt kran spirtovoi kontrabandi: Radioobrashcheniye Prezidenta Rossiyskoy Federatsii B. N. Yeltsina" [Turn off the tap of alcohol contraband: Radio address of president of the Russian Federation Boris Yeltsin], *Rossiyskaya gazeta*, 13 September 1997, 1–2.

6. Simpura and Moskalewicz, "Alcohol Policy in Transitional Russia," 40.

7. Ibid., 45.

8. Nemtsov, *Alkogol'naya Istoriya Rossii*, 120.

9. Simpura and Moskalewicz, "Alcohol Policy in Transitional Russia," 45.

10. Yury Zarakhovich, "Russian 'Water,' Machismo and National Decay," *Eurasia Daily Monitor* 6, no. 137 (17 July 2009).

11. For a summary of the scientific evidence at the end of the 1990s, see McKee, "Alcohol in Russia."

12. Like "social problems," the identification of certain demographic trends as constituting a "demographic crisis" is a matter of interpretation. The notion of a "demographic crisis" is thus a social construct.

13. Vishnevsky and Bobylev, *National Human Development Report Russian Federation 2008*, 51.

14. Ibid., 18.

15. Ibid., 59–66.

16. Khaltourina and Korotayev, "Alcohol and Narcotics as Factors of the Demographic Crisis," 21. The major role played by alcohol in Russia's high rate of deaths from external causes is also evidenced by the dramatic decline in such mortality during the antialcohol campaign of the Gorbachev era. During the campaign, alcohol consumption fell by 25 percent, and at the same time male mortality rates fell by 12 percent. Male mortality from accidents and violence decreased by 36 percent, from alcohol poisoning

by 56 percent, and from pneumonia by 40 percent. After the antialcohol campaign came to an end, these indicators once again rose sharply. Ibid. See also Leon et al., "Huge Variation in Russian Mortality Rates 1984–94."

17. Nemtsov, *Alkogol'naya Istoriya Rossii*, 266.

18. Ibid., 269.

19. Andrey Korotayev and Daria Khaltourina, "Russkiy vodochnyy krest" [The Russian vodka cross], *Ekspert*, 8 May 2006, 78.

20. This early history of RAOZ is related by Demin himself in Demin and Demina, "Opyt grazhdanskogo obshchestva v reshenii problemy zloupotrebleniya alkogolyem v Rossiyskoy Federatsii," 361.

21. Demin, *Alkogol' i zdorov'ye naseleniya Rossii, 1900–2000.*

22. In Russian state policymaking, a *kontseptsiya* or "policy concept" is a short document outlining the main strategy and aims of government policy in a particular area. *Kontseptsii* typically establish long-term goals over a set period of time, often a decade.

23. There is virtually no information about this project in the public domain; searches of the Eastview database indicate that its development was never reported in the press, and no respondents mentioned it. I became aware of its existence only because of a brief mention of it by industry expert Pavel Shapkin at a press conference. "Situatsiya na alkogol'nom rinke: perviye itogi zakonodatel'nykh izmeneniy" [The situation on the alcohol market: Initial results of the legislative changes], press conference, RIA Novosti Press Centre, Moscow, 19 October 2012, accessed 11 November 2014, http://pressria.ru/media/20121019/600926565.html.

24. Nemtsov, *Alkogol'naya Istoriya Rossii*, 288.

25. Roizen, "How Does the Nation's 'Alcohol Problem' Change from Era to Era?," 61.

26. Rebrykov, "O vliyanii zakonodatel'stva na potrebleniye alkogolya v Rossii," 144.

27. Oleg Shchedrov, "Russia's Medvedev Praises Gorbachev's Anti-alcohol Campaign," Reuters, 17 July 2009.

28. "Rozhdeniye sverkhnovoy" [Birth of a supernova], interview with Andrey Yakovlev, *Ekspert-Ural*, No. 18 (190), 16 May 2005, accessed 28 November 2014, http://www.expert-ural.com/25-0-3155/.

29. Vladimir Shlapentokh, "Russia's Demographic Decline and the Public Reaction," 951.

30. Ibid., 956.

31. Vladimir Velikovskiy, "Russkiy krest" [Russian cross], interview with Sergey Zakharov, *Politicheskiy zhurnal*, No. 13 (16), 12 April 2004, accessed 28 November 2014, http://www.politjournal.ru/index.php?action=Articles&dirid=67&tek=1062&issue=28.

32. "Programma Kommunisticheskoi partii Rossiyskoy Federatsii" [Program of the Communist Party of the Russian Federation], 2008 revision, reproduced in *Sovetskaya Rossiya*, No. 137, 11 December 2008, 2.

33. Nemtsov and Milov, *Putin. Itogi,* 12.

34. Davis, "Commentary: The Health Crisis in the USSR," 1404.

35. Evgeniya Chaykovskaya, "CIA: Russia's Population Statistics Worse Than Official Version," *Moscow News*, 10 October 2011.

36. "Strategy 2020" is the anecdotal name for the updated version of the *Kontseptsiya of Long-Term Socio-economic Development of the Russian Federation until 2020*, prepared in accordance with a 2011 decree of the Russian government.

37. "Kak TsRU i Rosstat informiruyut svoi pravitel'stva" [How the CIA and Rosstat inform their governments], *Nezavisimaya gazeta*, 7 October 2011, 2.

38. "The Kind of Russia We Are Building. Speech by V. V. Putin at the Presentation of the Annual Message from the President of the Russian Federation to the Federal Assembly of the Russian Federation, July 8, 2000, Moscow," *Current Digest of the Post-Soviet Press* 28, no. 52 (9 August 2000), 5.

39. *Sobraniye zakonodatel'stva Rossiyskoy Federatsii*, No. 40, 1 October 2001, 8655–61.

40. Shlapentokh, "Russia's Demographic Decline and the Public Reaction," 957.

41. "Message to the Federal Assembly of the Russian Federation. Text of President Vladimir Putin's Address to the Deputies of the Federal Assembly, Delivered in the Kremlin on April 25, 2005," *Current Digest of the Post-Soviet Press* 17, no. 57 (25 May 2005), 5.

42. Ibid., 955–56.

43. Ibid., 957.

44. "Rezolyutsiya Tserkovno-obshchestvennogo foruma 'Dukhovno-nravstvenniye osnovi demograficheskogo razvitiya Rossii'" [Resolution of the Church-Public Forum "The spiritual and moral basis of Russian demographic development"], 18–19 October 2004. Reproduced on Sedmitza.ru, website of the Church-Academic Centre "Orthodox Encyclopaedia," accessed 17 November 2014, http://www.sedmitza.ru/text/429865.html.

45. "Poslaniye V. Putina Federal'nomu Sobraniyu Rossiyskoy Federatsii" [V. Putin's address to the Federal Assembly of the Russian Federation], *Stolitsa plius*, 13 May 2006.

46. Kim Murphy, "The Vanishing Russians: A Dying Population," *Los Angeles Times*, 8 October 2006.

47. *Sobraniye zakonodatel'stva Rossiyskoy Federatsii*, No. 42, 15 October 2007, 10382–91.

48. According to official data, this target was met early. Average life expectancy exceeded seventy years for the first time in 2012. *Rossiyskiy statisticheskiy yezhegodnik 2014* (*Russian Statistical Yearbook 2014*) (Moscow: Rosstat), table 4.20, 88.

49. "Improvement of Demographic Situation Is Russia's Main Task—Zubkov," Itar-Tass, 17 January 2008.

50. "Russia Government Sets Population Growth as Top Priority," Itar-Tass, 29 November 2012.

51. Most notably, in 2007 maternity benefits were significantly increased and a maternal capital (*materinskiy kapital*) program was introduced, whereby mothers were granted a lump sum equivalent to a few thousand dollars upon the birth of a second and subsequent children. Federal law No. 256-F3 of 29 December 2006 "O dopolnitel'nykh merakh gosudarstvennoy podderzhki semyey, imeyushchikh detey" [On additional measures of state support for families with children], published in *Rossiyskaya gazeta* No. 297, 31 December 2006, 4.

52. "Message to the Federal Assembly of the Russian Federation," 5.

53. Levintova, "Russian Alcohol Policy in the Making," 502.

11. The New Antialcohol Network

1. The second sentence is a reference to the "Common Cause" program of antialcohol programs and advertising developed by the Russian Orthodox Church and aired on Russia's national TV channel *Perviy Kanal* (First Channel). Nina Petlyanova, "Soobrazili na svoikh" [Divided up between themselves], *Novaya gazeta*, No. 23, 4 March 2011.

2. See Evans Jr., "Vladimir Putin's Design for Civil Society," for a scholarly account of this tendency.

3. Berridge, *Marketing Health*, 167–77.

4. Thom, *Dealing with Drink*, 200.

5. Schrad, *The Political Power of Bad Ideas*, 127.

6. Charles Clover, "Putin and the Monk," *Financial Times*, 26 January 2013.

7. Zygar, *All the Kremlin's Men*, 234.

8. Ibid. While not all models of Russia's informal governing elite include Father Tikhon, some accord him a prominent position. For example, in Evgeniy Gontmakher's "Planets" model of Putin's elite, Father Tikhon appears in the first circle of planets closest to Putin. Cited in Ledeneva, *Can Russia Modernise?*, 59–60.

9. Public Chamber of the Russian Federation, "O Palatye" [About the Chamber], accessed 2 November 2013, http://www.oprf.ru/about.

10. James Richter, "Putin and the Public Chamber."

11. Public Chamber of the Russian Federation, *Zloupotreblenie Alkogolem v Rossiyskoy Federatsii.*

12. Maria-Lousia Tirmaste, "Dmitry Medvedev posovyetuyetsya s prezidentom" [Dmitry Medvedev seeks presidential advice] *Kommersant*, 8 September 2010, accessed 9 November 2014, http://www.kommersant.ru/doc/1499877?fp=.

13. Andrey Korotayev and Daria Khaltourina, "Russkiy vodochnyy krest" [The Russian vodka cross], *Ekspert*, 8 May 2006, 72–78.

14. Ibid., 75.

15. "Tok-shou Obshcheye Delo: detskiy alkogolizm" [Talk show Common Cause: Child alcoholism], *Perviy Kanal* (First Channel), 28 February 2009, accessed 11 November 2014, http://www.1tv.ru/sprojects_editions/si=5761.

16. All of the public service advertisements shown in the winter 2009 campaign can be viewed on the Common Cause website at "Proekt 'Obshchee Delo'. Roliki sotsialnoy reklamy" [The "Common Cause" project. Public service advertisements], Pravoslavie. ru, 18 February 2009, accessed 29 August 2009, http://www.pravoslavie.ru/jurnal/29500 .htm. One important detail that remains unknown is how the partnership with *Perviy Kanal* came about (was it an independent editorial decision by the channel, or was external influence brought to bear?), and who exactly paid for the prime-time advertising space.

17. "Arkhimandrit Tikhon (Shevkunov): 'Razmakh p'yanstva v Rossii nikogda ne bil stol' chudovishchnym'" [Archimandrite Tikhon (Shevkunov): "The extent of alcohol abuse in Russia has never been so terrible."], Pravoslavie.ru, 14 May 2009, accessed 23 July 2009, http://www.pravoslavie.ru/press/30407.htm.

18. Public Chamber of the Russian Federation, *Zloupotreblenie Alkogolem v Rossiyskoy Federatsii*, 12.

19. Ibid., 46–48.

20. "Rezolyutsiya XIII Vsemirnogo russkogo narodnogo sobora 'O neotlozhnykh merakh po zashchitye ot alkogol'noy ugrozy'" [Resolution of the XIII World Russian People's Congress "On urgent measures for protection against the alcohol threat"], 23 May 2009, reproduced at Pravoslaviye.Ru, accessed 17 November 2014, http://www.pravoslavie.ru/news/30515.htm. Pravoslaviye.Ru is a Russian Orthodox web portal run by Father Tikhon Shevkunov.

21. Ibid.

22. Ibid.

23. "Obrashcheniye Kongressa Tserkovno-obshchestvennogo soveta po zashchitye ot alkogol'noy ugrozy k rukovodstvu Rossiyskoy Federatsii" [Appeal of the Congress of the Church-Public Council for protection against the alcohol threat to the leadership of the Russian Federation], 20 February 2012, reproduced at Pravoslaviye.Ru, accessed 14 November 2014, http://www.pravoslavie.ru/jurnal/51689.htm.

24. White, "The Political Parties," 89–90.

25. Lyudmila Alexandrova, "Alliance of State and Church Grows Tighter," ITAR-TASS, 2 June 2010.

26. This strange anomaly was a remnant from Soviet times, when it was decided that pure alcohol (ethanol) for drinking could be legally sold at retail in certain regions of the Far North of Russia, owing to the supposed logistical difficulties of delivering less concentrated forms of alcohol. Amazingly, in spite of the obvious public health risks, this practice was brought to an end only by the 2011 amendment of Law 171.

27. Amending the 2011 alcohol control bill such that beer could no longer be sold in kiosks and other forms of nonstationary outlet. How Zvagelskiy achieved this in spite of substantial opposition from within the government is detailed in chapter 13.

12. Medvedev and the Antialcohol Initiative

1. Nataliya Antipova, "Dmitry Medvedev nachinayet antialkogol'nuyu kampaniyu" [Dmitry Medvedev is starting an antialcohol campaign], *Izvestiya*, 1 July 2009.

2. "Antialkogol'naya kampaniya nomer dva" [Antialcohol campaign number two], *Sankt-Peterburgskiye vedomosti*, 13 August 2009, 3.

3. Andrew Osborn, "Medvedev Risks a Sore Head in War on Vodka Drinking," *Daily Telegraph*, 15 September 2009, 20.

4. Simon Shuster, "Russia's Medvedev Launches a New War on Drinking," *Time*, 23 August 2009, accessed 25 August 2009, http://content.time.com/time/world/article/0,8599,1917974,00.html.

5. "Nachalo soveshchaniya o merakh po snizheniyu potrebleniya alkogolya v Rossii" [The start of discussions on measures to reduce alcohol consumption in Russia], Kremlin.ru, 12 August 2009, accessed 13 August 2009, http://news.kremlin.ru/transcripts/5171.

6. "Excerpts from Transcript of Meeting on Measures to Reduce Alcohol Consumption in Russia," Kremlin.ru, 12 August 2009, accessed 13 August 2009, http://www.kremlin.ru/eng/text/speeches/2009/08/12/1845_type82912type82913_220798.shtml.

7. "Dmitry Medvedev utverdil perechen' porucheniy Pravitel'stvu po itogam soveshchaniya o merakh po snizheniyu potrebleniya alkogolya" [Dmitry Medvedev has approved a list of instructions to the government following the meeting on measures to reduce alcohol consumption], Kremlin.ru, 11 September 2009, accessed 13 March 2010, http://news.kremlin.ru/news/5428.

8. Like the United States, Russia has a federal system of government. There have been eighty-three federal subjects since a merger process of some smaller subjects was completed in 2008. In 2014 the Russian Federation constitutionally adopted Sevastopol and the Republic of Crimea as the eighty-fourth and eighty-fifth federal subjects, but these are still regarded by the international community as part of Ukraine.

9. *Sobraniye Zakonodatel'stva Rossiyskoy Federatsii*, No. 2, 11 January 2010, 777–84.

10. Intriguingly, I have not been able to find any government statement or press report from 2012 or 2013 on whether this target had been met.

11. Vladimir Emel'yanenko, "Rasstrel'naya Komanda" [Firing squad], *Profil'*, No. 47 (602), 15 December 2008, accessed 26 July 2009, http://www.profile.ru/items/?item =27715.

12. "Over 3 Million Russians Abuse Drugs and Alcohol—Ministry," Itar-Tass, 12 November 2008.

13. Medvedev, for example, stated at the Sochi meeting that "our first task should be to stop the rise in alcohol consumption among young people. This is absolutely essential." It is also notable that the first of the Common Cause broadcasts on First Channel was dedicated to underage drinking.

14. Swedish Council for Information on Alcohol and Other Drugs (CAN), *The 2011 ESPAD Report*, 12.

15. "Proveryat' dokumenty pri pokupke alkogolya razreshili zakonodatel'no" [The right to check documents when a customer purchases alcohol has been legally established], *E'konomicheskie novosti*, 21 December 2010.

16. Federal Law No. 253-F3 of 21 July 2011 "On the introduction of amendments to the separate legislative acts of the Russian Federation in respect of strengthening measures to prevent the sale of alcoholic beverages to minors," *Rossiyskaya gazeta*, No. 161, 26 July 2011, 11.

17. FZ No. 193-F3 "O vnesenii izmenyeniy v stat'i 3.5 i 14.16 Kodeksa Rossiyskoy Federatsii ob administrativnykh pravonarusheniyakh" [On the amendment of articles 3.5 and 14.16 of the Code of Administrative Offences of the Russian Federation], 12 November 2012, *Parlamentskaya gazeta*, No. 39, 16 November 2012, 27. See also "Putin Signs Law to Increase Fines for Selling Alcohol to Minors," Interfax, 13 November 2012.

18. Elena Denisenko, "Slovo i delo" [Words and deeds], *Ekspert*, 1 February 2010.

19. Anna Ryabova, "Vladimir Pekarev nal'yot investoram" [Vladimir Pekarev pours for investors], *Kommersant*, No. 124p, 13 July 2009.

20. Irina Parfent'eva, "Propivochniy minimum" [The minimum you can squander on booze], *Kommersant*, No. 196, 25 October 2007.

21. To my knowledge, this document is not in the public domain. A copy of it was passed to me by one of my respondents. I have no reason to doubt that the document is genuine, but at the same time it has not been possible to independently verify its authenticity.

22. Elizaveta Nikitina, "Minfin sobirayetsya vernut' sukhoy zakon" [Ministry of Finance intends to return to prohibition], Slon.ru, 10 June 2010, accessed 2 July 2010, http://www.slon.ru/blogs/nikitina/post/408142/?sphrase_id=66865.

23. Georgiy Panin, "Vodku ostavili v pokoye" [Vodka left in peace], *Rossiyskaya Gazeta*, 1 July 2010.

13. Alcohol Policy as Battleground: The 2011 Alcohol Law

1. Shaun Walker, "End of a Drinking Culture? Russia Accepts That Beer Is Alcoholic," *Independent*, 20 July 2011, accessed http://www.independent.co.uk/life-style/health-and-families/health-news/end-of-a-drinking-culture-russia-accepts-that-beer-is-alcoholic-2317798.html. On the notion that beer could be sold like a soft drink, see "Russia Finally Declares Beer Alcohol, Not Foodstuff," *Huffington Post*, 21 July 2011, accessed http://www.huffingtonpost.com/2011/07/21/russia-declares-beer-alcohol_n_906297.html; Fred Weir, "Why Russia Finally Decided That Beer Is Alcohol," *Christian Science Monitor*, 20 July 2011, accessed https://www.csmonitor.com/World/Europe/2011/0720/Why-Russia-finally-decided-that-beer-is-alcohol.

2. The bill bore the unwieldy title of "On the amendment of the Federal Law 'On the state regulation of production and turnover of ethyl alcohol and alcohol containing products' and repeal of the Federal Law 'On the restriction of retail sale and consumption (drinking) of beer and beverages produced on its basis' (in terms of improving state regulation of production and turnover of ethyl alcohol and alcohol products, as well as beer and beverages, manufactured on its basis)" O vnesenii izmeneniy v Federal'nyy zakon 'O gosudarstvennom regulirovanii proizvodstva i oborota etilovogo spirta, alkogol'niy i spirtosoderzhashchey produktsii' i priznanii utrativshim silu Federal'nogo zakona 'Ob ogranicheniyakh roznichnoy prodazhi i potrebleniya (raspitiya) piva i napitkov, izgotavlivaemyh na ego osnove' (v chasti sovershenstvovaniya gosudarstvennogo regulirovaniya proizvodstva i oborota etilovogo spirta, alkogol'noj i spirtosoderzhashchey produktsii, a takzhe piva i napitkov, izgotavlivaemykh na ego osnovye), 22 July 2011, *Sobraniye zakonodatel'stva Rossiyskoy Federatsii*, No. 30, 25 July 2011 (Part 1), 9538–67.

3. EGAIS (the Unified State Automatic Information System) is the centralized electronic system that records data on alcohol production in individual enterprises and sends them to the government. Alcohol-producing enterprises are required to install the necessary electronic equipment, at considerable cost. The system caused a market crisis when it failed to operate properly when introduced in 2006, leading to halted production and retail shortages, and it has continued to be plagued by technical problems. See chapter 6.

4. The ministries' positions were revealed in internal documents leaked by Elizaveta Nikitina, "Zakon o trezvom budushem" [Law for a sober future], Slon.ru, 2 December 2009, accessed 11 December 2009, http://slon.ru/articles/201384/?sphrase_id=154857.

5. Natal'ya Litvinova, "Proverka na krepost" [Test of strength], *Ekspert*, No. 20 (754), 23 May 2011.

6. Oleg Trutnev, "Pivo popalo v plokhuyu kompaniyu" [Beer's fallen into bad company], *Kommersant*, 25 September 2014, http://www.kommersant.ru/doc/2574343.

7. "Populizm ili real'naya bor'ba za zdorov'e natsii?" 99.6 Finam FM.

8. This was in fact the harmonization of a restriction that most regional governments had already implemented of their own accord: over sixty of Russia's eighty-three federal subjects already had some kind of restrictions on the sale of alcohol at night. Setting a federal norm would compel those that had not introduced such restrictions to do so, while allowing those that had tighter restrictions than the federal norm to retain them. The vast majority of existing regional restrictions applied only to spirits or, at most, to spirits and wine. They did not tend to apply to beer.

9. "Gosduma uzhestochit regulirovaniye alkogol'noy otrasli" [State Duma to toughen regulation of the alcohol industry], *Ekonomicheskiye novosti*, 19 January 2011.

10. Aleksei Batashov, "Strong Beer Restricted in a Not-So-Strong New Law," *Business and Economic Reports*, 25 February 2011.

11. PET stands for polyethylene terephthalate. The acronym PET is commonly used in the packaging industry to refer to packaging—typically bottles—made from this material.

12. Brewing executives claim that Kazakhstan's ban was introduced for protectionist reasons: to protect its domestic producers from cheap Russian competition, and because its ruling elite has interests in the glass industry.

13. Ledeneva, *Can Russia Modernise?*, 253.

14. Litvinova, "Proverka na krepost."

15. Ibid.

16. *Sobraniye zakonodatel'stva Rossiyskoy Federatsii*, No. 30, 25 July 2011 (Part 1): 9538–67.

14. The Campaign Is Over, but the Battle Continues

1. Maria Kunle, "Pivo postavyat na uchyot cherez god" [Beer to be monitored in a year's time], *Vedomosti*, No. 3856, 22 June 2015.

2. Union of Russian Brewers, "Gosduma rassmotrit zakonoproekt o vvedenii EGAIS na pivovarennykh predpriyatiyakh v marte" [State Duma to consider bill on introducing EGAIS to breweries in March], 21 January 2015, http://www.beerunion.ru/press _office/news/18687/.

3. Russian law contains a very strict definition of what constitutes "beer." Beverages that are brewed from over 20 percent nonmalted materials (such as wheat, corn, and rice) are categorized as beer-based beverages. The famous Western brands Guinness, Hoegaarden, and Corona fall into this category.

4. Oleg Trutnev, "Pivo popalo v plokhuyu kompaniyu" [Beer's fallen into bad company], *Kommersant*, 25 September 2014, http://www.kommersant.ru/doc/2574343.

5. "Gosduma otklonila zakonoproekt o litsenzirovanii proizvodstva i oborota piva i pivnykh napitkov" [The State Duma has rejected a bill on licensing the production and circulation of beer and beer-based beverages], Profibeer.ru, 28 September 2015, accessed 1 October 2015, http://profibeer.ru/main/6503/.

6. The original version of bill No. 280796-6 would have banned all alcohol from sale in PET containers of any size. The government's official response (dated 16 Decem-

ber 2013) proposed a ban on alcohol in PET containers larger than 1.5 liters, and to "consider" putting a limit on the strength of beverages allowed to be sold in PET containers. The revised version of bill No. 280796-6 (which actually passed first reading in the Duma on 10 June 2014) provided for an eventual ban on the retail sale of alcohol over 4 percent abv in PET containers altogether, and under 4 percent abv only in containers of 0.5 liters or less.

7. Maria Kunle, "Pivovarov lishayut plastikovoy tary" [Brewers deprived of plastic containers], *Vedomosti*, 9 June 2015, https://www.vedomosti.ru/business/articles/2015/06 /09/595728-pivovarov-lishayut-plastikovoi-tari.

8. "MER: zapret PET-tary mozhet privesti k rostu bezrabotitsy" [MER: A ban on PET containers could lead to a rise in unemployment], RIA Novosti, 24 August 2015, accessed 26 August 2015, http://ria.ru/economy/20150824/1203955266.html#ixzz3o1m5smyk.

9. "Soyuz Rossiyskikh Pivovarov: Prinyatoye ogranicheniye ob'yoma PET-tary—eto razumnyy kompromiss, dostignutyy v dialoge pivovarov s gosudarstvom" [Union of Russian Brewers: The adoption of restrictions on the volume of PET containers is a reasonable compromise, arrived at through dialogue between brewers and the government], Union of Russian Brewers press release, 24 June 2016, accessed 22 August 2016, http:// beerunion.ru/press_office/press_releases/21593/.

10. *Sobraniye zakonodatel'stva Rossiyskoy Federatsii*, No. 26, 27 June 2016, article 3871.

11. Interfax, "Proizvoditeli PET obsudyat posledstviya vvedeniya zapreta plastikovoy upakovki dlya piva," 16 February 2015, http://www.interfax-russia.ru/Moscow/news .asp?id=583285&sec=1668.

12. Anna Zmanovskaya, "Minpromtorg khochet vernut' alkogol' na stadioni I v kioski" [Minpromtorg wants to return alcohol to stadiums and kiosks], *Izvestia*, 15 January 2016.

13. Oleg Trutnev, "Pivo otdelyat ot vodki" [Separating beer from vodka], *Kommersant*, No. 212, 16 November 2016, 7

Conclusion: What Alcohol Tells Us about Russian Politics

1. On the scope for synthesis by combining several theories of the policy process, see Cairney, *Understanding Public Policy*, 265–89.

2. Dearing and Rogers, *Agenda Setting*, 1–2.

3. Rent seeking is not "unnatural" or "deviant" economic behavior but a logical consequence of profit seeking, the behavior that underpins the capitalist order. A purely competitive market does not offer large profits—indeed, in economic theory, in a perfectly competitive market, no firm makes a profit, since another firm will always enter the market to capture a share of any available profit. It is therefore in companies' interests to try to eliminate or restrict competition artificially. Thus, the profit motive that underpins free markets at the same time serves to undermine those markets. The costs of lobbying represent a social loss because they are nonproductive; that is, they do not create wealth but consume it. See Simmons, *Beyond Politics*, 187–89.

4. Cairney, *Understanding Public Policy*, 204.

5. Nordlinger, *On the Autonomy of the Democratic State*, 7–8.

6. Cairney, *Understanding Public Policy*, 180–81, 203; Sabatier, "An Advocacy Coalition Framework," 131; Jenkins-Smith et al., "The Advocacy Coalition Framework," 191.

7. Andrey Korotayev and Daria Khaltourina, "Russkiy vodochnyy krest" [The Russian vodka cross], *Ekspert*, 8 May 2006, 76.

8. Ledeneva, *Can Russia Modernise?*, 223.

Bibliography

Accounting Chamber of the Russian Federation. "Otchyot o rezul'tatakh kontrol'nogo meropriyatiya 'Proverka effektivnosti ispol'zovaniya federal'noy sobstvennosti, peredannoy federal'nomu gosud arstvennomu unitarnomu predpriyatiyu "Rosspirtprom", za 2005–2006 gody'" [Report on the results of the inspection measure "Audit of the efficiency of the use of federal property transferred to the Federal State Unitary Enterprise 'Rosspirtprom,' for 2005–2006"], 2008.

Accounting Chamber of the Russian Federation. "Otchyot o rezul'tatakh proverki effektivnosti i tselesoobraznosti upravleniya FGUP 'Rosspirtprom', v tom chisel obespecheniya postupleniy chaste pribyli, ostayushcheysya posle uplaty nalogov i inykh obyazatel'nykh platezhey, v federal'niy byudzhet, a takzhe effektivnosti i tselesoobraznosti uchrezhdeniya i upravleniya dochernimi predpriyatiyami" [Report on the results of the audit of the effectiveness and appropriateness of the management of FSUE "Rosspirtprom," including revenue generation of the profits remaining after payment of taxes and other obligatory payments to the federal budget, as well as the effectiveness and appropriateness of the establishment and management of subsidiary companies], 2003.

Babor, Thomas. *Alcohol: No Ordinary Commodity: Research and Public Policy.* Oxford: Oxford University Press, 2010.

Baltika Breweries LLC. "Sustainability Report 2015." Available at http://eng.baltika.ru /i/msg/7326/baltika_sustainability_report_2015.pdf.

Barnes, Andrew. *Owning Russia. The Struggle over Factories, Farms, and Power.* Ithaca, NY: Cornell University Press, 2006.

Berridge, Virginia. *Marketing Health: Smoking and the Discourse of Public Health in Britain, 1945–2000.* Oxford: Oxford University Press, 2007.

Black, John, Nigar Hashimzade, and Gareth D. Myles., eds. *A Dictionary of Economics.* 4th ed. Oxford: Oxford University Press, 2012.

Bobrova, Natalia, Robert West, Darya Malyutina, Sofia Malyutina, and Martin Bobak. "Gender Differences in Drinking Practices in Middle Aged and Older Russians." *Alcohol and Alcoholism* 45, no. 6 (2010): 573–80.

Bunton, R. "Regulating Our Favourite Drug." In *New Directions in the Sociology of Health*, edited by P. Abbott and G. Payne, 104–17. London: Falmer, 1990.

Cairney, Paul. *Understanding Public Policy: Theories and Issues.* New York: Palgrave Macmillan, 2012.

Christian, David. *Living Water: Vodka and Russian Society on the Eve of Emancipation.* Oxford: Clarendon, 1990.

Cohen, Stephen. *Bukharin and the Bolshevik Revolution: A Political Biography, 1888–1938.* Oxford: Oxford University Press, 1980.

Colen, Liesbeth, and Johan F. M. Swinnen. "Beer-Drinking Nations: The Determinants of Global Beer Consumption." In *The Economics of Beer*, edited by Johan F. M. Swinnen, 123–39. Oxford: Oxford University Press, 2011.

Connor, Walter D. "Alcohol and Soviet Society." *Slavic Review* 30, no. 3 (1971): 570–88.

Cook, Philip J., and Michael J. Moore. "The Economics of Alcohol Abuse and Alcohol-Control Policies." *Health Affairs* 21, no. 2 (2002): 120–33.

Dafflon, Denis. *Youth in Russia—The Portrait of a Generation in Transition.* Bienne, Switzerland: Swiss Academy for Development, 2009. Accessed 20 July 2009. http://www .sad.ch/images/stories/Publikationen/sad-youth-in-russia.pdf.

Daucé, Françoise. "Dzhinsa." In *Global Encyclopaedia of Informality: Towards an Understanding of Social and Cultural Complexity*, Vol. 2, edited by A. Ledeneva, 284–87. London: UCL Press, 2018.

Davis, Christopher. "Commentary: The Health Crisis in the USSR: Reflections on the Nicholas Eberstadt 1981 Review of *Rising Infant Mortality in the USSR in the 1970s*." *International Journal of Epidemiology* 35, no. 6 (2006): 1400–1405.

Dawisha, Karen. *Putin's Kleptocracy.* New York: Simon and Schuster, 2015.

Dearing, J. W., and E. M. Rogers. *Agenda Setting.* London: Sage, 1996.

Deconinck, Koen, and Johan F. M. Swinnen. "From Vodka to Baltika: A Perfect Storm in the Russian Beer Market." In *The Economics of Beer*, edited by Johan F. M. Swinnen, 288–307. Oxford: Oxford University Press, 2011.

Demin, A. K., ed. *Alkogol' i zdorov'ye naseleniya Rossii, 1900–2000* [Alcohol and the health of the Russian population, 1900–2000]. Moscow: Russian Association for Public Health, 1998.

Demin, A. K., and I. A. Demina. "Opyt grazhdanskogo obshchestva v reshenii problemy zloupotrebleniya alkogolyem v Rossiyskoy Federatsii: deyatel'nost' Rossiyskoy assotsiatsii obshchestvennogo zdorov'ya" [The experience of civil society in resolving the problem of alcohol abuse in the Russian Federation: The activity of the Russian Association for Public Health]. In *Alkogol'naya Katastrofa i vozmozhnosti gosudarst-vennoy politiki v preodolenii alkogol'noy sverkhsmertnocti v Rossii* [The alcohol crisis and possibilities for state policy to overcome alcohol-related hypermortality in Russia], edited by D. A. Khaltourina and A. V. Korotayev, 356–72. Moscow: The Russian Academy of the State Service to the President of the Russian Federation, 2008.

Downs, Anthony. *Inside Bureaucracy*. Boston: Little, Brown, 1967.

Eberstadt, Nicholas. "Drunken Nation: Russia's Depopulation Bomb." American Enterprise Institute for Public Policy Research, 2 April 2009. Accessed 1 June 2009. http://www.aei.org/article/100331.

———. "The Health Crisis in the USSR." *New York Review of Books*. 1981. Reprinted in *International Journal of Epidemiology* 35, no. 6 (2006): 1384–94.

———. "Russia's Peacetime Demographic Crisis: Dimensions, Causes, Implications." The National Bureau of Asian Research, NBR Project Report, May 2010.

Eberstadt, Nicholas, and Apoorva Shah. "Russia's Demographic Disaster." *Russian Outlook*. American Enterprise Institute for Public Policy Research, May 2009. Accessed 1 June 2009. http://www.aei.org/docLib/RO percent20Special percent20Edition percent20Eberstadt-g.pdf.

Evans, Alfred B., Jr. "Vladimir Putin's Design for Civil Society." In *Russian Civil Society: A Critical Assessment*, edited by Alfred B. Evans Jr., Laura A. Henry, and Lisa McIntosh Sundstrom, 147–58. New York: M. E. Sharpe, 2006.

Fituni, Leonid. "Economic Crime in the Context of Transition to a Market Economy." In *Economic Crime in Russia*, edited by Alena Ledeneva and Marina Kurkchiyan, 17–30. London: Kluwer Law International, 2000.

Forsyth, Gillian. "Samizdat." In *Global Encyclopaedia of Informality: Towards an Understanding of Social and Cultural Complexity*, Vol. 1, edited by A. Ledeneva, 250–53. London: UCL Press, 2018.

Frye, Timothy. "Capture or Exchange? Business Lobbying in Russia." *Europe-Asia Studies* 54, no. 7 (2002): 1017–36.

Gaidar Institute for Economic Policy. "Analiz tekushchego sostoyaniya nalogooblozheniya alkogol'noy otrasli v Rossii i otsenka posledstviy povysheniya stavok aktsiza na alkogol'nuyu produktsiyu" [Analysis of the current taxation structure of the alcohol industry in Russia and assessment of the consequences of the increase in excise rates on alcoholic products]. PowerPoint presentation, October 2011, Gaidar Institute for Economic Policy, Moscow.

———. "Issledovaniye aktsiznoy nagruzki na otdel'niye kategorii alkogol'nykh produktov (vino, pivo, krepkiy alkogol') v raznykh stranakh mira" [Study of the excise burden on separate categories of alcoholic products (wine, beer, spirits) in various countries worldwide]. PowerPoint presentation, June 2013, Gaidar Institute for Economic Policy, Moscow.

Galeotti, Mark. "The Mafiya and the New Russia." *Australian Journal of Politics and History* 44, no. 3 (1998): 415–29.

Gil, Artyom, Olga Polikina, Natalia Koroleva, David A. Leon, and Martin McKee. "Alcohol Policy in a Russian Region: A Stakeholder Analysis." *European Journal of Public Health* 20, no. 5 (2010): 588–94.

Gorbachev, Mikhail. *Zhizn' i reformy, kniga 1.* Moscow: Novosti, 1995.

Gusfield, Joseph R. *Contested Meanings: The Construction of Alcohol Problems.* Madison: University of Wisconsin Press, 1996.

——. *Symbolic Crusade: Status Politics and the American Temperance Movement.* Urbana: University of Illinois Press, 1963.

Handelman, Stephen. *Comrade Criminal: Russia's New Mafiya.* New Haven, CT: Yale University Press, 1995.

Harper, Timothy. *Moscow Madness: Crime, Corruption, and One Man's Pursuit of Profit in the New Russia.* London: McGraw-Hill, 1999.

Heath, Dwight B. "Why We Don't Know More about the Social Benefits of Moderate Drinking." *Annals of Epidemiology* 17 (2007): S71–S74.

Hellman, Joel S., Geraint Jones, and Daniel Kaufmann. "Seize the State, Seize the Day: State Capture and Influence in Transition Economies." *Journal of Comparative Economics* 31 (2003): 751–73.

Hendley, Kathryn. "The Role of Law." In *Return to Putin's Russia: Past Imperfect, Future Uncertain.* 5th ed., edited by Stephen K. Wegren, 83–102. Lanham, MD: Rowman and Littlefield, 2013.

Herlihy, Patricia. *The Alcoholic Empire: Vodka and Politics in Late Imperial Russia.* Oxford: Oxford University Press, 2002.

Himelstein, Linda. *The King of Vodka: The Story of Pyotr Smirnov and the Upheaval of an Empire.* New York: Harper Collins, 2009.

Hoffman, David E. *The Oligarchs: Wealth and Power in the New Russia.* New York: Public Affairs, 2002.

Hough, Jerry F., and Merle Fainsod. *How the Soviet Union Is Governed.* Cambridge, MA: Harvard University Press, 1979.

Institut Sotsiologii Rossiyskoy Akademii Nauk [Sociological Institute of the Russian Academy of Sciences]. *Potrebleniye alkogolya v Rossii. Sotsiologicheskiy analiz* [Alcohol consumption in Russia: A sociological analysis], *Informatsionno-analiticheskiy byulleten'* No. 1. Moscow: Institut sotsiologii RAN, 2011.

Ivanets, N. N., and M. I. Lukomskaya. "The USSR's New Alcohol Policy." *World Health Forum* 11, no. 3 (1990): 246–52.

Jargin, Sergei V. "On the Causes of Alcoholism in the Former Soviet Union." *Alcohol & Alcoholism* 45, no. 1 (2010): 104–5.

Jenkins-Smith, Hank C., Daniel Nohrstedt, Christopher M. Weible, and Paul A. Sabatier. "The Advocacy Coalition Framework: Foundations, Evolution, and Ongoing Research." In *Theories of the Policy Process.* 3rd ed., edited by Paul A. Sabatier and Christopher M. Weible, 183–222. Boulder, CO: Westview Press, 2014.

Khaltourina, Daria A., and Andrey V. Korotayev. "Alcohol and Narcotics as Factors of the Demographic Crisis." *Sociological Research* 47, no. 3 (2008): 18–31.

——. *Alkogol'naya Katastrofa i vozmozhnosti gosudarstvennoy politiki v preodolenii alkogol'noy sverkhsmertnocti v Rossii* [The alcohol crisis and possibilities for state policy to overcome alcohol-related hypermortality in Russia]. Moscow: The Russian Academy of the State Service to the President of the Russian Federation, 2008.

——. "Potential for Alcohol Policy to Decrease the Mortality Crisis in Russia." *Evaluation & the Health Professions* 31, no. 3 (2008): 272–81.

Korolenko, Caesar, Vladimir Minevich, and Bernard Segal. "The Politicization of Alcohol in the USSR and Its Impact on the Study and Treatment of Alcoholism." *Substance Use & Misuse* 29, no. 10 (1994): 1269–85.

Krasikov, A. "Commodity Number One (part 1)." In *The Samizdat Register*, edited by Roy Medvedev. London: Merlin Press, 1977: 93–115.

Kryshtanovskaya, Ol'ga, and Stephen White. "Inside the Putin Court: A Research Note." *Europe-Asia Studies* 57, no. 7 (2005): 1065–75.

Ledeneva, Alena. *Can Russia Modernise? Sistema, Power Networks and Informal Governance*. Cambridge: Cambridge University Press, 2013.

——. "Cronies, Economic Crime and Capitalism in Putin's Sistema." *International Affairs* 88, no. 1 (2012): 149–57.

——. *How Russia Really Works: The Informal Practices That Shaped Post-Soviet Politics and Business*. Ithaca, NY: Cornell University Press, 2006.

——. "Introduction: Economic Crime in the New Russian Economy." In *Economic Crime in Russia*, edited by Alena Ledeneva and Marina Kurkchiyan, 1–15. London: Kluwer Law International, 2000.

——. *Russia's Economy of Favours: Blat, Networking, and Informal Exchange*. Cambridge: Cambridge University Press, 1998.

——. "Telephone Justice in Russia." *Post-Soviet Affairs* 24, no. 4 (2008): 324–50.

Leon, David A., Laurent Chenet, Vladimir M. Shkolnikov, Sergei Zakharov, Judith Shapiro, Galina Rakhmanova, Sergei Vassin, and Martin McKee. "Huge Variation in Russian Mortality Rates 1984–94: Artefact, Alcohol, or What?" *Lancet* 350, no. 9075 (1997): 383–88.

Leon, David A., Lyudmila Saburova, Susannah Tomkins, Evgueny Andreev, Nikolay Kiryanov, Martin McKee, and Vladimir M. Shkolnikov. "Hazardous Alcohol Drinking and Premature Mortality in Russia: A Population Based Case-Control Study." *Lancet* 369, no. 9578 (2007): 2001–9.

Levada, Yury. "Homo Praevaricatus: Russian Doublethink." In *Contemporary Russian Politics, a Reader*, edited by Archie Brown, 312–22. Oxford: Oxford University Press, 2001.

Levin, Boris M. "Main Factors of Alcohol Consumption under Conditions of Rapid Social Changes." In *Demystifying Russian Drinking: Comparative Studies from the 1990s*, edited by Jussi Simpura and Boris Levin. Stakes National Research and Development Centre for Welfare and Health, Research Report 85. Helsinki, Finland: Stakes, 1995: 33–58.

Levine, M. B. "The 1985 Alcohol Reform in the USSR: A Special Case of Rejected Moral Reform." PhD diss., McMaster University, Hamilton, Ontario, 1999.

Levintova, Marya. "Russian Alcohol Policy in the Making." *Alcohol & Alcoholism* 42, no. 5 (2007): 500–505.

Ligachev, Yegor. *Inside Gorbachev's Kremlin*. New York: Random House, 1993.

Lipman, Masha, and Michael McFaul. "'Managed Democracy' in Russia: Putin and the Press." *International Journal of Press/Politics* 6, no. 3 (2001): 116–27.

Mäkelä, K., and M. Viikari. "Notes on Alcohol and the State." *Acta Sociologica* 20: (1977): 151–79.

Mauss, A. L. "Science, Social Movements, and Cynicism: Appreciating the Political Context of Sociological Research in Alcohol Studies." In *Alcohol: The Development of*

Sociological Perspectives on Use and Abuse, edited by P. M. Roman, 187–204. New Brunswick, NJ: Rutgers Center of Alcohol Studies, 1991.

McKee, M. "Alcohol in Russia." *Alcohol and Alcoholism* 34 (1999): 824–29.

McKee, Martin, and Richard Rose. *Smoking and Drinking in Russia, Ukraine and Belarus.* Studies in Public Policy No. 337. Glasgow: Centre for the Study of Public Policy, University of Strathclyde, 2000.

Mesquita, M. "Reiderstvo." In *Global Encyclopaedia of Informality: Towards an Understanding of Social and Cultural Complexity,* Vol. 2, edited by A. Ledeneva, 296–300. London: UCL Press, 2018.

Mitchell, William C., and Randy T. Simmons. *Beyond Politics: Markets, Welfare, and the Failure of Bureaucracy.* Oxford: Westview Press, 1994.

Mitrokhin, Nikolay. "The Russian Orthodox Church in Contemporary Russia: Structural Problems and Contradictory Relations with the Government, 2000–2008." Presentation given at the Post-Soviet Press Group, SSEES, UCL, London, 25 March 2009.

——. *Russkaya pravoslavnaya tserkov': sovremennoye sostoyaniye i aktual'niye problem* [The Russian Orthodox Church: Its contemporary condition and topical problems] Moscow: Novoye Literaturnoye Obozreniye, 2004.

Morris, Jeremy. "Drinking to the Nation: Russian Television Advertising and Cultural Differentiation." *Europe-Asia Studies* 59, no. 8 (2007): 1387–1403.

Nemtsov, A. V. *Alkogol'naya Istoriya Rossii: Noveyshiy Period* [A history of alcohol in Russia: The modern period]. Moscow: Librokom, 2009.

Nemtsov, Boris, and Vladimir Milov. *Putin. Itogi. Nezavisimyi Ekspertnyi Doklad* [Putin: The results: An independent expert report]. Moscow: Solidarnost', 2008.

——. *Putin i Gazprom. Nezavisimiy Ekspertniy Doklad* [Putin and Gazprom: An independent expert report]. Moscow: Novaya gazeta, 2008.

Nikolayeva, M. F. "Opyt sotsiologicheskogo izucheniya sotsial'no-priemlemykh praktik alkogol'nogo potrebleniya v Pskovskoy oblasti" [Experience of the sociological study of social practices of alcohol consumption in the Pskov region]. *Materialy Chetvertoy Mezhdunarodnoy Nauchno-Prakticheskoy Konferentsii "Alkogol' v Rossii"* [Materials of the Fourth International Scientific and Practical Conference "Alcohol in Russia"], 174–81. Ivanovo, Russia: Filial RGGU v g. Ivanovo, 2013.

Nordlinger, Eric A. *On the Autonomy of the Democratic State.* Cambridge, MA: Harvard University Press, 1981.

North, Douglass. *Institutions, Institutional Change and Economic Performance.* Cambridge: Cambridge University Press, 1990.

Orttung, Robert W. "Business and Politics in the Russian Regions." *Problems of Post-Communism* 51, no. 2 (2004): 48–60.

Orwell, George. *Nineteen Eighty-Four.* London: Penguin, 1949 [1989].

Ovcharova, Elena, and Nataliya Travkina. "Problemy litsenzirovaniya na alkogol'nom rynkye" [Problems of licensing in the alcohol market]. *Zakon* 9 (2011): 138–46.

Pavlovsky, Gleb. "Russian Politics under Putin." *Foreign Affairs* 95, no. 3 (May/June 2016). Accessed 22 July 2016. https://www.foreignaffairs.com/articles/russia-fsu/2016-04-18/russian-politics-under-putin.

Petrov, Nikolay. "Kak v kaple vodki: politika, finansi, regionalizm" [The vodka factor: Politics, finance and regionalism]. *Ezhegodnoye Prilozheniye k Politicheskomu Almanakhu Rossii* (2000): 140–64.

Phillips, Laura L. *Bolsheviks and the Bottle: Drink and Worker Culture in St Petersburg, 1900–1929.* DeKalb: Northern Illinois University Press, 2000.

Pokhlebkin, William. *A History of Vodka.* New York: Verso, 1992.

Popova, Svetlana, Jürgen Rehm, Jayadeep Patra, and Witold Zatonski. "Comparing Alcohol Consumption in Central and Eastern Europe to Other European Countries." *Alcohol & Alcoholism* 42, no. 5 (2007): 465–73.

Pravda, Alex. "Ideology and the Soviet Policy Process." In *Ideology and Soviet Politics*, edited by Stephen White and Alex Pravda. Basingstoke: MacMillan, 1988: 225–252.

Pravitel'stvo Rossiyskoy Federatsii [Government of the Russian Federation]. *Kontseptsiya realizatsii gosudarstvennoy politiki po snizheniyu masshtabov zloupotrebleniya alkogol'noy produktsiey i profilaktike alkogolizma sredi naseleniya Rossiyskoy Federatsii na period do 2020 goda* [A plan for the implementation of state policy for decreasing the scale of abuse of alcoholic products and prevention of alcoholism among the population of the Russian Federation for the period to 2020], Decree No. 2128-r, 30 December 2009.

Pridemore, William Alex. "The Role of Alcohol in Russia's Violent Mortality." *Russian Analytical Digest*, No. 35 (February 2008): 6–9.

———. "Vodka and Violence: Alcohol Consumption and Homicide Rates in Russia." *American Journal of Public Health* 92 (2002): 1921–30.

Pridemore, William Alex, Mitchell B. Chamlin, Maria T. Kaylen, and Evgeny Andreev. "The Effects of the 2006 Russian Alcohol Policy on Alcohol-Related Mortality: An Interrupted Time Series Analysis." *Alcoholism: Clinical and Experimental Research* 38, no. 1 (2014): 257–66.

Public Chamber of the Russian Federation. *Zloupotreblenie Alkogolem v Rossiyskoy Federatsii: Sotsial'no-Ekonomicheskiye Posledstviya i Meri Protivodeystviya* [Alcohol abuse in the Russian Federation: Socio-economic consequences and means of combating it]. Moscow, 2009.

Putin, Vladimir Vladimirovich. *First Person: An Astonishingly Frank Self-Portrait by Russia's President.* New York: Public Affairs, 2000.

Rebrykov, V. A. "O vliyanii zakonodatel'stva na potrebleniye alkogolya v Rossii. Pozitsiya rossiyskogo parlamenta, politicheskikh partiy, imeyushchiyesya rekomendatsii po vyrabotke i realizatsii mer, vliyayushchikh na potrebleniye alkogolya" [On the influence of legislation on alcohol consumption in Russia. The position of the Russian parliament, political parties, having recommendations on the development and implementation of measures affecting alcohol consumption]. In *Alkogol' i zdorov'ye naseleniya Rossii, 1900–2000* [Alcohol and the health of the Russian population, 1900–2000], edited by A. K. Demin, 143–55. Moscow: Russian Association for Public Health, 1998.

Reitan, Therese C. "The Operation Failed, but the Patient Survived. Varying Assessments of the Soviet Union's Last Anti-alcohol Campaign." *Communist and Post-Communist Studies* 34 (2001): 241–60.

Richter, James. "Putin and the Public Chamber." *Post-Soviet Affairs* 25, no. 1 (2009): 39–65.

Rochlitz, Michael. "The Raider and the Modernizer—Economic Modernization, State-Business Links and Property Rights in Post-Crisis Russia." Higher School of Economics, Moscow, 28 February 2010.

Roizen, Ron. "How Does the Nation's 'Alcohol Problem' Change from Era to Era? Stalking the Social Logic of Problem-Definition Transformations since Repeal." In *Altering the American Consciousness: Essays on the History of Alcohol and Drug Use in the United States, 1800–2000* edited by Sarah Tracy and Caroline Acker, 61–87. Amherst: University of Massachusetts Press, 2004.

Room, Robin. "The Idea of Alcohol Policy." *Nordic Studies on Alcohol and Drugs* 16 (English supplement) (2004): 7–20.

Ryzhkov, N. I. *Desyat let velikikh potraseniy*. Moscow: Kniga, 1995.

Sabatier, Paul A. "An Advocacy Coalition Framework of Policy Change and the Role of Policy-Oriented Learning Therein." *Policy Sciences* 21 (1988): 129–68.

Sakwa, Richard. *Putin: Russia's Choice*, 2nd ed. London: Routledge, 2008.

Schrad, Mark Lawrence. *The Political Power of Bad Ideas: Networks, Institutions, and the Global Prohibition Wave*. Oxford: Oxford University Press, 2010.

———. *Vodka Politics: Alcohol, Autocracy, and the Secret History of the Russian State*. Oxford: Oxford University Press, 2014.

Segal, Boris. *The Drunken Society: Alcohol Abuse and Alcoholism in the Soviet Union: A Comparative Study*. New York: Hippocrene Books, 1987.

Shabalin, V. V. "P'yanka, vypivka, popoyka (fonovye praktiki rayonnoy nomenklatury)" [Drinking revelry, drinking bout, bacchanalia (background practices of the regional nomenclature)]. In *Materialy Vtoroy Mezhdunarodnoy Nauchno-Prakticheskoy Konferentsii "Alkogol' v Rossii"* [Materials of the Second International Scientific and Practical Conference "Alcohol in Russia"]. Ivanovo, Russia: Filial RGGU v g. Ivanovo, 2011: 19–25.

Sharafutdinova, Gulnaz. *Political Consequences of Crony Capitalism inside Russia*. Notre Dame, IN: University of Notre Dame Press, 2010.

Shlapentokh, Vladimir. *Public and Private Life of the Soviet People*. Oxford: Oxford University Press, 1989.

———. "Russia's Demographic Decline and the Public Reaction." *Europe-Asia Studies* 57, no. 7 (2005): 951–68.

Shleifer, Andrei, and Daniel Treisman. *Without a Map: Political Tactics and Economic Reform in Russia*. Cambridge, MA: MIT Press, 2000.

Simmons, Randy T. *Beyond Politics: The Roots of Government Failure*. Oakland, CA: The Independent Institute, 2011.

Simmons, Randy T., Ryan M. Yonk, and Diana W. Thomas. "Bootleggers, Baptists, and Political Entrepreneurs: Key Players in the Rational Game and Morality Play of Regulatory Politics." *Independent Review* 15, no. 3 (2011): 367–81.

Simpura, J., and J. Moskalewicz. "Alcohol Policy in Transitional Russia." *Journal of Substance Use* 5 (2000): 39–46.

Spector, Malcolm, and John I. Kitsuse. *Constructing Social Problems*. New York: Aldine de Gruyter, 1977 [1987].

Stone, Helena. "The Soviet Government and Moonshine." *Cahiers du Monde russe et so-vietique* 27 (1986): 359–80.

Swedish Council for Information on Alcohol and Other Drugs (CAN). *The 2011 ESPAD Report. Substance Use among Students in 36 European Countries.* Stockholm, Sweden, 2012.

Swinnen, Johan F. M., and Kristine Van Herck. "How the East Was Won: The Foreign Takeover of the Eastern European Brewing Industry." In *The Economics of Beer*, edited by Johan F. M. Swinnen, 248–63. Oxford: Oxford Univeristy Press, 2010.

Takala, I. R. *Veseliye Rusi. Istoriya alkogol'noy problemy v Rossii* [The joy of the Russians: A history of the alcohol problem in Russia]. Saint Petersburg: Zhurnal Neva, 2002.

Tarschys, Daniel. "The Success of a Failure: Gorbachev's Alcohol Policy, 1985–88." *Europe-Asia Studies* 45, no. 1 (1993): 7–25.

Thom, Betsy. *Dealing with Drink: Alcohol and Social Policy from Treatment to Manage-ment.* London: Free Association Books, 1999.

———. "A Social and Political History of Alcohol." In *International Handbook of Alcohol Dependence and Problems*, edited by Nick Heather, Timothy J. Peters, and Tim Stock-well, 15–31. Chichester: Wiley, 2001.

Tkatchenko, Elena, Martin McKee, and Agis D. Tsouros. "Public Health in Russia: The View from the Inside." *Health Policy and Planning* 15, no. 2 (2000): 164–69.

Transchel, Kate. *Under the Influence: Working-Class Drinking, Temperance, and Cultural Evolution in Russia, 1895–1932.* Pittsburgh, PA: University of Pittsburgh Press, 2006.

Treisman, Daniel. "Death and Prices: The Political Economy of Russia's Alcohol Cri-sis." *Economics of Transition* 18, no. 2 (2010): 281–331.

———. "Putin's Silovarchs." *Orbis* 51, no. 1 (2007): 141–53.

———. *The Return: Russia's Journey from Gorbachev to Medvedev.* New York: Free Press, 2011.

Treml, Vladimir G. *Alcohol in the USSR.* Durham, NC: Duke University Press, 1982.

———. "Drinking and Alcohol Abuse in the USSR in the 1980s." In *Soviet Social Prob-lems*, edited by Anthony Jones, Walter D. Connor, and David E. Powell, 119–36. Lon-don: Westview, 1991.

Treml, Vladimir G. "Soviet and Russian Statistics on Alcohol Consumption and Abuse." In *Premature Death in the New Independent States*, edited by Jose Luis Bobadilla et al., 220–238. Washington, DC: National Academy Press, 1997.

Tullock, Gordon. "Rent Seeking." In *The New Palgrave Dictionary of Economics*, 2nd ed., edited by Steven N. Durlauf and Lawrence E. Blume. London: Palgrave Macmillan, 2008.

Vishnevsky, Anatoly G., and Sergei N. Bobylev. *National Human Development Report Russian Federation 2008: Russia Facing Demographic Challenges.* Moscow: United Na-tions Development Programme, 2009.

Volkov, Vadim. "Organised Violence, Market Building, and State Formation in Post-Communist Russia." In *Economic Crime in Russia*, edited by Alena Ledeneva and Ma-rina Kurkchiyan, 43–61. London: Kluwer Law International, 2000.

———. *Violent Entrepreneurs: The Use of Force in the Making of Russian Capitalism.* Ithaca, NY: Cornell University Press, 2002.

Wegren, Stephen K., and Andrew Konitzer. "Prospects for Managed Democracy in Russia." *Europe-Asia Studies* 59, no. 6 (2007): 1025–47.

Weissman, Neil. "Prohibition and Alcohol Control in the USSR: The 1920s Campaign against Illegal Spirits." *Soviet Studies* 38, no. 3 (1986): 349–68.

White, Stephen. *After Gorbachev*. Cambridge: Cambridge University Press, 1993.

———. "The Political Parties." In *Developments in Russian Politics 6*, edited by Stephen White, Zvi Gitelman and Richard Sakwa, 80–95. New York: Palgrave Macmillan, 2005.

———.*Russia Goes Dry: Gorbachev, Alcohol and the Policy Process*. Cambridge: Cambridge University Press, 1996.

———. *Understanding Russian Politics*. Cambridge: Cambridge University Press, 2011.

Wilson, Andrew. *Virtual Politics: Faking Democracy in the Post-Soviet World*. New Haven, CT: Yale University Press.

Wilson, James Q. *Bureaucracy: What Government Agencies Do and Why They Do It*. 2nd ed. New York: Basic Books, 1989 [2000].

Yakovlev, Andrei. "The Evolution of Business—State Interaction in Russia: From State Capture to Business Capture?," *Europe-Asia Studies* 58, no. 7 (2006): 1033–56.

Zaigraev, Grigory G. "Gosudarstvennaya politika kak factor alkogolizatsii naseleniya" [State policy as a factor in the alcoholization of the population]. *Sotsiologicheskie Issledovaniya* 24, no. 4 (1997): 109–16.

———. "P'yanstvo v Rossii kak real'naya ugroza natsional'noy bezopasnosti" [Drunkenness in Russia as a real threat to national security]. *Sotsiologicheskie Issledovaniya* 8 (2001): 74–84.

Zaridze, David, Paul Brennan, Jillian Boreham, Alex Boroda, Rostislav Karpov, Alexander Lazarev, and Irina Konobeevskaya. "Alcohol and Cause-Specific Mortality in Russia: A Retrospective Case-Control Study of 48,557 Adult Deaths." *Lancet* 373 (2009): 2201–14.

Zudin, A. Yu. "Rezhim V. Putina: konturi novoy politicheskoy sistemi" [The regime of V. Putin: Contours of the new political system]. *Obshchestvennye nauki i sovremennost'* 2 (2003): 67–83.

Zygar, Mikhail. *All the Kremlin's Men: Inside the Court of Vladimir Putin*. New York: PublicAffairs, 2016.

Index

Kovalchuk, Yury, 64
KPRF. *See* Communist Party of the Russian Federation
Krasikov, A., 20, 208n11
Kristall distillery, 48, 52, 57, 60, 63
Kudrin, Aleksey, 58, 154–55

Law, 171, 148
  2011 amendment of, 3, 8, 87, 98, 108, 145, 151, 158–72, 227n26
Lenin, Vladimir, 13
Levada, Yury, 110
life expectancy, 1, 119, 124, 126, 128, 129, 180, 225n48
Ligachev, Yegor, 27, 122–23
lobbying, 7, 83–87, 88, 97–98, 114, 154–55, 160–61, 163–64, 165–69, 173–74, 181, 182–83
Luzhkov, Yury, 48

mafiya, 6, 32, 33, 34–35, 36–37
Marx, Karl, 11
Matviyenko, Valentina, 61, 68–69, 178
Medvedev, Dmitry, 46, 74, 129, 140–41, 147, 148, 156, 176
  alcohol policy instructions, 8, 147–48, 149–50, 159, 162t13.1, 166, 171, 182, 185
  antialcohol initiative of (*see* antialcohol initiative (2009–2012))
  antialcohol rhetoric, 1, 116–17, 123, 147, 152, 228n13
Milov, Vladimir, 64, 125
minimum pricing, 71, 83, 106, 114, 148, 153–54, 181
Ministry for Economic Development (Minekonomrazvitiya), 72, 161, 176, 178, 183
Ministry of Agriculture, 52, 71, 72
Ministry of Finance (Minfin), 72, 154–57, 178, 181, 184
Ministry of Health and Social Development (Minzdrav), 66, 103, 144, 149, 161
Ministry of Internal Affairs (MVD), 35, 161, 162
  in the USSR, 23
Ministry of Trade (Minpromtorg), 161, 162–63, 168, 178, 183
monopoly. *See* state monopoly on alcohol
moonshining. See *samogon*

National Sports Federation (NSF), 31, 36
National Union for the Protection of Consumer Rights, 176
Nemtsov, Alexandr, 91, 102–3, 118, 121–22
Nemtsov, Boris, 64, 125
New Economic Policy (NEP), 15
Nicholas II, Tsar, 11–12
North Ossetia, 37–38, 78

OBSA. *See* Society for the Struggle with Alcoholism
Obshcheye Delo. *See* Common Cause project
oligarchs, 6, 44–45, 46, 112
Onishchenko, Gennady, 88, 90–92, 103
opinion polls. *See* public opinion
Orwell, George, 18

Pavlovsky, Gleb, 65
per capita consumption. *See* consumption of alcohol, average per capita
populism, 112–15, 177
"power vertical", 6–7, 47. *See also* Putin, Vladimir: reestablishment of federal control
price liberalization, 33
Public Chamber of the Russian Federation, 132, 136–37, 142, 145
  Alcohol Abuse in the Russian Federation report (2009), 88, 132, 136–37, 139–40
public health, 3, 20–21, 71, 83, 117–18, 130, 180
  public health activists, 7, 66, 120–22, 132–33, 136–39, 142–46, 180, 182, 184, 185
public opinion, 4–5, 52, 100–2, 104–15, 150–51, 180–81
Putin, Vladimir, 44, 50–51, 53, 55, 64, 66, 114, 122–23, 155, 180
  associates and inner circle, 55–57, 58–59, 61, 64, 66, 92–93, 134–36
  discussion of demographic and alcohol problems, 127, 128–30
  monocentric regime of, 112–13, 124
  reestablishment of federal control, 6, 43, 44–47
Putinka vodka, 59–61

RAR. *See* Rosalkogolregulirovaniye
regional authorities, 6–7, 33, 44, 47, 148, 159, 166, 228n8, 230n8

Zubkov, Viktor, 56–57, 71, 74, 79, 129, 135, 168

Zvagelskiy, Viktor, 7, 66, 73–74, 94–96, 97–99, 163–65, 175–76

alleged vodka interests of (*see* Vodka Artel "Yat")

clashes with brewing industry, 98–99

perceived as "vodka lobbyist," 85, 97–98

relationship with public health activists, 145–46

relationship with RAR, 8, 165, 183, 185

role in 2011 alcohol control bill, 8, 165, 167–70

Zyuganov, Gennady, 125